Beyond Gifted Education

Beyond Gifted Education

Designing and Implementing Advanced Academic Programs

Scott J. Peters, Ph.D.,
Michael S. Matthews, Ph.D.,
Matthew T. McBee, Ph.D., and
D. Betsy McCoach, Ph.D.

PRUFROCK PRESS INC.
WACO, TEXAS

Library of Congress Cataloging-in-Publication Data

Peters, Scott J., 1983-
 Beyond gifted education : designing and implementing advanced academic programs / by Scott J. Peters, Michael S. Matthews, Matthew T. McBee, & D. Betsy McCoach.
   pages cm
 ISBN 978-1-61821-121-7 (pbk.)
 1. Gifted children--Education--United States. I. Matthews, Michael S., 1968- II. McBee, Matthew T., 1980- III. McCoach, D. Betsy. IV. Title.
 LC3993.9.P48 2013
 371.95--dc23
                    2013017456

Copyright ©2014, Prufrock Press Inc.

Edited by Lacy Compton

Cover design by Raquel Trevino

Layout design by Allegra Denbo

ISBN-13: 978-1-61821-121-7

Printed in the United States of America.

At the time of this book's publication, all facts and figures cited are the most current available. All telephone numbers, addresses, and websites URLs are accurate and active. All publications, organizations, websites, and other resources exist as described in the book, and all have been verified. The authors and Prufrock Press Inc. make no warranty or guarantee concerning the information and materials given out by organizations or content found at websites, and we are not responsible for any changes that occur after this book's publication. If you find an error, please contact Prufrock Press Inc.

Prufrock Press Inc.
P.O. Box 8813
Waco, TX 76714-8813
Phone: (800) 998-2208
Fax: (800) 240-0333
http://www.prufrock.com

Table of Contents

Preface

It is one of the most frequently addressed topics in gifted education journals and newspaper articles about the field. Every handbook and text-book on gifted education devotes one or more chapters to the topic. It is a central concern of parents and, increasingly one on which they will spend money in the hopes of gaining an edge for their child over the competition. In some states, it is the only mandated activity for gifted education and in others, the largest line-item in the budget. And yet it remains as controversial and, in many quarters, as poorly understood as ever. What is it? Identification. Many of us who have worked to help schools develop better, fairer identification policies have concluded that these efforts are unlikely to succeed as long as they are tied to the word *gifted*. The question "Who are the gifted children in this school?" leads to policies and practices quite unlike the question "Who are the children who are currently mismatched with the level of instruction they are receiving?" or even "Who are the children who show talent in this domain that we might help them develop?" Although many have objected to current policies, few have offered specific guidelines for new ones. This book bridges that gap.

The authors begin by boldly announcing that their approach differs radically from gifted education as currently practiced, so radically that they give it a different name: *advanced academics*. Identification of the cognitive, motivational, and personality traits that might uniquely characterize gifted learners is left for psychologists to investigate and debate. For practitioners, identification should refer to "a formalized system that sets out to determine which students have needs that are not being met by the standard curriculum of a given school or district" (p. 15). The goals and processes for identifying students in need of advanced academic programming are described in greater detail in Chapters 2 and 3. To identify is to predict that a student will succeed (or at least not suffer harm) in a particular instructional program. It is local, not only to the school, but to the particular academic program at that school. At one extreme, students might be allowed self-identify by opting to enroll in a class or participate in a program. At the other extreme, the system can offer (or require) a multi-step, multimeasure assessment that is designed either to prevent unqualified students from entering the program and/or to encourage qualified but unwilling students to participate in it. But it is decidedly not about imposing a more permanent label such as *gifted*.

The consequences for curriculum and school organization are described in successive chapters devoted to Total School Cluster Grouping (Chapter 4), acceleration (Chapter 5), and enrichment (Chapter 6). Then the final three chapters revisit identification, this time addressing knottier issues that are often ignored or mishandled. Underrepresentation is tackled in Chapter 7. Specific guidance is offered on how to use assessment data to achieve better representation of underrepresented groups, a problem that is made much easier when the goal is to identify those who are (or might be) mismatched, not to confer an enduring label. Common pitfalls in identification policies are enumerated an illustrated in Chapter 8. And Chapter 9 gives a nontechnical introduction to procedures for combining multiple measures, a topic that is as poorly understood as it is critical for the success of any identification system that relies on more than one data point for each student.

This book will delight some, annoy others, but challenge all. It offers a radical, but needed, perspective on what gifted education without gifted students might look like.

David Lohman
The University of Iowa
April 2013

Introduction

1

Gifted or advanced education is focused on providing appropriate education for those students who need it. Regardless of whether or not we call them gifted, students exist in every school who could do more than they are currently being asked to do. Every school has those students who would benefit—academically, socially, and motivationally—from additional challenge. This book is about how to find and serve those children. However, before we begin this complicated trek, we first address how the perspective we offer differs from that of traditional gifted education. To do so we will, in places, offer some seemingly harsh critiques of gifted education. We have all dedicated our careers to the field, and we believe passionately in championing the cause of challenging all learners. We only offer criticisms to the service of this cause, while simultaneously offering suggestions for change and improvement.

Determining whether or not a child meets a formal definition of giftedness is not a particularly useful thing to do from the point of view of the stakeholders in K–12 education—students, teachers, administrators, and parents. Instead, we believe that it is much more educationally helpful to determine which children are not being well-served by the existing curriculum and then design programs to meet their needs. Identification, when it is necessary at all, then becomes focused on answering the question,

"Who can thrive in the advanced academic program(s) we've designed?" instead of "Who is gifted?" In place of the old "gifted education" approach, we will provide a new framework that is logical, clear, and free of some of the internal contradictions and atheoretical practices that have been part of the practice of gifted education for many decades. Although our position stands in contrast to many years of practice, we believe it is supported by theory and is also far more defensible than current practice. We believe that the adoption of the framework we describe in this book would result in vastly improved K–12 educational experiences for bright students. Furthermore, our framework securely grounds programs and policies for gifted students within the context of major current educational initiatives such as the Common Core State Standards and Response to Intervention (RtI).

It is time that we, as passionate advocates of gifted education in K–12 schools, recognize that some (but not all) of the criticism directed at our field is legitimate. We have been unable to provide evidence-based arguments against these criticisms. As a result, advocates of gifted education have been less persuasive of policy makers, K–12 educators, and funding agencies than any of us would like. The history of the field is characterized by the slow assimilation of, and reform around, legitimate criticisms from the outside. For example, the historical concept of giftedness was essentially synonymous with high IQ, whereas now the widespread consensus in the field is that giftedness is a multidimensional construct that cannot be adequately measured by a single IQ score (Borland, 2005; Worrell, 2009). This book should be understood as another instance of the same historical trend within the field.

Finally, this book does not provide a step-by-step procedure or a "canned" program for using these ideas. This book is far more in the spirit of a persuasive essay whose goal is to reframe discussion and debate around gifted education. The principles presented in this book argue for advanced educational opportunities that are intensely local, that is, that are closely tailored to the needs and values of a particular setting at a particular time. Providing a canned program for implementation of our ideas would represent a violation of the very principles we espouse. These ideas place much of the burden of responsibility on local district and school personnel to develop appropriate programming for their advanced learners. This perspective is consistent with a philosophical viewpoint that believes teachers are professionals and experts in whose care we entrust the development of our children. Teaching is not, and should not be, a turnkey operation that anyone with a pulse can simply walk into a classroom and do!

Defining Giftedness, Talent, and Advanced Academics

What can be said most confidently about conceptual definitions of giftedness, talent, and high ability is that they are widely inconsistent. In fact, there is so much disagreement on the topic that even a workgroup of the National Association for Gifted Children (NAGC) had much difficulty agreeing on a definition. The two most general types of conceptual definitions revolve around typical academic skills (those important to student success in traditional K–12 school subjects) and those specific tasks that are not as directly related to traditional academics. For example, Renzulli (2005) referred to children who excel in academic subjects as the "schoolhouse gifted," and he observed that the schoolhouse gifted are not necessarily the same group of children who exhibit adult creative productivity. Some in the gifted education community have taken this as evidence that we, as a field, have been focusing on the wrong individuals or the wrong goals (e.g., Subotnik, Olszewski-Kubilius, & Worrell, 2011). We disagree. Whether a child will or will not become an eminent adult is irrelevant to K–12 instruction; we hope many children will, but it simply is not possible to predict with accuracy which children will attain eminence as adults. Adult eminence is tangential to whether or not that child will spend his entire year sitting through coursework or instruction in content that he has already mastered. Schools are designed to help children develop expertise in a rather circumscribed set of disciplines and skills, and this book focuses on helping schools conceptualize programming to foster more advanced levels of development in those domains.

Because the approach we describe is so different from what is usually practiced under the rubric of gifted education, we consciously have decided to give it a different name. We refer to our approach as *advanced academics*. We clarify the precise meaning of the term in later chapters of the book. To summarize succinctly, gifted education is about identifying and serving a distinct class of individuals—the gifted. Advanced academics is about providing students who are not challenged by the ordinary curriculum and instruction with faster, deeper, and more rigorous instruction than they would receive within their typical academic experience, regardless of whether or not they are formally identified as gifted. Many students in need of such instruction may have been identified as gifted, but many others who also need and can benefit from such instruction have not. To better contrast our approach against other ideas, next we review some influential definitions of giftedness that inform current practice.

Defining Gifted and Talented

The current federal definition of "gifted and talented" comes from the 1993 *National Excellence* report created by the U.S. Department of Education:

> Children and youth with outstanding talent perform or show the potential for performing at remarkably high levels of accomplishment when compared with others of their age, experience, or environment. These children and youth exhibit high performance capability in *intellectual, creative, and/or artistic areas, possess an unusual leadership capacity, or excel in specific academic fields [emphasis added].* They require services or activities not ordinarily provided by the schools. Outstanding talents are present in children and youth from all cultural groups, across all economic strata, and in all areas of human endeavor. (p. 3)

What is interesting to note about this definition is that the term *gifted* is conspicuously absent and instead the term *outstanding talent* is included. Although having a national-level definition might seem convenient for the sake of consistency, given the absence of any federal mandate for its use, identification, or programming, this definition serves as little more than guidance for states and districts. In practice, taking a closer look at the state-level definitions reveals many stark similarities.

Also at the national level are multiple conceptual definitions offered by the National Association for Gifted Children, the official current form of which is as follows:

> Gifted individuals are those who demonstrate outstanding levels of aptitude (defined as an exceptional ability to reason and learn) or competence (documented performance or achievement in top 10% or rarer) in one or more domains. Domains include *any structured area of activity with its own symbol system (e.g., mathematics,*

music, language) and/or set of sensorimotor skills (e.g., painting, dance, sports) [emphasis added]. (NAGC, 2010b, p. 1)

This recent NAGC definition is broader and more inclusive than that of the U.S. Department of Education (1993) report and includes a wider range of skills and abilities than are typically addressed in public schools. Even if a school were to adopt this definition verbatim, the school still would have to decide which content areas or domains it would serve under the purview of advanced (specific) academic programming. In addition, this definition specifies the percentage of individuals at 10% or fewer. It is likely that most percentages used in conceptual definitions are arbitrary. Therefore, it is somewhat unusual to mandate that no more than 10% of some unknown group could be considered gifted and/or talented in any single area without first considering what the "other" people can or will do. However, because the NAGC definition does not specify a norm group, the terms *outstanding* and *exceptional* remain open to interpretation by the end user.

State-Level Definitions

Fortunately, a conceptual definition of giftedness turns out to be not all that important when it comes to fostering advanced academic skills. In other words, we don't need a fixed percentage or a psychological framework in order to provide students in need with subject-specific advanced content. However, many states do provide some structure and/or mandate when it comes to anything falling under the guise of "gifted" education. Because of this, programs for advanced academics should, when possible, align with any required state definitions or mandates that relate to gifted education. At the time of the 2010–2011 *State of the States in Gifted Education* report, 41 (out of 45 states responding) states had an official state definition for giftedness (NAGC & Council of State Directors of Programs for the Gifted [CSDPG], 2011). However, only 32 of these required that their definition be followed, allowing individual schools and districts much latitude in defining and identifying giftedness. For example, the State of Wisconsin dictates that gifted and talented students can and must be identified in five areas: intellectual, specific academic area, leadership, creativity, and visual and performing arts (Wisconsin Administrative Rule PI 8.01(2)(t)2, 2012; see https://docs.legis.wisconsin.gov/code/

admin_code/pi/8/01/2). Such state-level guidance in the form of a mandate makes gifted/advanced academic programming easier than if a given state had no formal definition or did not require adherence to such a definition. In theory, all Wisconsin schools must identify students in these five areas and then provide these learners with appropriate services. This is similar to the other 31 states that require either identification or services, or both (NAGC & CSPDG, 2011). However, just because a state has a formal definition and a mandate to identify and serve does not mean the mandate is universally followed or that all areas of the mandate receive equal attention. Some Wisconsin schools have no gifted program even if they do identify students, and many others only identify high-ability learners in math and language arts.

The situation is similar in other states; for example, a recent survey of the high school gifted coordinators across the state of Indiana revealed that although Indiana mandates that all school districts have a gifted and talented coordinator, only 75% of respondents indicated such a position or person existed (Peters & Mann, 2009). Given that the surveys were sent to the person listed by the state as the gifted coordinator, it's clear that having a state mandate does not always assure action. Furthermore, although states such as Wisconsin and Indiana specify that multiple measures must be used in student identification, both stop short of requiring specific assessments to be used, again leaving that decision to the school or district.

States such as Georgia have a conceptual definition similar to Indiana and Wisconsin. In Georgia, a gifted student is defined as

> A student who demonstrates a high degree of intellectual and/or creative ability(ies), exhibits an exceptionally high degree of motivation, and/or excels in specific academic fields, and who needs special instruction and/or special ancillary services to achieve at levels commensurate with his or her abilities. The abilities manifest in a collection of traits, aptitudes and behaviors that, when taken together, are indicative of gifted potential. (Georgia Department of Education, 2012, p. 7)

Although this definition is similar to Wisconsin's in that it includes general intellectual, creative, and specific academic abilities, the Georgia definition does not include leadership or visual art abilities (although these perhaps could be considered part of creative talent). However, Georgia

does allow for a high degree of motivation as being sufficient to identify gifted ability in these areas, whereas high ability or achievement are
required in the other two states mentioned. Although Georgia leaves some
freedom to local districts to decide criteria for identification, the state does
specify initial eligibility criteria based on the five areas of their conceptual
definition. Students in Georgia then have two pathways to identification.
They can either receive high scores on a nationally normed measure of
mental ability (99th percentile in K–2, 96th percentile in 3–12) and on
achievement tests (90th percentile or "superior" rating), or they can follow
an alternate path that involves additional tests of creativity and motivation.
For a discussion of some of the inherent issues and complexities with such
a system, see McBee, Peters, and Waterman (in press).

The *State of the States* (NAGC & CSDPG, 2011) report is a biannual
survey of gifted education policies across the country. In the 2010–2011
report, 45 states responded to a wide range of questions regarding gifted
education practice in their respective states. As mentioned above, 41 of
the responding states reported having a formal definition of giftedness.
Of these, the most common area of giftedness listed was intellectual
giftedness (34 states) followed by creatively gifted (26), performing and
visual arts (25), academics (23), and specific academic areas (21). Other
areas listed less frequently included leadership, culturally diverse, English
language learners (ELL), disabled/twice-exceptional, highly gifted, and
underachieving.

Within the *State of the States* (NAGC & CSDPG, 2011) report, 45
states responded to the question regarding identification practices. Of
those states, 33 required the use of specific identification practices (such as
in Georgia, as outlined above). Such requirements included multiple criteria (20), IQ tests (16), achievement tests (13), a menu of state-approved
tests from which schools can choose (10), and nominations (8). However,
even when specific criteria are required for the local schools, often the
process and procedures are not specified. Only eight states mandate a specific process be followed, while seven states allow for collaborative decision
making by the state and local district. In 15 states, schools are completely
free to create an identification process. For example, how "multiple measures" are to be used in a state that requires such a practice (e.g., Arkansas,
Indiana) is not specified, leaving each local district or school to decide
what combination of measures to use and/or how to combine them. In
another example, eight of the 33 states responding require nominations as

part of the specific methods of identification: Some list specific tools that are approved or recommended, but others do not. The same can be said for virtually all of the various required methods. Even though a class or type of assessment (e.g., IQ test) might be required, the definition specifies neither which particular test to use, nor the manner of its use. Because of this widespread emphasis on local control in education, the roles of the district coordinator, school board, and other local stakeholders can be extremely important in fostering effective identification and programming for academically advanced students.

Some areas of giftedness and talent are easier to assess and evaluate than others. In fact, several states specifically name the local education agency (school or district) as the deciding body for matters related to conceptual definition. For example, both North Carolina and Florida require locally developed plans to guide gifted identification and programming, although in both cases, these plans are reviewed at the state level for their compliance with the state rule.

In conclusion, states vary widely in their definitions of giftedness and their identification of students for gifted or advanced programming. With regard to identification, some states do not specify content areas at all (leaving terms like *specific academic area* to be operationalized by the district or school), other states specify content areas but not how these areas should be assessed, and still others specify the types of assessments but stop short of naming specific assessments to be used. Interested parents or professionals should investigate state-level policies before attempting to create a new framework or program for a specific school or district. *In some cases, the advanced academic approach is sufficiently different from gifted education that schools may not need to worry about whether the advanced academics program is in compliance with the state's gifted education policy, especially for students not currently identified as gifted or in settings where gifted status is not tied to funding. After all, advanced academics are not gifted education!*

Local Definitions

In cases where a state lacks an official definition or specifically leaves the decision to the local education agency (LEA), the decision falls on local school personnel. This situation obviously allows the greatest flexibility for implementing advanced academic programs.

Whenever advanced academic programs are being contemplated, the first step should be a needs assessment. What skills, aptitudes, and dispositions need additional development, in the form of educational programming, as justified by local values and unmet student need? This final point is very important. If student need is being met by the general education curriculum, such that even the highest performing students are challenged and engaged, then *it is unnecessary to create an advanced academic program in that area.* This may seem like a trivial issue, but when defining gifted or advanced, a major consideration needs to be what content is offered as standard or grade level in the given district, school, or grade. The need for specialized academic programming arises from a mismatch between a given student and his or her environment. Therefore, when a school board or group of individuals sets out to define advanced academics in a local setting, both existing local curriculum (and its accompanying student needs) and the characteristics of the local student population must be taken into account. Using a national perspective for comparison is likely to result in a large mismatch between the type of content and level of skills students need and what is actually being delivered. Lohman (2006) illustrated this issue with the example of a high-achieving school where an average student's achievement is around the 95th percentile relative to the national average. At this school, the content offered as standard or grade level would be much more advanced than that offered at a more typical, average-performing school district.

Even in the world of increasingly strict content standards, wide variation within a single school district is common. In average performing school districts, a subject such as Algebra I might be viewed as advanced, honors, accelerated, or gifted for eighth graders. However, in the high-achieving schools referenced above, Algebra I might be considered grade-level content for seventh graders. As Renzulli (2005) argued, "Even in schools where achievement levels are below national norms, there still exists an upper-level group of students who need services above and beyond those that are provided for the majority of the school population" (p. 271). Thus, supplementary advanced academic services should focus on *needs that are not being met as part of the general curriculum of a local school or district,* rather than on a statewide or national grade-level standard. This local-norm perspective is critical if a program is to best connect with local students' levels of need. This also means that some students who would be in an advanced academic program at one school would not have a need for such a program in a different school, and that some students within a given school might be in need of a program one year, but not the following year.

Needs change across time and across schools, and programming should be responsive enough to change with them. When national standards or national norms are used for gifted and talented identification, a few schools will end up having 0% or 100% of their students being classified as gifted. Although the 100% instance might seem very appealing (what a wonderful thing to have 100% gifted students), the idea is rather absurd. If 100% of the students in a school are identified as in need of "advanced academics" (meaning they require more challenging curriculum than is being offered by the standard curriculum), then the standard curriculum is simply inadequate! It is impossible to specify on an a priori basis a desirable percentage of students who should be receiving advanced academic opportunities in a given school. However, when the percentage grows steadily over time (as we have seen it do), schools need to reconsider what level of content they offer as their standard, grade-level curriculum. In other words, when large numbers of students need advanced academics, this suggests there are deficiencies in the standard curriculum. Rather than shunting those students into special programs, the standard curriculum needs to be upgraded.

Where Does Giftedness Begin?

Often state or district policy identifies a set percentage of students as gifted. The use of these percentages may be arbitrary, but it is also likely that these target percentages were based on intelligence test percentiles (e.g., an IQ of 130 = approximately 2.5% of a population) and are rooted in the historically fixed percentages of some special education diagnoses (i.e., intellectually disabled, which traditionally has required an IQ score below 70, in addition to other criteria). Although those students in need of more challenge beyond the standard curriculum should by definition be *somewhat* rare, in this book we will not argue for any specific percentage of a population as being in need of advanced academic programming. Instead, *the percentage of students served by advanced programming should be directly proportional to the number of students whose needs cannot readily be met in the general education classroom as it currently exists in a particular setting.* In a district with a large portion of above-grade-level students, the percentage of the population labeled as in need of such programs could actually be relatively small (e.g., 1%–2%) because the high-achieving nature of the school population requires that most needs typical of high-ability students are met as part of the general curriculum. Such a situation might occur in a high-performing high school serving an affluent population, where nearly all students take several honors, AP, or above-grade-level classes and go on to college. In this instance there (ideally) would be services that would not necessitate a label or advanced program because they already exist for most students as part of the general curriculum (so that, because the need is being met, no special program is required). The opposite could also be true. In a very large school in which the majority of students are low performing, the percentage of students identified for advanced academic services could be relatively high (e.g., 10%–15%) because these students are unlikely to have their needs met in the general education curriculum. Such a case could exist in a middle school where most students take pre-algebra in eighth grade, and algebra and geometry are not offered until high school. In this setting, some middle school students who are ready for advanced algebra, geometry, and trigonometry are unlikely to have their needs met in the general education classroom and are more likely to need special services.

These examples run contrary to the popular wisdom that says high-performing districts can expect to have a larger percentage of identified high-need students and low-performing districts would have a smaller percentage of such students, although such scenarios are also possible. When *educational need* is locally defined based on the students enrolled in a particular school or district and the standard curriculum of that district, the percentages of students who require academic programming outside of the standard grade-level curriculum varies. For this reason, our use of particular percentages in the examples does not imply that any set number or percentage is the "right number" for any advanced academic program.

A point that arises throughout this book is that predetermined percentages (or cutoffs) that only serve to arbitrarily limit the number of students who can receive a service should be avoided. The use of percentages can lead to a fixed number of spaces being set aside for a given program; this puts the needs of schools ahead of the needs of their students, rather than focusing on students' needs as they differ from year to year and grade level to grade level. In contrast, percentages can be very useful for the purpose of comparing the ethnic, gender, racial, ELL, and socioeconomic status (SES) makeup of the identified student population. If dominant cultural

groups are overly represented in the population served by advanced programming, additional services might be necessary or the administrators
and staff of the local school might consider reevaluating the philosophical,
cultural, and practical base of their existing program. Because score discrepancies are correlated with cultural, ethnic, and especially economic status on nearly every existing measure of academic achievement or academic
aptitude (Valencia & Suzuki, 2001), it may not be realistic to expect that
students who are identified based on their performance on such measures
should be representative of overall student population in a given school.
Nevertheless, we suggest, existing discrepancies usually are far more lop-
sided than test scores alone would predict. We return to this issue in more
depth in Chapter 7.

Does It Really Matter if a Student Is Gifted?

So what is giftedness and who are the gifted? These two questions
have driven eight decades of educational philosophy, research, and practice.
Even today, more than 90 years after the 1922 publication of Terman's
seminal work, scholars still have not coalesced on a consensual, paradig-
matic definition of the term. This lack of a common definition of the term
gifted (and the related term *talented*) is frequently decried by researchers in
the field (e.g., Lohman, Korb, & Lakin, 2008), for whom the lack of definitional consistency leads to great difficulty in synthesizing research results
across studies. Furthermore, varied and inconsistent definitions don't tell
us what to do with those students for whom the standard content or curriculum is inappropriate. Teachers need to know "Who needs more challenging math on Monday?" and "What do I do during reading time for my
kindergarten students who can already read chapter books?" In the context
of K–12 schooling, these are the questions that matter.

The lack of definitional consistency for the term gifted suggests there
may be other fundamental flaws and logical inconsistencies in current
educational practice. As we detailed in a recent paper (McBee, McCoach,
Peters, & Mathews, 2012) the concept of giftedness does not really answer
the educationally relevant question of "Who needs harder math problems?"
Although it might seem like the gifted students would be those with unmet
needs (and some scholars have argued that giftedness *itself* creates need), in
our experience this is simply not the case. Every student who attends the
North Carolina High School for Science and Math, for example, could be

considered gifted according to the field's most common definitions of that term. Does that imply that the education they are receiving is automatically inadequate—that they need more by virtue of being gifted? Do only neighborhood schools need a gifted program? What about a high-poverty school in which no students meet the criteria for being identified gifted? Are we prepared to argue that none of those students can and should be doing more than what they are asked to do academically? In many cases, there will be substantial overlap between those students who would be identified as gifted under traditional definitions and those who would be determined to have unmet academic needs, but this overlap is not perfect. Furthermore, the very term gifted, due to its long history, carries with it many unhelpful and unavoidable connotations in the minds of teachers, parents, children, and the academy. Replacing the concept of giftedness with the much more contextual notions of *academic need* and *advanced academic programming* removes an invisible intellectual straightjacket that has tied our hands and blinded our eyes to obvious changes our schools must make to support high-achieving or potentially high-achieving students.

We realize that our last few paragraphs may have alarmed the reader. It is critical at this point to clarify what we mean. We do *not* argue that bright children do not exist—we have collectively worked with many extraordinarily bright students whose minds work in qualitatively different ways and whose cognitive skills far surpass their physical and emotional development. It is precisely for this reason that we argue explicitly, forcefully, and passionately that many children in our schools need a great deal more challenge, opportunity, and intellectual rigor than is provided in the typical K–12 setting. Discarding the concept of giftedness on the part of parents, teachers, researchers, and advocates for gifted children is the very best thing that can happen to the gifted child when it comes to the educational experiences he or she receives in K–12 schools, provided other appropriate changes are made in order to meet bright children's educational needs.

The Case for Separating Advanced Academics From Gifted Studies

Gifted education has grown out of several fields and represents a truly multidisciplinary arena. Although psychologists dominated the first era of research and theory on giftedness, today gifted education is a mélange of several branches of psychology (primarily educational, cognitive, and developmental) and education. Some of the long-running lack of consistency in definitions and theoretical conceptions must surely result from the diversity of perspectives brought by people who approach the study of giftedness from varying intellectual traditions.

Psychologists have contributed perhaps more theory than any other single constituent groups. However, psychologists have, in aggregate, quite different priorities and interests than educators. Psychologists interested in high ability often aim to understand and predict eminent achievement in adulthood. Psychologists yearn for a common definition of giftedness that is constant across settings and domains (and therefore consistent across studies), hoping to operationalize the construct of giftedness in the same way that they approach constructs such as depression. For example, to determine whether someone is depressed or not, his or her symptoms are compared against an operational definition that is defined objectively with respect to some external criteria. Whether or not someone is classified as depressed is not at all affected by whether that person happens to be the most or least melancholy person in his or her social context. In this way, and unlike definitions of giftedness, depression is a criterion-referenced construct as opposed to a norm-referenced construct.

Educators, on the other hand, may be tolerant of much less rigid definitions—a fact that has challenged researchers in the field for some time. Educators' primary concern must be with providing optimal services and education to students. Advanced academics should focus on designing, implementing, evaluating, and improving instructional models, program design, and curriculum for those students who need more—the question of whether a psychologist might define that student who needs more as *gifted* is completely irrelevant. Advanced academics, therefore, is a completely needs-based and *school-based* construct that stems directly from historical conceptions of gifted education with their focus on student need. Therefore, assessing the degree to which a student's level of academic need matches with his or her currently provided level of education becomes the key feature of any "identification" system. Although insights, discoveries, and theory from high-ability psychology may occasionally be applicable to advanced academics, there should be no attempt to force this connection. Indeed, the progress of our field has been stunted precisely *because* of our insistence on theoretical unification across subfields. The psychological focus on understanding talent, creativity, and eminence (which we refer to as high-ability psychology) is still incredibly important as a scientific discipline and undoubtedly requires additional research. But schools should have a different focus, a focus on advancing students' academic skills. Although there are many important areas of human endeavor worthy of investigation from a psychological point of view, not all content areas or domains can be the purview of K–12 schools. Instead, schools focus on a semistandardized set of academic skills, and some students demonstrate far greater proficiency in those areas than their grade-level peers, necessitating the provision of programs or services to meet their advanced academic needs. The term advanced academics that we promote throughout this book is meant to capture educationally relevant, academically oriented, needs-based programming geared toward students who have already mastered the grade-level curriculum or who have the capability of doing so far faster than their chronological peers.

The notion that giftedness is a stable trait has naturally led to a great deal of concern and attention in our field being directed to the effort of *finding the gifted.* The common misconception is that if we could just create or purchase the right test, then we would be able to find those gifted kids. The prevailing "trait" theory of giftedness has naturally led to the labeling of children as a primary concern. Labeling is only useful to the degree that it provides diagnostic information, and perhaps to a lesser extent as a means of directing funding toward specific needs. The label *gifted*, just like the label *tall*, provides little diagnostic information. We believe that effort expended in the interest of finding children who *need more* educationally than their peers is a better investment of resources—indeed this is what tests in schools are supposed to be for; however, *identifying* the gifted has been dramatically overemphasized and has crowded out other more educationally relevant efforts, such as what to do with these children once they are identified. We know of schools that have spent 100% of their gifted education funding for a year on a single test, only to have no funds remaining for programming. In the state of Connecticut, the identification of gifted students is mandatory; however, school districts are not required to provide programming or services for gifted students. We find such policies and practices absurd.

Legitimate Critiques of Gifted Education

Gifted education is under constant attack by critics with a variety of perspectives. As a field, we have frequently failed to provide convincing counterarguments to some of these criticisms. In this section, we explore common criticisms of gifted education; some of this discussion continues in Chapter 8. If gifted education is to grow beyond the niche program that it so often is, often surviving on the thinnest margins of public support, then the field must change the way that it operates so that these critiques can be honestly addressed.

Why Do We Set the Identification Cutoff Where It Is? Is the Child Who Scores One Point Below the Cutoff Really so Different From the One Who Scores One Point Above?

A child must exhibit a score or scores above some cutoff(s) in order to be identified as gifted. These cutoffs vary, in some cases dramatically, from state to state and district to district. For example, for a child to meet the "intellectual ability" aspect of the state of Georgia's mandated definition, students must score above the 96th percentile on an appropriate test. This prompts the question, "What is so special about the 96th percentile?" As it turns out, there is *nothing* special about the 96th percentile. It's simply an arbitrary cutoff. Proponents of the status quo would argue that you have to draw the proverbial line somewhere, and that the act of "line drawing" is not unethical.

Is there any evidence that a child at the 95th, 92nd, or 90th percentile on mental ability would be unable to keep up with the "top 4%ers" in the advanced educational services that (should) follow identification? If we had evidence that a cut score at the 96th percentile actually *does* discriminate between those who can and those who cannot succeed in an advanced educational program, then perhaps that cutoff would be justified. But such evidence does not exist. So a cutoff-based system that sorts children into the gifted and nongifted without sufficient thought and/or evidence for the creation of the cutoff appears to bestow a desirable label on some students but not others. This practice cannot be defended convincingly, and it only reinforces the image that gifted education is an optional luxury. Instead, cutoffs or identification criteria should be based on the demands of the programming or intervention. We will address this topic in depth in Chapters 3 and 9.

Why Do Gifted Students Get to Do Fun Activities While the Other Students Do Worksheets?

Another criticism addresses what children actually do in gifted education programs after they have been identified. There are two general classifications of service provided in gifted education: acceleration and enrichment. Academic acceleration involves moving through the typical curriculum at a faster rate, whereas enrichment involves more in-depth study of topics within the curriculum and/or the study of topics that are outside the regular curriculum. A vast amount of research has supported the effectiveness of acceleration (Colangelo, Assouline, & Gross, 2004), but there is much weaker evidence supporting the efficacy of enrichment (although to be fair, enrichment programs are much more difficult to evaluate). Nonetheless, programs such as resource rooms and differentiation in the regular classroom were the most common types of gifted education programming reported in the *State of the States* report (NAGC & CSDPG, 2011). Ironically, schools appear overwhelmingly to prefer offering enrichment-like services to acceleration, even though there is far stronger evidence supporting the practice of acceleration. Why is enrichment more popular than acceleration? Enrichment maintains the status quo, the chronological delivery of curriculum. Gifted children in an enrichment-only program follow the same timeline and pace through the curriculum as their nongifted peers. Often when schools have provided acceleration, due to inadequate coordination across grades and schools, students may rapidly advance through content in some subjects or grades only to slam into an administrative brick wall in a later grade, at which point it is all too common that they are required to repeat material that has already been mastered. This does not happen with enrichment. In short, acceleration is much more complex from a logistical and administrative standpoint. Because in many settings the dominant proportion of care, concern, and energy is expended on the effort of identifying children, the question of "identifying them for *what*" (see Chapter 2) too often becomes an afterthought, when it should in fact be the most important question under consideration.

One rationale for acceleration is that gifted students are capable of learning more rapidly than their peers (Davis, Rimm, & Siegle, 2011); therefore, they can master material with less instructional time and less practice. The rationale for enrichment stems from common conceptions of giftedness: (a) that the gifted have wide and intense interest in intellectual topics; (b) that the gifted possess a proclivity to make spontaneous connections across subjects and domains; and (c) that the gifted engage in higher order thinking skills and these skills can be honed through the enrichment process. We will return to this topic in depth in Chapter 6.

The term *enrichment* encompasses a wide variety of programming. However, generally, enrichment entails the coverage of topics not usually encountered in the usual curriculum, frequently through individualized or small-group instruction or independent study, and often involving open-ended projects leading to products or performances (Davis et al., 2011). Often, these projects allow the exercise of creativity in ways that are rarely available in the usual curriculum, with its prescribed learning goals and state-mandated assessments. For most students, enrichment activities are far more enjoyable than "business as usual" instruction. For these reasons, enrichment is a hallmark of many gifted education programs. However using enrichment as the core of a gifted education program is potentially problematic: Although gifted students are likely to benefit from an enriched curriculum, there is no evidence that *only* gifted children benefit from enriched curriculum. Most, if not all, children would prefer to be involved in enrichment activities instead of the endless drill and practice of basic skills that characterizes so much of contemporary American education. If enrichment is to have a place in a program of advanced academics (and we believe that it should!), the program should be designed such that not all children can thrive in it due to its challenging demands. We will address this point in detail in Chapters 3 and 6. The perception that gifted students are allowed to have fun and be creative, while other students must endure monotony, undermines support for gifted education.

One might suspect that a central reason for the dominance of enrichment as gifted education programming is simply because of its convenience to the school and district, which does not have to engage in the troublesome coordination of effort required for integrated and meaningful acceleration opportunities or for focusing more attention on the match between student need/readiness and the curriculum. Also, acceleration typically requires a larger commitment to "dosage"—the amount of time and energy devoted to the intervention by the school—than does enrichment; enrichment frequently is implemented with small dosages of one hour per week or less (i.e., in pull-out or coteaching program models). One of the authors of this book actually participated in an enrichment program that was comprised of two afterschool trivia competitions each semester in middle school and a single field trip each year in high school. In short, schools frequently default to enrichment because it is easy and convenient for them to implement; it often doesn't involve specialized training, students enjoy their time in the program, and parents are happy because the school has recognized their child's giftedness and is appearing to be responsive to their child's needs. There's also little chance of harm to the child. These programs are not deemed ineffective because often there is no stated purpose or goal for the program, and there are no formal assessments or evaluations of the program's efficacy. With so little risk also comes little potential for reward.

The State of Gifted Education

How should we characterize the state of gifted education today? Only one word is sufficient: Gifted education is in *crisis*. Many schools currently do nothing for gifted students. Of the schools that do provide services, many end that "service" at identification. Well-articulated programs of reasonable dosage are the exception, not the rule. The best evidence we have today regarding the overall effectiveness of gifted education programs was provided in a recent study performed by Adelson, McCoach, and Gavin (2012). Using the most rigorous statistical techniques and a very large, nationally representative dataset (the Early Childhood Longitudinal Study), the researchers compared children in gifted education programs and matched children who did not participate in gifted education. The result? There was no difference in students' academic performance in math or reading whether they were in gifted programs or not. Two potential takeaway messages form this research are that current gifted education programming is not influencing academic achievement and/or that programming is so inconsistent that some programs work while others do not.

Similarly Bui, Craig, and Imberman (2011) performed a rigorously designed study to estimate academic effects of gifted education. There were no differences for those students identified as gifted versus those who were very similar but were not identified in math or reading. There was an effect for science achievement, but there were no effects in other academic areas. Some proponents of gifted education argue that the effects of gifted education are not well measured by achievement tests. However, in the world of increasingly stringent standards and accountability, increased achievement at least must be considered. In the end, the status quo is not well-supported by current research.

What is gifted education without giftedness? Focusing on the delivery of advanced academics allows for the development of a model that is less fundamentally unfair, that responds to local needs with tailored and responsive programs, and is centered around what students *do* (behavior) rather than who they *are*. Gifted education without giftedness is called advanced academics.

Identification for What?

2

Perhaps no single step in the process of gifted and talented identification is more overlooked than answering the following question:

"For what program are we identifying students?"

Before any identification or assessment system can be devised, we must determine the purpose of the program and what it is that the identification seeks to find. The traditional model in gifted education has been to:
1. adopt a definition of giftedness,
2. identify the gifted, and
3. provide an educational intervention.

We describe a much different approach; an approach that is focused on *advanced academics*. In the advanced academic framework, we:
1. design or identify the program we want to offer,
2. think locally and in the present tense about student need,
3. identify those who have a need for and would succeed in the program, and
4. regularly review student progress.

An identification plan or policy cannot be developed in isolation from the programming or curriculum that will be provided to those students who are identified. We repeat this message throughout the book because we believe it is one of the most often misapplied parts of gifted or advanced academic programming: *It is impossible to design an identification system unless we know, specifically, for what type of program or service we are identifying students.* There is no point in having an identification system for which the corresponding academic need—that is, the content area(s) or domain(s) that programming would address—are ones that the school is not prepared to serve. This might seem obvious, but we have seen many districts spend their time and money to identify students but then provide little to no programming for the students they have spent such effort to identify. Being identified as gifted should not be a reward, but rather should be the outcome of a formal observation identifying a need that is not being met (see the definition discussion later in this chapter). Identification is a formalized system (see Chapter 3) that sets out to determine which students have needs that are not being met by the standard curriculum of a given school or district.

We (the authors) have been approached by frustrated teachers, parents, and administrators and asked what should be done to identify gifted students. Unfortunately, adding to the frustration of people looking for a simple answer, our most frequent answer is that "it depends." In essence, ethically defensible identification decisions cannot be made unless programming decisions already have been answered by local education leaders, administrators, and teachers, with (when applicable) appropriate attention to state-level education regulations. The programming a school wants to provide must be determined first. To make decisions about programming, stakeholders need to understand (a) current curriculum offerings of a local school or district, (b) current levels of student mastery or need, (c) what state regulations require when it comes to gifted and talented education, and (d) whether the planned advanced academics program needs to be in compliance with gifted education policies at all. Once these initial programming questions have been answered with sufficient detail, only then should attention turn to the process of selecting students for the program. This process, as outlined above, essentially operationalizes the term advanced academics in our model. Figure 2.1 represents this process in graphical form.

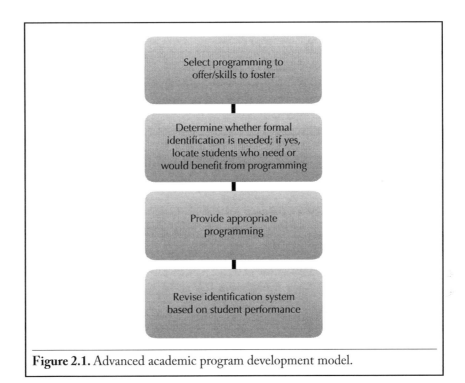

Figure 2.1. Advanced academic program development model.

Design the Program First

The traditional model for gifted education begins with identifying gifted students. Although this approach is understandable from the psychologist's point of view, the concept of *giftedness* lacks detailed diagnostic information about the specific areas of academic need possessed by the student and whether or not the student is an appropriate match to a given program. Telling a teacher that a child is gifted tells that teacher very little about what to do with that child.

Once freed from thinking that we must "find the gifted," we suddenly are able to adopt a different perspective. By beginning with program design, rather than the identification of students, we can begin to address many existing (and justified) critiques of gifted education. Specifically, an important critique of gifted education is that the identification cutoffs chosen are often arbitrary and are not connected with the available gifted education programming, assuming there is some. The advanced academics paradigm addresses that critique by ensuring that the identification or student selection process is designed to predict success *in the specific program*

being offered. Identification should be based on the principle of beneficence, both for students and for the program itself. Beneficence for students means protecting them from experiencing abject failure. Therefore,
we guide students away from programs where their probability of failure
is high. It also means that when the program cannot accommodate all
interested students, the admission decision is driven on the basis of pre-
dicted probability of success in the program (or in other words, by student
need for the program). Beneficence for programs means that identification
is sometimes required to protect the integrity of a program. This topic is
addressed in detail in Chapters 3 and 9.

Questions to consider when designing the program include:

- In what areas do we (the school community) want to devote additional resources? What areas do we want to foster?
- What will be the nature of the program? Is it primarily acceleration? Is it enrichment? Is it some combination of these, or something altogether different?
- What content area(s) will the program serve?
- What are the goals of the program? In other words, how will we
  (the school community) know if the program was successful?
- How much intensity ("dosage") will be required in order for the
  program to have a reasonable chance of meeting its goals?
- What administrative barriers may impede the success of the program? How will these be reduced, removed, or modified?
- What resources will be needed, in terms of time, space, materials, and personnel, for the program? What resources actually are
  available?
- Given that available resources will always be limited, is there a
  maximum number of students that can be accommodated by the
  program? How does the program's capacity compare to the number of students who may potentially benefit from the program?
- Will the program feature tiered classrooms or levels of service
  analogous to Response to Intervention tiers?
- What does successful completion of the program look like? How
  will progress be measured? How will/can nonthriving students be
  removed from programming once placed?

Answering these questions will be more difficult for some types of
programs than for others, but these questions must be answered clearly

for any contemplated intervention. For example, these questions generally will be easier to answer for acceleration programs than for enrichment programs. Given that enrichment is typically enjoyable and educational for most students, it may be reasonable to assume that interest in the program may greatly exceed the number of students that can be served, necessitating some type of identification process. But for this identification process to satisfy the principle of beneficence, it must *predict success in the program.* Otherwise it is arbitrary, exclusionary, and therefore unethical. Luckily, as we demonstrate in Chapter 3, a formalized identification system is not always required.

When deciding on the program goal(s), it is very important that these goals be specific and measurable. The widespread adoption of vertically equated growth scales for achievement tests may be fortuitous here. For example, if the program is math acceleration, one goal might be that "students in the program will show at least 1.5 years of growth in math per instructional year." This goal is specific and is measurable for all students. Further, the goal provides an organizing principle for the structure and curriculum of the program itself; if 1.5 years of growth are needed, the curriculum for the program must sample topics and learning objectives for the current grade—presuming this is where students are; recall (b) above, the need for knowledge of current levels of student mastery—as well as topics and learning objectives for half of the next grade, if not more. In other words, topics and objectives are not selected on the instructor's whim —there is a philosophy and a purpose behind what is being done.

The necessary dosage of a program may be quite difficult to estimate. In these cases, the "sports rule" should be used. The sports rule works like this—if you wanted to field a successful sports team, how much practice and game time would be required each week? One would be hard-pressed to find a football coach who only devotes one hour per week to practice, and yet such low dosage is the norm rather than the exception in gifted education. It is ironic that such low dosages are tolerated in educational programs, the raison d'être of schools, even though they would never be tolerated in school-sponsored competitive sports.

To continue with the math acceleration example, identifying and removing administrative barriers means ensuring that the program is integrated at the school and district policy levels, with adequate buy-in from relevant administrators and teachers, to ensure that students can continue their progression through the curriculum to its logical conclusion. If the acceleration program in mathematics is to begin in elementary school, it is likely that participating students will be ready to take Algebra 1 much earlier than it is typically offered. However, many school districts have formal or informal policies restricting Algebra I to students in eighth grade or higher. Unless a solution is found, students may either exhaust the math curriculum before they reach grade eligibility to take algebra, leaving them with years of no math at all, or worse, they might be forced to drop back into the regular math curriculum that they had mastered long ago.

Moreover, some states specifically forbid early entrance to kindergarten or early graduation (NAGC & CSDPG, 2011). Therefore, if the Algebra 1 barrier is removed, another barrier to consider is that students may exhaust the high school's complement of AP courses long before 12th grade. In this case, removing administrative barriers means providing opportunities for students to continue learning mathematics after completing AP Calculus. Possibilities here would include dual-enrollment college courses, online programs, independent studies, and mentorships. Additionally, if there is a large enough group of students and sufficient faculty expertise, the high school may wish to offer college-level mathematics classes itself.

Think Locally and in the Present Tense

When designing a program of advanced academics, the focus should be intensely local. What program serves the needs of the students in *this* school? What level of instruction would be required to challenge and engage the students in *this* classroom who are coasting through the standard curriculum? What types of educational programming are valued the most in *this* community? Decades of tradition and practice in gifted education have conditioned its advocates to think in terms of identifying the "gifted." According to this status quo, if a child is gifted, then he is gifted forever and everywhere. He remains gifted regardless of the classroom environment in which he is placed—even if that classroom is meeting his needs, his *giftedness itself* creates special needs that require curricular intervention. Because this system has been the dominant paradigm for so long, and the paradigm under which many of us were trained, it can be difficult to break out of this way of thinking. But breaking out is something that we must do in order to create advanced academic programs that make sense.

The advanced academic perspective, rather than considering the child's *absolute* level of ability, focuses deeply on the match between the child and her instructional environment. In this view, *it is not high ability itself that creates a need for intervention; rather, it is a mismatch between the child's ability and the pacing, depth, and content of the instruction provided that creates the need for intervention.* Because of this critical fact, we must take the current instructional environment into account when identifying students for programming. A child may require intervention in one school, class, grade, year, or subject, but not in another, depending on the degree of child-to-context compatibility. Perhaps one school has a class that meets a child's needs but in another school, her needs would only be met by an advanced academic program. Alternatively, perhaps Mrs. Johnson is very skilled at differentiating up to challenge a wide range of students whereas Mr. Alexander is not. As a result, more of Mr. Alexander's students might need advanced academic programming.

Identify Those Who Have a Need for and Can Succeed in the Program

The proper role of identification is to allocate opportunity for special programming in such a way as to optimally benefit students while protecting them from needless failure. Although identification issues traditionally have been the predominant concern in gifted education, in advanced academics the role of identification is far less prominent. In some cases, where the program capacity exceeds or is equal to the size of the population of interested students, and where consequences of failure are mild, formal identification may not be required at all (think of student self-selection into music, business, and career technical education in high school). In other cases, where the consequences of failure within the program (the potential risks) are substantial, effective identification becomes critical. That said, justifiable identification must *always be explicitly linked to the program itself* and to qualities and characteristics that predict success in the program. Indeed one of the failures of traditional gifted education programs is their attempt to identify for global giftedness (or g) but then program for domain-specific talent. We have seen many such programs.

We believe that identification carried out solely on the basis of general characteristics and arbitrary cutoffs is unethical and indefensible. As an illustration, consider the Supreme Court case of *Griggs v. Duke Power Co.* In that decision, the court ruled that when employers use tests to make employment or promotion decisions, those tests must be "reasonably related" to the job requirements. In other words, using the results of an IQ test to determine who may be promoted to a management position is only allowable if evidence shows that high-IQ individuals perform better in the position than low-IQ individuals do. Similarly, when assessments are adopted as part of an identification system for an advanced academic program, they should be "reasonably related" to the program in question. Therefore, they should predict success or failure in the program. When creating identification systems, educators should ask themselves what evidence exists that the system will locate students who have a need for a particular program and which students will be successful in that program.

Regularly Review Student Progress

The program, whatever it may be, should allow for the frequent review of student progress. When programs are designed with specific and measurable goals at the programmatic and student levels, this process becomes much easier. Indeed, a lack of sufficient evidence regarding the effectiveness and measurable outcomes of gifted programming is a tremendous barrier when it comes to advocacy. Students who repeatedly fail to make even minimal progress should be discontinued and allowed to transition back to the standard curriculum in the most graceful way possible. The program should be designed such that discontinued students experience a "soft landing"—resuming their participation in the usual curriculum in the least-disruptive manner.

Regular documentation of student progress also serves another important end; it provides evidence of the program's impact on student learning. In an era of budget cuts, programs that cannot justify their existence with evidence can expect to find themselves on the chopping block.

Guidelines for Program Design

This book will focus primarily on locating students who are most in need of and would benefit the most from advanced academic programming that is related to the content areas and skills most commonly addressed in American schools. Both of these considerations must be taken into account, because if students are identified who are in need, but then the district provides programming in which they will not be successful, there is a mismatch between program and service just as there was before the student was even identified. At the same time, if we place students in a program in which they will be successful, but that has not been targeted toward their specific needs, the program in unlikely to have any meaningful impact. We focus on the creation of advanced academic programs that correspond to the subjects usually taught in K–12 schools and do so with two acknowledgments. First, we recognize the importance of skills and talents that fall outside the purview of what is taught and addressed in school. Second, we fully recognize that the population of students currently labeled gifted often do have widespread unmet academic need that spans many subjects as well as potential or realized talents in domains that are not part of the usual curriculum (such as painting or computer programming). Although these students would also benefit from talent development in those noncurricular domains, we feel that the focus of teachers' efforts generally should be on meeting students' *academic* needs. Similarly, teachers are certainly on the front line in dealing with students' social, emotional, behavioral, and psychological issues every day within the classroom setting. However, intensive needs in the psychological, emotional, social, or behavioral realm are best addressed in conjunction with counselors and school psychologists, whether or not the student is gifted or academically advanced.

Furthering a Needs-Based, Developmental Perspective on Giftedness and Talent

Regardless of one's conceptual definition of giftedness, the term gifted provides little to no specific diagnostic information about a student's current academic needs. Just because two students are identified as gifted does not mean that these students have the exact same needs. Schools commonly label students as special education/not special education or gifted/nongifted. Although use of these labels is widespread and they help schools address state reporting requirements and receive dedicated funding for these groups of learners, these broad labels contain little diagnostic information. Although labeling special and gifted education students helps from an organizational perspective, doing so "can also reinforce the perverse human tendency to misrepresent a characteristic that varies continuously" (Lohman, 2006, p. 10). Put another way, when attaching labels to objects, individuals start to view those objects as falling into mutually exclusive, all-or-nothing categories, as opposed to viewing what we are labeling as a single point on a continuum.

Because the purpose of gifted and talented identification is to identify student needs and then address them with services, a categorical (all students are either gifted or not gifted) definition is not very helpful. As we have stated before, it doesn't tell us who needs more math (i.e., advanced academics) on Monday. The degree to which a student can develop excellence in any given domain or demonstrates a need for advanced academic programming in a domain is not dichotomous (i.e., yes or no). This categorical gifted/not gifted focus is likely one of the culprits that has led the field to focus so heavily on identification over assessment of students needing appropriate programming. Lohman (2006) put this point quite eloquently:

> We are not interested in identifying bright kids in order to congratulate them on their choice of parents or some other happenstance of nature or nurture. Rather, the goal is to identify those children who either currently display or who are likely to develop excellence in the sorts of things we teach in school. (p. 7)

The categorical label of gifted does not inform the educator, parent, or administrator about what it is that the student needs, or the programs in which he or she would be successful. To remedy this deficit, we suggest that the act of identifying a student should look more like a needs assessment—determining a student's specific needs so that he or she can be matched with appropriate programming. Sometimes a single identification tool can accomplish both tasks, while at other times additional information might be needed to better understand the nature of the student's need. For example, a student with a score of 189 on the Measures of Academic Progress (MAP) might be functioning far beyond what is currently being taught in his or her classroom (signifying a need not being met). Because of this, school professionals could compare the student's current level of performance (need) and place that student in a classroom where that need is better met. This may be done by comparing the student's current level of mastery with a curricular map of courses in his or her district (see Chapter 4). However, in other instances, the match is not as clear. A student who has a score of 155 on a standard IQ test is clearly very bright, but where or how to best meet that student's academic needs is less clear because IQ tests contain no information about curricular levels. Therefore, the MAP provides a link between identification and programming for advanced academics; the IQ test (by itself) does not.

The developmental perspective (Horowitz, Subotnik, & Matthews, 2009) focuses on how students' gifts and talents are mitigated or augmented by normal developmental stages and life events, and this focus implies that students' needs will change over time. A gifted label cannot be permanent and cannot be *unilateral*: Not all students who are labeled as gifted require the same things in order to receive an appropriate educational experience. Just as not all gifted students require the same services, a given individual (gifted or not) does not automatically need the same services year after year. Just because a student is identified or labeled as gifted or as in need of advanced academic programming and requires special services one year, does not mean he or she will automatically *need* services the next year. His or her needs can, and likely will, change as he or she develops physically and cognitively. These needs also depend on the current educational placement and how well that placement meets the student's current level of academic readiness.

Gifted education is similar to special education in that it is fundamentally concerned with students who fall outside traditional developmental stages and growth curves (hence the term exceptionality). In special education, these differences are addressed through Individualized Education Plans (IEPs), and a few states and schools have adopted this model with gifted education through Differentiated Education Plans (DEPs; NAGC & CSDPG, 2011). The philosophy behind such plans, and one of the reasons they are successful, is that they are programs individualized to meet students' needs.

Even in the absence of IEPs or DEPs, gifted services and programming must be based on students' needs. Therefore, it is completely conceivable that during some years a gifted student would need special services not provided in the general curriculum, while in other years he or she would not. As curriculum, instructional staff, and students change with the passage of time; educational labels and services should be flexible enough to change with them. Some years the standard grade-level curriculum will be enough for a given student, whereas other years advanced academic programming might be needed. For instance, if a kindergarten student is already reading fluently while the rest of the class is learning their letters, such a student likely would require special academic programming to meet his or her needs. However the need for specialized services might change in first grade. For example, if the school has a multiage grade 1/2 classroom or if the kindergarten teacher is able to teach many of her students to read chapter books in a single year, then the following year our original student might no longer need special/gifted services *because his or her needs now are being met in the general education setting.* We believe this goal is easier to accomplish under the guise of advanced academic programming than when using the gifted terminology because the term gifted tends to be perceived as a stable trait, rather than a sign of an immediate need. In the advanced academic perspective that we espouse, teachers, parents, and students should all expect programs and services to change from year to year as the needs of the students change. Parents often become very upset if they are told that their child was gifted one year but is no longer gifted the next year, but these parents may be more understanding of fluctuating academic need. The fluctuating need essentially represents a differing degree of mismatch between a student's ability and his or her regular classroom environment, which is as much a function of the context as of the student.

The Process: Philosophical Decisions

Background. With local curriculum in hand, the interested educator or committee can proceed to deciding what content areas and student skills are in need of special programming. In other words, what counts as part of advanced academics? This is no easy task, as it encompasses philosophical, cultural, and practical considerations. It is philosophical because local community members, teachers, parents, students, and all other stakeholders must decide what areas they value enough to foster through specific advanced programming. For example, the science, technology, engineering, and math (STEM) disciplines have gained national and international attention as high-need areas. The 2009 National Assessment of Educational Progress Science Report Card found that only 34% of fourth-grade and 21% of twelfth-grade students scored above proficient in science (National Center for Educational Statistics [NCES], 2011). Such statistics make a compelling case for subjects and content areas such as science being an emphasis area in an advanced academic program. Some might take this as a sign that no advanced program in STEM areas is needed—after all, very few students are above proficient. But the NCES level of advanced is unrelated to what is being taught in the general education classroom of a local school. Whether or not an advanced program in STEM is needed depends solely on whether or not there are students who could do more than they are currently being asked to do. Therefore, a district might choose to emphasize talents in the STEM areas with regard to their definition of what is included as advanced academic programming. In the same fashion, a rural district with a strong agricultural base might include 4-H or other natural resource-related curricula as worthy of special programming and services, despite this traditionally being a nonacademic curricular focus. Regardless of the rationale, a philosophical decision needs to be made as to which skill areas will be supported by advanced programming and services, which will be addressed through enrichment programming, which will be encouraged or fostered through outside organizations and mentors, and which are completely outside the purview of public education. Even in states with explicit conceptual definitions of giftedness, these local decisions guide the specific academic areas addressed by the program.

So far we have discussed two different terms: needs and values. Needs identify students' abilities and skills that are not currently being fostered by the standard education curriculum. Values identify the content areas, domains, or skills that the local school or district decides to devote resources toward developing in students. Renzulli (2005) argued that one of the purposes of gifted education is "to increase society's supply of persons who will help to solve the problems of contemporary civilization by becoming producers of knowledge and art rather than mere consumers of existing information" (p. 249). Viewed from this perspective, all content areas are valuable, but some are in greater demand or are of greater value, due to current issues and problems facing the world community, than others. Therefore, the local school community must decide what domains will be fostered through its advanced academic programming based on both local value and local need.

Sometimes needs and values overlap: Students who have a high need for advanced math and science content happen to reside in a district that provides advanced math and science programming. However, there are instances where a need exists in an area that the school does not address. For example, a student who is very skilled in woodworking may have exhausted all available courses on the topic; however, the school may not provide any advanced programming to further meet his or her needs. In this case, the district (with input from key stakeholders, we hope) has decided not to invest additional resources into woodworking. This discussion illustrates the two masters that advanced academic programming seeks to serve: Student need is the driving focus, but only within the context of skills and domains that the school has decided are part of its mission to develop. Again, this perspective stands in stark contrast to the philosophies underpinning some gifted and talented programs. Schools will never be able to address every need that every student has—it's just not possible. Therefore, a values-based decision needs to be made with regard to what areas will receive additional attention and which will be left to the assistance of resources outside the school setting.

What to do. The philosophical decision is twofold, with both components being equally important to consider. First, the decision about which programs and services are to be included in a definition and then served under a program for advanced academics should be based in part on the needs of students that are not being met within the existing curriculum. In some cases, this requires the school or district to conduct a needs assessment or gap analysis (see Chapter 3) of what programs are missing and/or what needs are not already being met. Such assessments are similar to formative assessments in that they help guide instruction and programming directly in response to students' needs. The second component is truly a philosophical value-based decision, wherein stakeholders must decide whether each area of needs and skills is to be fostered directly, indirectly, or not at all in the school setting. As mentioned above, the reason for this step is that not all needs can be addressed by schools. Student abilities always outnumber available services and resources. Programs should not exist solely because they deal with a content area that has not been mastered by students. For example, just because many students can't speak Chinese does not mean that Chinese language should be the focus of special programming—however, if local values include a strong connection to Chinese culture, then it may be an appropriate option for special programming because the philosophical decision of what programs, services, and content areas are to be served under the banner of advanced academics must take local values into account.

Of course, every public school also has standards and regulations under which it must operate. Because of this, stakeholders do not need to proceed blindly into this process. Instead, existing state content standards can serve as a guide for what content areas (at a minimum) should be included under an advanced academic program.

The Process: Cultural Decisions

Background. The second decision is a cultural one. Schools are increasingly diverse, as is society at large. In 2008, Briggs, Reis, and Sullivan conducted a review of promising practices for culturally, linguistically, and ethnically diverse gifted learners. Successful programming as identified by these authors took a wide perspective on talent that included skills valued by the populations served. Thus, certain cultural practices, skills, or behaviors might be included in a gifted program in one school that would be unheard of in another. Such culturally relevant pedagogy (see Castellano & Frazier, 2010) is important for the student-school connection as well as for high levels of minority student success in school as a whole. Therefore, an operating definition of what is included as advanced academics should not depend solely on what skills are important to the world or country as a whole, but should also consider skills valued by the local community and local culture.

In 2009, Yoon and Gentry reviewed the current status of ethnic and racial representation in the United States using various federal datasets. Their findings confirm what has been known since the mid-1970s: Students from African American, Native American, Latino/a, and low-income families are underrepresented in programs for gifted and talented students. Partially, this is due to limitations of student identification as traditionally practiced; however, it is also the case that many gifted and talented programs do not include a local perspective that consciously values the skill sets of the local community. Even if a group of stakeholders makes the philosophical decision that academics in the form of math and science should be the primary focus of a local advanced academic program, these same stakeholders need to also consider local, culturally specific content areas that might be valued by the populations being served by that particular school. This should not be taken to mean that nondominant cultural groups lack skills in traditional academic areas such as math and science. However, extra effort may be required for school staff to identify these or other skill areas in cultural groups that are different from their own. This will be discussed in depth in Chapter 7.

Gifted and talented programming and identification also need to be culturally responsive. For example, the Paradise Valley (Arizona) School District has a large Hispanic and ELL population. Because of this distinct cultural composition, in addition to International Baccalaureate programs at all levels, honors courses in traditional academic areas, and cluster grouping in the elementary grades, Paradise Valley provides a nonverbal core honors program at the middle school level. This program was created explicitly to foster the skills that were present and valued in a large portion of the district's population and to help those students further develop their skills in traditional academic areas. It did this by identifying students as they completed their sixth-grade year using one of two nonverbal aptitude tests. Identified students were then placed in project-based courses taught by teachers who were dual-licensed in bilingual and gifted education. The goal of this program was to prepare ELLs for the advanced academic curriculum of high school over the course of their seventh- and eighth-grade years. Thus, the program leveraged student strengths to enhance academic achievement. In other words, programs and services took cultural values and interests into account when creating a full-service educational program. Programming focused both on depth (below- and above-grade-level courses in traditional academic areas) as well as on breadth (a wider range of services and content areas beyond just academics). This second point is especially important for programs among culturally diverse districts, as having culturally relevant programming has been shown to increase student success, as it did for the Paradise Valley district. By incorporating these features into the program for advanced learners, this school district is better able to foster the skills of all students while at the same time increasing the representation rates of an often-overlooked group of students in advanced academic programming.

What to do. In 1999, Peterson published an article describing her conversations with cultural leaders regarding what they see as gifted or talented among members of their communities. Perspectives varied widely, especially among Native American and Hispanic groups who downplayed the idea of individual achievement but instead focused on the good of the group. Given such a range of what is valued within school communities, administrators and school boards need to consider (a) how they can include those values in the K–12 school setting as a whole (including in the advanced academic program), and (b) how school officials can work within the diverse cultural values and beliefs of their students in order to further develop traditional academic skills. The nonverbal honors core course described above offers a perfect example of this second consideration.

Two questions need to be asked in order to accomplish the cultural connection of diverse students to an advanced academic program. First, stakeholders need to find out how best to connect the cultures of the populations they serve with the overall goals of the K–12 school. This is critical for all aspects of education. Just as 4-H or other agricultural skills might be important to a local community because of their professions, so might a specific kind of art be important to a given cultural group. Schools should strive to incorporate such locally valued domains into both the general and the advanced academic curriculum. Second, if underrepresentation is occurring in an existing program, stakeholders need to investigate why. In the case of students categorized as ELL, often the problem is a language barrier. Once underrepresentation and its suspected causes have been established, the school can determine how best to mitigate this barrier. Such an example was presented above with mitigation by means of a specific nonverbal honors program. Other examples of targeted interventions for underrepresented students might include additional levels of service in order to provide scaffolding to students, modified identification procedures in order to better locate students who have skills but are not demonstrating them well (Chapter 4), feeder programs that accelerate students' learning and develop prerequisite skills, and even social-emotional support and counseling in order to help underachievers or students who have a variety of challenges in their lives that prevent them from focusing on advanced academics. The most important takeaway is that the problem of underrepresentation will not solve itself. It requires explicit action on the part of school officials.

The Steps: Practical Decisions

Background. The final decision is a practical one. Although many educators and parents would love to see all student skills and abilities fostered in school, not all can be addressed directly within the confines of the current educational structure. Although it's true that technology is allowing for a wider range of independent studies, mentorships, and enrichment courses, schools can't be responsible for everything. For financial, logistical, and simple space reasons, not all skills, regardless of their worth, can be developed within advanced academic programming. If specific content domains are not specified at state or federal levels, then local school personnel must decide which skills the district is able to address with additional programming. "Programs would do a better job of identifying talented children if they started with a clear understanding of the types of expertise that they seek to develop and the kinds of instruction that they can offer" (Lohman, 2006, pp. 46–47). School and community members need to ask themselves (while taking state and local laws and regulations into consideration), what skills and content areas fall under the purview of K–12 schools and which should be left to outside organizations? In addition, they also need to consider what kinds of programs and services they are in a position to offer.

Logistical and practical considerations will always be a factor; however, technology and creativity can expand advanced academic options, even in small or remote schools. For example, Stoughton High School in Wisconsin (see Palmer, 2009) addressed this issue by offering a wide range of different independent study courses and mentorships for credit, the majority of which took place outside of the school walls. Students, in collaboration with the high school gifted coordinator, were able to design a "course" that not only fit their interest area and skill set, but was also targeted toward meeting goals of the general school curriculum. Mentors or facilitators were then recruited (over the course of several years) from the local community to help guide students through content that was far beyond something a school could offer within its own walls.

What to do. Once a group of stakeholders has decided on a general conceptual idea of what to include in its programming for advanced academics (after taking into account relevant philosophical orientations and cultural factors), specific conversations need to take place with school administrators regarding what the school is able to support. Most times, this conversation also should involve the school board, as more money might be required for programming, teacher training, or extra staff, depending on the programming required. Additional assessment tools might also be needed in order most effectively to identify students' needs. Part of this decision also requires that stakeholders have a general idea of students' needs, as this is a major factor of consideration when making the practical decision of what services the school will be able to support.

The Process
of Identifying
Students in Need of
Advanced Academic
Programming

3

As outlined in Chapter 2, the purpose of student identification is to locate those students who have academic needs that are not being addressed as part of the general curriculum or who have talents that the school and local community have decided to foster. Thus, the purpose of student identification is to identify students *for* a specific program or intervention.

The first thing to consider is the *role* of identification. In the old *gifted education* paradigm, educators used psychoeducational assessments to identify members of a class of persons—the gifted. This notion was based on a conception of giftedness as a stable characteristic that people either possess or do not possess. However, giftedness is not a highly visible or unambiguous phenomenon. Educated, neutral laypeople (or even experienced teachers) might reasonably be expected to disagree regarding who is gifted and who is not. Therefore, formalized assessment, consisting of the administration of objective intelligence tests, achievement tests, or other related measures, was required in order to identify the gifted.

Instead of trying to identify giftedness as a stable trait, we instead assess students' need for a particular program as well as their probability of success in the program. *The overarching goal is to better match instruction and teaching with the student's current level of mastery and need.* Thus, the new *advanced academics* paradigm ignores the controversial question of who is or is not gifted, or even if such a thing as giftedness exists. Instead, academic needs form the cornerstone on which programs and services are built. Academic need, of course, is not a property of individuals, but rather emerges from an *interaction* between a student and a particular academic environment—a particular teacher, subject, curriculum, and peer group. As such, academic need is not expected to be a stable trait across contexts, schools, or teachers, but rather a (hopefully) temporary condition that arises when the instructional pacing, depth, and/or content are not sufficiently rigorous as to require full engagement and effort from the student. Academic need implies that the student is not being educated to his or her full potential. Unmet academic need carries a personal cost for the student—in the form of lost motivation, unrealized potential, boredom, etc.—as well as a societal cost in the form of lost opportunity and reduced productivity. The alleviation of academic need, therefore, requires an intervention in the form of an advanced, accelerated, or enriched instructional program.

The fundamental nature of the identification process in advanced academics is that it is *predictive.* The goal of the assessment is to predict success in a program rather than to attach a label to a student. Some students will perform well and others will not, so we would like to know in advance which students will do well in the program we seek to provide and which will struggle. In this way, we can provide the services or programs to those students who will experience the greatest benefit (i.e., those who have the greatest need), and protect students who are unlikely to be successful from the frustration and negative consequences of failure. After placing the student in the advanced academics intervention, we can observe how that student actually performs in the program, which provides us with valuable information about the likely success of future participants who share similar characteristics to those learners who have participated in the past.

An acknowledgement of this predictive nature of identification leads to four maxims of assessing students for advanced academic programs:

1. The value of the assessment process lies only in its ability to accurately predict performance in the program—to tell us who likely will and who likely will not be successful.
2. The best predictor of future performance is usually past performance.
3. A prediction is worth far less than an actual observation of performance.
4. Motivation is the great equalizer.

The third point may seem blatantly obvious, but it is violated so often in educational and vocational settings that it is sometimes called "predictor-criterion confusion." For example, many universities consider prospective students' SAT scores when making admissions decisions. The value of the SAT score is that it predicts which students will succeed or are a good match for the programs the university offers and which ones will fail (though in fact the predictive power for failure is consistently found to be weak to nil, but we digress). Imagine a university with a policy of only admitting students with a minimum SAT score of 1200. However, due to some administrative error, a student with a score of 900 is accidentally admitted. That student does reasonably well, passing all of his courses and earning all of the credits needed for graduation. On graduation day, the university realizes its error. The student didn't actually qualify to attend the university. Therefore, the university refuses to issue a diploma to that student, *even though the student was clearly able to do the work.*

The absurdity in this example is obvious. If the whole purpose of administering the SAT to prospective students is to increase the accuracy of predictions regarding success or failure, then surely *actual* success or failure should take precedence over a prediction. When the predictor (the SAT, in this case) is held in higher regard than the criterion that it is supposed to predict (undergraduate performance), the situation is bizarrely illogical. Therefore, the utility of assessments should be evaluated in this context: An assessment that helps us to make a better prediction about students' outcomes in the program is useful; one that adds nothing to our predictive ability is not, especially if that assessment cost a significant amount of time and money.

Some programs may not need a formal identification policy or system. The most common alternative to formalized identification is open enrollment or self-identification. For example, high-school-level arts or drama courses are not typically "identified" for, but rather students self-identify into these courses due to personal interest and motivation. The primary logic behind such a system is that students self-select if they have interest and believe they have the necessary prerequisite learning to be successful. A similar analogy could be drawn with sports programs. Only those students who want to play and who think they are good enough to play try out. If those self-perceptions turn out to be inaccurate, then the student doesn't make the team or withdraws after a short period of time. The benefit is that there are likely to be few false positives in such a system;

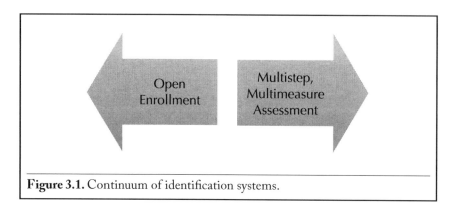

Figure 3.1. Continuum of identification systems.

students who self-enroll are likely to be highly motivated and to possess the qualities needed to succeed. This means there will be fewer students in such courses or programs who are not ready or who are uninterested in the content. The downside is that there will be a higher level of false negatives; some students who could benefit from such courses or programs do not enroll for reasons such as lack of knowledge regarding the availability of such courses or because they have not experienced the content enough to know whether or not they might be interested.

In general, identification systems can be placed on a continuum from open enrollment to complex multiple-criteria systems, as depicted in Figure 3.1. Contrary to popular belief, there are times where schools do need to serve as gatekeepers to some advanced academic programs. Where on the continuum a program's identification system should fall depends on factors we will discuss next.

Open enrollment under the umbrella of advanced academics has the benefit of the school being relatively uninvolved in who "gets identified" and who does not. Complex formalized assessment systems (such as the use of testing and associated cut scores) can be used in two ways: (a) to prevent unqualified students from entering programs, and (b) to encourage qualified but initially unwilling students to participate—that is, to let them know the program might be a good match for them. In most cases, however, formalized assessment systems are far more involved in keeping kids out than in helping kids get in, a process that can be traumatic to students and can provoke conflict with parents. When open enrollment is appropriate, the school is relieved of the burden of saying "no." Open enrollment also removes the ever-present downside to using standardized instruments in a formal identification policy: identification errors. Every assessment in education, be it an intelligence test, an achievement test, or a portfolio evaluation, contains measurement error to varying degrees. Measurement error causes imperfection and inconsistency in scores. A child earning a full-scale IQ score of 123 today might get a 118 next week and a 126 the week after that, even though her underlying intelligence did not change. Because in formalized assessment systems placement decisions are made on the basis of error-contaminated scores, these decisions have the potential to be imperfect. Some unqualified students will be admitted (false positives), and some qualified students will be left out (false negatives).

Whereas a major concern for traditionally formalized assessment procedures (i.e., using full-scale IQ scores for identification) is false negatives[1], false positives are a major concern for open-enrollment programs. In other words, some students could enroll even though the content of the course or program is far beyond their need or level of readiness. This sometimes happens in open-enrollment Advanced Placement (AP) courses when students enroll out of a desire to show potential colleges and universities that they have AP experience, even though the content is beyond their current level of need or readiness. This is not a problem if the rigor of the course is maintained. Such a case is similar to that of the sports team example from earlier—students for whom the level of content is not appropriate would drop out of the class in favor of a classroom having a more appropriate level of challenge. Unfortunately, what is more likely is that a concerned AP teacher would provide extra aid and assistance to struggling students, perhaps in the process ignoring the needs of students who can master this level of rigor and thereby negating the purpose of the AP course, which is to provide more challenging content to those who need it.

There is plenty of room between the extremes of open enrollment and multiple-measure identification systems for the use of other identification options to make sure that students are best matched with appropriate programming. For example, many standardized assessments exist in the areas of math, science, and reading comprehension. Because these assessments have a high accuracy in measuring students' current level of content mastery (see examples in the following chapters) and also are relatively accurate in predicting future performance in an area, then a formal identification system utilizing standardized tests can be useful. In other content areas or domains, the same cannot be said. For example, the ability to identify current levels of mastery or student need in the creative arts has proved to be far more challenging, labor intensive, and often far more subjective

---

1   False positives are also a concern under formalized assessments.

than identification of need in the traditional academic areas. In addition, for content areas not included in state or federal mandates, high-quality assessments are far less commonly used in schools or even available at all. As a general comment, educators should consider using all data they have available that might indicate which students have needs for a certain program or intervention. But this does not mean that, for example, reading tests should be used to identify students for programs in which reading achievement is not critical.

We will now proceed through each of the remaining steps as a way to highlight a process for gifted and talented identification. The steps are as follows:

1. Determining what is "advanced academics" in our setting, and deciding what skills or content areas we (a school) want to foster through differentiated educational services for students in need. What level of need do we believe cannot be met by the standard, grade-level curriculum?

2. Deciding what content areas/types of programming are in need of formalized identification, and which areas can be left open to access by all learners.

3. Selecting those measures that can best identify student need for advanced academic programming; what measures will we use for predicting student success in the program?

4. Determining what sources of data we can systematically collect that will enable us to make accurate predictions regarding student success in the program.

5. Evaluating how we might combine multiple measures in a statistically defensible way.

6. Deciding how often we need to reassess placement decisions. How do we assess the performance of the identification process itself?

Process

Because Step 1 should already have been decided earlier on, we will start with thinking through Step 2. Unless there are relatively severe consequences of failure if an inappropriate placement is made, it is our position that the identification system should be structured so that, when inaccurate placement decisions are made, they are biased toward the inclusion of less-qualified students rather than the exclusion of qualified students. In other words, err on the side of inclusion for most programs. However, the specific nature of the program and the consequences of failure in this setting may modify this general principle. As all assessment systems produce false positives and false negatives, the question becomes, "How are these consequences balanced?" The rationale for our general principle is that perhaps those students who were identified who were in fact false positives will experience the programming and will either decide it is not enjoyable due to the inappropriate match of level of readiness and program or experience failure in the program and be discontinued. However, these unqualified students might actually damage the integrity of the program if teachers reduce the challenge of the instruction[2] in order to accommodate the less-qualified students or if those students are harmful to a program's culture. School counselors and teachers can also help facilitate this process by discouraging enrollment for students who do not appear to be well-suited for the given program, although careful attention must be devoted to avoid inadvertently including systemic bias against specific groups of learners in this advising process. Of course, some students may wish to leave a program for which they are well-suited due to a desire to underachieve; teachers and counselors should encourage such students to persevere in the most advanced setting possible, with the understanding that no student should be forced into a program against his or her will.

Consider AP U.S. History as an example "program" a school has decided to offer for those students who are advanced in this content area and are ready for more challenge. Under the school's plan, students may self-enroll in the course (with parent permission); there is typically no barrier to registration. In some years, there is one section of the course and in other years, there are two, depending on student need and interest. In addition to self-identification, student grades in past history/social science and language arts courses are examined, along with aptitude assessment data and teacher ratings, to locate additional students who might benefit from taking AP U.S. History. This demonstrates the use of assessment data to find more students—an emphasis on inclusion. Students who want to self-enroll can do so, but the school will also take measures to make sure it does not miss those students who might benefit from the course (it would be a good match with their need) but for whatever reason do not enroll

---

2   We are not negating the value of differentiated instruction to accommodate the lower readiness of marginally qualified students via scaffolding; this in fact is vital, and we discuss it in more detail in the chapter on underrepresentation.

I High Need High Interest	**II** Low Need High Interest
III High Need Low Interest	**IV** Low Need Low Interest

Figure 3.2. Interest versus need.

(potential false negatives). When it is desirable to institute formal, multiple-criteria identification systems with maximum inclusivity, the "or" rule for making placement decisions may be appropriate (as we will describe in Chapter 9).

To help design a system to locate as many of the students in need of a particular program as possible, we suggest using a 2 x 2 table (or something similar), looking at interest in the topic (or motivation toward further learning of the topic, as measured by self-enrollment) and level of mastery/need in the content area (see Figure 3.2). This distinction is particularly important in an identification system where students have the ability to self-enroll. If some students will be identified as potential beneficiaries of the program based on their own self-assessment, then considerations must be made for those who (a) have the need, but not the interest and (b) have the interest, but not the need (whether true low need or level of mastery or measured low need or level of mastery). This is important because our stated goal is to locate all students who have a *need* for a given program. Once need has been established, the issue of interest can be addressed. Student interest is relatively simple to assess through the process of open enrollment. This is based on the idea that if students are interested in a given content area, they will elect to enroll in a program in this area. Of course, interest is not the only factor in a student decision, but it will catch a number of students.

An open-enrollment or self-identification policy will likely identify the students who are more "schoolhouse gifted" or whose abilities are in general more apparent. These are students who have likely been fairly successful in school before and who would enjoy additional challenge. Students identified under this system are most of those in Cell I, a majority of Cell

II, and probably only some of Cell III of Figure 3.2. Odds are that a few students from Cell IV would be identified under this system as well; we will address them in turn.

To make this an inclusive-focused identification system, the trick now is to locate those students in Cell I who have not already been identified/self-selected (and find out why); those students in Cell III (assuming their disinterest is not so severe as to refuse programming—something we'll address later); and also any additional students in Cell II who might want to challenge themselves despite not initially appearing to be ready for such content. To continue the example, Figure 3.3 presents hypothetical percentages of each group who *might* be identified via self-selection under this system. Each cell of Figure 3.3 includes whether or not students are high or low interest, high or low need, the total number of students who actually fall in that cell, the percentage of students who were identified via self-enrollment, and the total number of students identified.

We will pretend for a moment that the school in question has the capacity to offer two AP U.S. History classes that are able to accommodate roughly 60 students (provided there is enough need to offer two sections of the course). We will further pretend that the school has 260 students in the overall pool, and that students who do not enroll in the AP course are served in general U.S. History coursework that is offered during the same periods as the AP course. Based on the hypothetical self-identification percentages presented in Figure 3.3, 47 students would self-identify for this particular advanced academic program. However, some students in need were missed (e.g., we want to identify everyone in Cell I, but we didn't), and some students who did not have a need were identified (e.g., all of Cell IV and Cell II—false positives). A formalized, inclusion-focused assessment system can help to encourage the enrollment of needful students who fail to self-enroll and can discourage the enrollment of students who are unprepared and therefore likely to fail.

Before we discuss the addition of a formalized identification component, we should consider what might happen if we stopped where we are—thereby relying solely on self-identification. There are two technical issues (one real and one potential) with this practice. First, relying completely on self-identification would not be in alignment with the NAGC Pre-K–Grade 12 Programming Standards (NAGC, 2010a; see Appendix A). Ideally, *all* students should comprise the initial pool, not just those who happen to self-identify. It might seem like self-selection accomplishes this,

I	II
I	**II**
High Need	Low Need
High Interest	High Interest
80% of 30 students	70% of 10 students
24 identified	7 identified
III	**IV**
High Need	Low Need
Low Interest	Low Interest
30% of 20 students	5% of 200 students
6 identified	10 identified

Figure 3.3. Hypothetical student identification numbers by interest and need.

but in practice the group that self-identifies is likely to miss a number of students. The second (potential) issue is that many states require some kind of formal assessment system with regard to identification. Because of this, it is unlikely that self-identification alone would pass muster. Relying on self-identification will only locate those students who are *likely* to self-identify. This may seem like a silly point, but think about which students (and their parents and peer groups) are likely to self-identify—those from dominant cultural groups, those who are more proactive/aggressive, those who come from more educated families, and those for whom advanced programming is more socially encouraged. This is why self-selection can often serve as a great initial screener or start to an identification system (it can help catch some of the low-hanging fruit), but it is unlikely to be sufficient on its own; it fails to include some specific categories of learners.

The percentages in Figure 3.3 describe how many of the students in each cell might self-identify/self-enroll in our hypothetical program, assuming good awareness via advertising of the program's availability. Once these students have self-identified, a more traditional/formalized system should be implemented to (a) locate those students who are in need of the service but who did not self-identify (false negatives), and (b) to locate those students who did self-identify who actually might not be in need of the service (false positives). The simple starting point is that we would like any formal identification system to find the remaining 20% of Cell I (we are assuming that the program would be appropriate for all students of high ability and high interest). These students might have been missed simply because they were transfer students, because their parents never turned in the self-registration papers, or for various other unrelated or logistical reasons. It's important to note that many of these students can be found by simple diligence on the part of the teachers and school administration. Perhaps another 10% could be found by doing no more than extra advertising in school newsletters regarding paperwork being due. Therefore, perhaps the best initial method for ensuring the identification of high-need, high-interest students is to thoroughly advertise the program, making sure that all students know about the opportunity and understand what they need to do in order to sign up.

Cell IV represents those students who do not have a need for the program the school is offering. They do not have the requisite knowledge to benefit from the program and it is not an interest area for these students. Although the four cells appear equal in size, this cell would include the largest number of students (200 in our case—keep in mind that "low need" simply means their needs are being met by the standard curriculum in this area). It's hard to say exactly how many or what proportion of students would fall in this cell, because this would depend completely on what proportion of students in a given content area were not having their needs met by the general education curriculum. Perhaps the self-enrolled students from this condition did not actually understand what they were doing when they signed up, or perhaps they were pressured into enrolling by well-meaning parents or teachers. The optimal course of action for these students will vary depending on both the consequences of failure in the program for them as individuals and the consequences for the program (i.e., the robustness of the instructional culture and climate within the program). If the consequences of failure are mild, such that students who are unable to perform can simply be moved back into their regular instruction without undue disturbance, then perhaps the school should make no effort to remove these students, but if failure in the program carries significant consequences, then these students should be removed before the failure point if at all possible. Similarly, if the program is "fragile," such that the culture of achievement and the fast-paced instruction in the program is not robust and will quickly be undermined by struggling, disruptive, or uninterested students, then these students should be removed before this happens. However, we must acknowledge that some students will blossom unexpectedly when challenged—perhaps some of these students will succeed if given the chance. This is due to the motivation point mentioned earlier in our model. Once a formalized identification system is implemented, a program coordinator or instructor may want to speak with these students (10 in this example) to see why they enrolled and if they understand the level of rigor. These students may or may not be counseled out depending on the previously described factors. Most likely, many low-need, low-interest students will either chose to leave or will leave the program because it doesn't match with their needs, while some others will remain and be successful.

Cells II and III are more complicated than the others. This is because, despite having an ability to do something or a need for more content in a given area, some students are not interested (Cell III). Their interests might lie elsewhere, or they may prefer to continue in a program other than the one we are providing. Students from Cell III are typically the most frustrating for parents and teachers alike. This is the perfect place for formalized (by which we mean systematic, school-initiated) identification. Even something as simple as systematic examination of state achievement test scores in the content area could help locate some of these students. The formalized component of the identification system reveals these students as having high need or mastery, and yet they might not self-identify, or they might decline to participate in programming even when approached with the test data. Delisle (1992) has termed these students "selective consumers" because they are actively choosing not to participate in a program for which they have the ability, or in other words they are underachieving in a given content area. This is not an easy situation. What can be said is that students should never be placed in a program just because they have the ability or show a need. In some sense, "ability" and "need" are the same thing—they indicate a student who is not being properly challenged by the current curriculum and could benefit from more. For a variety of reasons, a parent might not want a student in the program, and forcing a student to enroll in a program against his or her wishes could actually do more harm than good, by decreasing motivation for future learning and also perhaps by encouraging the student to exhibit disruptive or nonparticipatory behavior in the program. Students in Cell III should be made aware that the program exists and that it is their choice (and their parents' choice) whether or not to enroll. The decision of how to proceed is an individual one that must be made thoughtfully. In this example, we have assumed that a formal identification system, in which these students are contacted based on their assessment data and encouraged to pursue the program, would "catch" some of these students (an additional 8 of 20), but that a few (4 of 20) still would decline to participate in the advanced programming.

The students in Cell II are in some ways more exciting than those in Cell I. These students are not especially outstanding in their ability or even high in their need, but they want the challenge and have an interest in the content. These are the students for whom a self-identification program really helps. A traditional assessment-based identification system would correctly show that these students do not stand out. That's because the assessments focus on content knowledge and ability—qualities these students don't currently possess at the superior levels that would place them in Cell I. However, they have interest and motivation—and motivation is the great equalizer. These are students who should be enrolled (whether formally or informally identified) in order to proceed with a trial placement into the program. After a trial period in the program, some will decide that despite their interest they are not ready, and they subsequently will move to a different level of instruction (and that's fine!). Others will rise to the challenge and make a metaphoric move into Cell I—the trial period allowed them the chance to demonstrate they really do have a high need and sufficient ability. Without providing these learners with the opportunity to try, educators have no way of knowing which of the Cell II students could become Cell I students. This is the most compelling rationale for including open-identification policies, and is also why the idea of a trial period in a particular program can be especially useful with potentially underachieving students.

One of the main purposes for gifted education programming is so that students can pursue an area in which they have a passion or an interest. The implicit rationale for this is that educators want to avoid stifling students' interests or holding them back in any way—the role of an identification system in serving as a gatekeeper to programs should happen *only if there is a high degree of risk, either to students or to a "fragile" program, associated with inappropriate placement.* Allowing for trial participation in advanced programming gives the message to students that the school wants them to challenge themselves and that such behavior should be encouraged. Table 3.1 presents the overall performance of our hypothetical system, from what source each student would be identified, and the total enrollment at the start of the program. It's important to note here that the "true" sample size in each cell would never be known. Here we include "true n" as an illustrative example only.

TABLE 3.1

Performance of Example System

Group	True *n*	Self-Identified	System Identified	Counseled Out	Errors
Cell I	30	24	3	0	3 FN
[1]Cell II	10	7	0	5	N/A
Cell III	20	6	8	0	6 FN
Cell IV	200	10	0	5	5 FP
Total ID		47	11	10	

Note. Total population size is 260; Total enrolled = 48, FN = false negative, FP = false positive.
[1]Some of these students subsequently would leave the program due to level of challenge

The combination of open-enrollment and a formalized identification system as just described leans more toward the inclusive and open side of the identification continuum. Part of this is due to the low level of risk associated with an inappropriate placement in an AP U.S. History class—something we again will address later on. Such an approach should work for diverse settings, with only the structure and restrictive nature of the formalized component changing.

Other programming options might be so advanced that allowing unprepared students to self-enroll would carry great potential for negative consequences (i.e., radical acceleration). Because of this, a more restrictive system might be necessary, one that does not allow as many Cell II and IV students to enroll. Perhaps even Cell III students should be admitted with caution due to the workload and difficulty of a particular program. This concept of potential risk and how to weigh it will be discussed later on in this chapter.

Choosing Data Sources to Assess Student Need

So far we have ignored the data sources that yielded the groups presented in Figure 3.3. Of course, the quality and appropriateness of these data sources are critical, as is the closeness of the match between the data and the program to be offered. In traditional academic areas of study, most schools have a wealth of achievement test data. This wealth of information (made available by federal mandates such as No Child Left Behind) means that nearly every school already has some (albeit limited) information with which to evaluate student need and/or mastery of grade-level content. At the same time, many of these state-level achievement tests do a poor job of assessing current levels of student mastery for those students who score far from the grade-level average. The Illinois Standards Achievement Test (ISAT; Illinois State Board of Education, 2009) is one such test, used by schools in Illinois to assess content mastery in reading, math, science, and social studies. To illustrate the drawbacks of using such assessments to assess above- or below-level students, we turn to an example of how we might determine academic need in math from fourth-grade ISAT math scores. "Grade-level" or "meets standards" scores for a fourth-grade student in math range from 200–246 on this particular test. It is in this range of scores that the test's conditional standard error of measurement, which simply quantifies the amount of measurement error, is the smallest; this shows that the measurement of math achievement is most precise for students scoring at grade level. For the ISAT, as for most tests, the further a score lies from "grade-level" or "average" performance, the less precise that score is, because the conditional standard error of measurement gets larger as scores get farther from this average range. This is because there just aren't many items written at the eighth-grade level for a fourth-grade test. Because of this, a fourth-grade level achievement test is not very accurate at measuring above- or below-grade-level skills.

A hypothetical student who scores in the middle of the "proficient" category for math in grade 4 received a score of 223; recall that the proficient category includes scores of 200–246. Taking into account the published standard error of 7 points, which represents the uncertainty of the student's true math ability due to the measurement error of the test at this score level, the student's actual score/achievement level is somewhere between 216 and 230 (the observed score of 223 +/- the 7 point standard error of measurement)[3]. This is the range in which the test is the *most* accurate. Again, for most tests, the standard error of measurement increases as observed scores move farther from the grade level for which the test was designed. Students in the "exceeds standards" category for the Math ISAT in 2010 had scores ranging from 247–355, with standard errors of measurement ranging from 8 for those students scoring a 247, to 48 points

---

3   And only 68% of students with a score of 233 would be expected to have true scores in this range. 95% of true scores can be found in a range of approximately ±2 times the standard error of measurement, here a range of 209 to 237.

for students scoring a 355. The measurement error for scores of the high-est performing students is almost five times that of grade-level/average students—for students in this range, the scores are five times less accurate when it comes to measuring what a particular students knows and can do. For a student scoring in the advanced range with a score of 288, the standard error is 15 points. This makes her actual math achievement likely to fall in a range of 273 to 303. Most state-level achievement tests are designed with the primary purpose of telling stakeholders whether a given student is achieving at or below grade level, so they are designed to yield maximum precision near the cut points that separate the below-, at-, and exceeds-grade-level categories. Unfortunately this reduces the usefulness of the test for making nuanced instructional decisions for students who are not at grade level.

Because of measurement error, a student could have earned a score of 300, but that student's true achievement could be quite different from this measured score. This becomes an issue when a coordinator goes to compare a student's score (a measure of need) to the current classroom content. If the coordinator sees that the current classroom can handle a student at score level of 300, then no change will be made. However, because of the imperfection in the test, that student's true score could be much higher (say 315)—a level at which the current classroom is not appropriate. This is a perfect example of why (as we stated earlier) all relevant data should be considered, while keeping in mind the limitations of each assessment. If higher levels of accuracy are needed in order to determine which students are most in need or are ready for an advanced program that a school wants to offer, out-of-level testing could be used, additional grade-level assess-ments could be administered, or the student could be placed in the pro-gram on a trial basis to see if she has the skills necessary to be successful. An easy way to get a more accurate measurement of student achievement is to use out-of-level testing, in which tests designed for older students are administered. In that case, the scores for high-achieving, above-grade-level students will lie closer to the average level of performance that the test was designed to measure. Research in the talent search programs has shown that this approach is psychometrically sound.

Standardized, state-level achievement tests are far less accurate for students scoring at the extremes (high or low). This does not mean such assessment tools have no use in evaluating student need (identifica-tion). Instead what should happen is a gifted coordinator, administrator, or classroom teacher should compare the score levels of students scoring above grade level to the content that is *currently being covered in the standard, grade-level classroom*. Most state achievement tests provide information regarding what a certain score actually means in terms of what students can do (diagnostic information). In other words, this diagnostic information tells you whether or not students with a score of 310 on the fourth-grade reading test can handle synthesizing multiple sources from different perspectives, or if that score indicates only the lower level skills of an understanding level of mastery. Such diagnostic information is often connected to state-level or Common Core State Standards that can then be used to determine whether there is a good match between student mastery and what that same student is being taught in the standard education classroom (i.e., what is offered in the typical, grade-level classroom of a particular school). If this information reveals that a student currently is able to complete multistep multiplication problems, yet his or her classroom will only teach this student addition and subtraction, a change such as a placement in an advanced academic program needs to be made. In this fashion, state-level achievement tests can be very useful—they can tell educators who is currently working above level. How far a given student is working above level is harder to evaluate in part because of measurement error, and in part because of restrictions in the test's content.

Empirical Example

An example highlights how a system like the one we described above might work in a real school. In this example, we will only consider the formal identification part of the overall system (skipping over the self-identification component). For this example, we use data from a previous study (Peters & Gentry, 2012) involving a highly diverse K–8 school in a large urban area. In this case, we use state achievement test data (on the same test described above). This measure is used as an example depicting the use of one specific measure of student need, not necessarily as best practice. Each district should decide what measures best assess need or program readiness, and then use assessments accordingly—never relying on a single measure. Chapter 9 will address how to use multiple measures appropriately. In the example that follows, we also begin to draw connections between advanced academics and the Response to Intervention model.

In this example, we will focus on fourth-grade students in the content area of reading. In addition, for the sake of simplicity, we will use a single score in the identification system. However, this process would be the same if multiple measures were used (see the "mean" combination rule), as we will discuss in a later chapter with a more complex example. For this particular achievement test (2009 test year), scores between 203 and 236 were interpreted as meeting grade-level expectations. It is important to note that meeting or exceeding grade-level standards should not automatically be used to determine who would benefit from a particular program or who has a need that is not being met. It is possible (though unlikely) that a fourth-grade student receiving a math score of 279 (a score that exceeds standards for eighth graders) could still be having his or her needs met already by a wonderful classroom teacher, hence negating the need for any additional programming. For this reason, *local* curriculum, as opposed to state-level measures of grade-level mastery, as well as the range of current student performance and readiness that a given classroom teacher can adequately differentiate for, need to be taken into account before deciding what cut score or percentile should be used for identification purposes. How these factors play into this decision is discussed further in the chapter on Total School Cluster Grouping (Chapter 4).

For this example, we will assume that a fourth-grade classroom teacher can differentiate up one entire grade level as well as down an entire grade level. This means he or she can adequately challenge students who are as low as basic third-grade reading performance and as high as ending fifth-grade reading performance. Students in this range can have their current reading-related needs met in the regular classroom (RtI Tier 1). On the upper end, scores of 247 or higher equate to "exceeds expectations" for a fifth-grade student. Because her score establishes that this student is not having her needs met or, more appropriately, that other programs or classes would better meet her needs, we now need to decide what to do. A quick look at the current level of performance of the students in the fifth-grade classroom next door would reveal if that class (in its reading instruction) would be a better match. If so (and if logistics permit), the solution seems akin to subject-level grade acceleration (see discussion of this topic in Chapter 5). Let us now take a look at the actual data of Thompson Academy (a pseudonym; Peters & Gentry, 2012).

The average score of fourth-grade students (n = 93) at Thompson is 223 with a range of 148–313. This translates to students in the fourth-grade classes who are below grade level even for third-grade students (far below the third-grade level), all the way to those scoring above grade level for eighth-grade students. As a side note, it's worth mentioning that this particular achievement test would tell us nothing about the students at the lowest or highest ends due to the measure's low test ceilings and high test floors. The standard deviation for this class of students is approximately 30 points. Based on our analysis of the curriculum and our assumption of the range for which teachers can differentiate, students who are nearly two grade levels advanced (i.e., whose scores exceed expectations for fifth-grade students) are those who are not having their needs met. *In this context, they are the students who need more because the standard curriculum of the school cannot meet their advanced needs.* This translates to a score of approximately 247 (see Figure 3.4). We say approximately because the standard error of measurement for these data is just over 3 points, necessitating some flexibility. This leaves us with 19 students scoring above 247, or roughly 20% of the class. This might seem high compared to traditional percentage-based definitions of giftedness (such as the top 5%). Such a policy would only identify those fourth-grade students who are scoring at "exceeds expectations" levels for eighth graders (272+). If such a definition were to be used, many students who are not having their reading-related academic needs met would still be underserved—those scoring between 247 and 272. This is why a local, needs-based position must be taken with regard to identification. It's also worth noting that most RtI systems suggest that roughly 80% of students can be served in the regular classroom (meaning that 10% on each end might need additional services), although this will vary greatly depending on the diversity of ability for the given school (Rollins, Mursky, Shah-Coltrane, & Johnsen, 2009).

One of the key issues with advanced academic programming is that many schools simply do not have enough students to warrant a stand-alone classroom or program. However, Thompson Academy had three fourth-grade classrooms in 2009 serving 93 students (roughly 31 per classroom). This arrangement would be perfect for a program such as Total School Cluster Grouping (Gentry & Mann, 2009; see Chapter 4), where the range of student ability in each classroom is narrowed in order to permit easier differentiation by the instructor. If instead of the full range of student ability (in this case, scores from 148–313), each teacher only has half of that (or even two-thirds), differentiation and targeted instruction becomes much easier to accomplish.

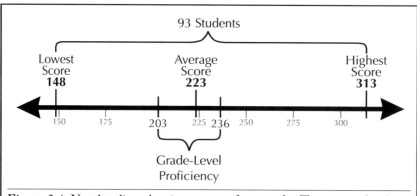

Figure 3.4. Number line showing range of scores for Thompson Academy fourth graders.

Further, not all of these students will have the same needs. For example, four students in the Thompson fourth-grade class scored above the "exceeds expectations" level for eighth grade (as high as this test goes!). It's possible that these students would have needs that were far above the rest of their "identified" peers and would require more substantial interventions such as multiple-grade acceleration in the area of reading (a Tier III RtI intervention). Even in a pull-out gifted program or using subject-based acceleration focused on reading designed for fourth graders reading at the sixth-grade level, these four students are unlikely to have their needs met. Multiple levels of services will be required in order to meet the needs of all learners.

The numbers and percentages involved with the identification system at Thompson happen to align closely with the RtI tiers of service. As mentioned earlier, approximately 20% of students were more than a full grade level advanced (fourth graders exceeding standards for fifth grade), and some of these were so advanced that they were exceeding standards for eighth grade. Figure 3.5 presents the RtI framework graphically.

Exactly what the Tier II and III interventions will look like for the students in need of remediation or additional challenge will depend on their measured need or level of readiness. For example, in Thompson Academy, four fourth-grade students scored at the "exceeds expectations" level for the average eighth grader. What this means is that the Tier II intervention (perhaps high-achieving cluster grouping or partial-grade acceleration), designed mostly for students working on fifth- to seventh-grade material as defined by Common Core State Standards, will work for many

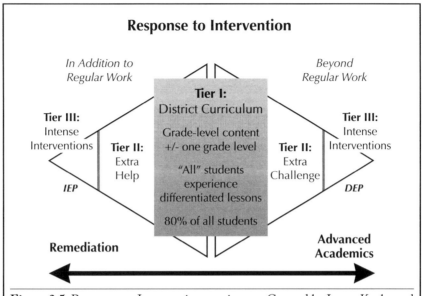

Figure 3.5. Response to Intervention continuum. Created by James Kueht and Ruth Robinson and used with their permission.

of the students who need more challenge, but will be insufficient for the four most advanced students. The four most advanced students (Tier III) are those who might benefit the most from more extreme interventions such as partial-grade or even full-grade acceleration (depending on their performance in other areas, as well as other considerations we detail in the chapter on acceleration). These learners likely would also benefit from mentorships, competitions, online replacement coursework, and independent study programs related to reading.

It should be clear by now that we are advocating for a system of advanced academics (and education in general) in which *the connection between student need and education is critical.* Rather than assuming a student needs a particular curriculum based solely on that student's age, we believe schools should make use of their data to make targeted educational decisions both within the classroom and for the school as a whole.

Returning to Instrument and Data Selection

Of course, state-level achievement tests have well-known limitations. In addition to the low ceiling effects and diagnostic efficacy mentioned earlier, such tests are only given a few times over the course of a student's K–12 career, often only annually even in the primary content areas of math and reading. Worse, the results from such tests do not often come back to the schools and teachers until several months after the tests were given. What this means is that by the time teachers or gifted coordinators have the data, most of it is stale and may no longer be indicative of current student need. Of course, a fourth-grade student who receives scores indicating mastery of eighth-grade level content is not going to regress back to fourth-grade level mastery in the span of a few months. The larger concern is obtaining a current understanding of student need and mastery. If the test was given 6 months ago, who knows what the student has learned or forgotten since?

Most state-level achievement tests do not represent the "state of the art" in the achievement test category (although some are very good). If a school has determined that an achievement test will yield good information regarding student need, then the question becomes, "How does the school decide which test instrument is best?" There are a few sources we want to reference that might help the confused or overwhelmed gifted coordinator to make good decisions regarding instrument selection. The first resource that every teacher should read is the *Code of Fair Testing Practices in Education* (Joint Committee on Testing Practices [JCT], 2004; see Appendix B). This document, while short and easy to read, provides an overview of everything a teacher, coordinator, or administrator should consider when selecting or using a standardized testing instrument. Of particular importance are special sections devoted to test users. An additional resource is Rudner's (1999) "Questions to Ask When Evaluating Tests" free online resource. This guide uses the Standards for Educational and Psychological Testing (American Educational Research Association [AERA], American Psychological Association [APA], & National Council on Measurement in Education [NCME], 1999) as a framework and walks stakeholders through the essential questions to ask and consider when selecting a testing instrument. Finally, perhaps the most detailed source of information about individual tests is the Buros *Mental Measurement Yearbook* (MMY; see http://buros.unl.edu). This resource is not free (unless your school or university has access through an online database), but it provides a searchable encyclopedia of test reviews. Nearly every major test has been evaluated and reviewed in the MMY by assessment experts with regard to test development, coverage, reliability, validity, scoring, and bias. For those who feel overwhelmed when trying to read test manuals, this is the resource for you.

Across all of this information, what makes a "good" achievement test is still fairly consistent. Some of the most important characteristics are as follows:

1. The test yields reliable and valid data concerning what you want to know.
2. The test provides timely scores concerning student performance.
3. The test requires as little interruption of instruction as possible.
4. The test has been shown to be appropriate for the group being assessed.
5. The test provides the necessary level of diagnostic and scoring information to be used for placement and instructional decisions.

The first point needs to be subjectively evaluated using the resources presented earlier. What constitutes "reliable" and "valid" data is not a simple thing to establish. However, this is exactly where the MMY reviews can come in handy. The second point is perhaps the most simple. In the world of today, technology should not require that teachers or schools wait 9 months to get test scores back. With computerized assessments, some results are reported instantly to the student and are then available in an online report to the classroom teacher. Such is the case with the Measures of Academic Progress (NWEA MAP®) and the Smarter Balanced Assessment System.

The benefits of computerized testing, such as the NWEA MAP and the new Smarter Balanced Assessment system, are numerous. Such tests are shorter in overall time required than paper-and-pencil tests because they are adaptive—the computer uses a student's response to one question in order to decide how difficult the next question should be. This not only makes these tests shorter (because students are prompted only with questions close to their performance level), but is also makes them more accurate (reliable and valid) with regard to the skills being covered. Accuracy is key when it comes to assessing student need. As mentioned earlier with regard to the ISAT, massive standard errors mean that educators can't tell exactly what students know once they are above grade level. With computer-adaptive tests such as the MAP, *standard errors are low and are very similar across the entire range of student scores.* This yields a far more detailed picture of what students actually know and are able to do. This final piece is the most important when it comes to student "identification" for advanced academic programming. If we cannot be confident that we know what students are currently able to do, due to limitations of our test, then we likewise cannot be confident in knowing what students should learn next.

Beyond tests of academic achievement, aptitude and ability tests are traditionally the most common in gifted education identification. Assessments of aptitude range from individually administered intelligence tests all the way to group-administered nonverbal ability tests. This huge range makes this category especially unwieldy. However, the criteria for a "good" aptitude test are the same as for an achievement test. What should be of primary concern when selecting any test is the degree to which the instrument measures current level of student mastery and also predicts need or readiness for a particular academic program.

Addressing Risk

So far we have considered program identification using only the variables of need and personal interest. We have also done so while placing the emphasis on inclusion rather than exclusion. However, as we mentioned earlier in this chapter in reference to Figure 3.1, deciding where on the continuum from open-enrollment to significant, substantial identification system a particular program should fall is a decision that also should be based on a third variable: risk. As used here, risk is an inherently subjective concept that refers to the potential negative outcomes or side effects that might result due to an incorrect student placement in an advanced-academic program. Considering risk, a coordinator might ask him- or herself these two questions: (a) "What might happen if this student is placed in the program by accident (meaning he or she doesn't really need it)?" and (b) "What might happen if this student is not placed in the program even though he or she really does need it?" To illustrate this concept, we will consider two examples. Weighing these two types of risk against one another allows the determination of what we call "relative risk."

The first example involves a standard pull-out enrichment program (see Chapter 6). This program is to take place for 45 minutes once a week for identified gifted or advanced academic fourth graders. Regardless of a student's level of need or readiness, the risk of an inappropriate placement is low. Missing out on the program for a student in need of more challenge is not likely to cause any serious harm beyond the lack of challenge that student is already experiencing during the majority of the school week. At the same time, participating in enrichment is likely to be good for all students, even those who might not be in need of additional challenge, with the real risk being limited to the few minutes each week that participating students miss out on needed grade-level instructional time. For these reasons, we can conclude that such an enrichment program would have low risk relative to many other programs, and therefore the coordinator does not have to be especially concerned regarding the possibility of an incorrect placement. The appropriate action would be to err on the side of inclusion, as we detailed earlier. Such a program could rely almost exclusively on open-enrollment identification or could use formalized identification systems solely as a means of inclusion.

The second example is more akin to a Tier III intervention: early entrance to kindergarten or college—both of which are forms of whole-grade acceleration (see Chapter 5). Acceleration is one of the most well-established, effective programs for gifted students (Steenbergen-Hu & Moon, 2011). However, the key caveat is that it must be implemented with care and only for those students who truly are in need of it. The very few negative outcomes related to acceleration have occurred only when students were accelerated before they were ready or without due diligence on the part of parents and school officials (Colangelo et al., 2004).

Again, we turn to the same two questions: (a) "What might happen if a student is accelerated by accident (meaning he or she doesn't really need it or isn't ready for it)?" and (b) "What might happen if a student is not accelerated even though he or she really does need it?" The risk for the first question is quite high. If a student is moved from finishing 10th grade (for example) straight to college as a 16-year-old, potential negative outcomes could result unless that student was 100% ready for the challenge. There is considerable risk. The same could be said for a 4-year-old starting kindergarten. As mentioned earlier, acceleration decisions made without due diligence to establishing readiness can result in negative outcomes such as unhappiness or intentionally low performance. We discuss readiness for whole-grade acceleration in detail in a later chapter.

The risk of not accelerating a student who is truly in need could also be quite substantial, although it is generally not as high as the risk of accelerating a student who is not ready. Imagine a student who has been working on calculus since she was 14 and who started reading college textbooks for fun at age 12. If this student, as a current 16-year-old, is sitting in typical grade-level courses, she is likely to be unchallenged and very bored. It's also likely that simple differentiation cannot meet her needs. If a school has an opportunity to send this student to college-level courses early, but chooses not to do so, the risk could be great. Being forced to sit through 2 more years of redundant content could have negative affective and motivational outcomes, as well as the loss of other potential advanced learning experiences for which she is ready now. It also represents a needless 2-year delay that will propagate throughout the student's remaining academic timeline and into her career. For this reason, even the choice not to allow drastic acceleration can have high potential risk. Programs with higher potential risk will simply require more conservative and comprehensive identification policies, whereas those with low relative risk might require no identification system at all. Such a comprehensive system is discussed with regard to the Iowa Acceleration Scale in Chapter 5.

The question now is how to approach relative risk thoughtfully—how should such information be used in an identification or programming decision? Unfortunately, the potential risk of a given program or intervention (such as enrichment programs or acceleration) can only be subjectively evaluated, and the risk likely will be different for each program and, to a lesser extent, even for each child. Some programs, such as most enrichment activities, carry very low potential risk for most students. They don't provide a great deal of measurable outcomes and therefore there isn't much risk to an incorrect placement.

Early entrance to college could have serious potential for relative risk for a student who is very academically advanced but who is also socially and emotionally immature. The issue of risk is more influential for the Cell II and III students—those for whom the decision is less clear. The simplest thing to reiterate is that *the higher the potential for risk, the more exclusive (as opposed to inclusive) an identification system should be.* Although our default position is to prioritize inclusion, this position changes as the risk of incorrect placement increases. Put simply, if there are programs or interventions that are potentially hazardous when used incorrectly, educators need to be very confident in our student placement decisions before moving forward. In addition, we should weigh the relative risks associated with incorrect decisions as we make placement decisions.

What does this philosophy and structure look like when applied to advanced academic identification and programming? Because our purpose is no longer to identify the "trait" of giftedness in students, we cannot recommend or suggest certain tools or specific methods for identification—it always depends. The assessments selected must be matched closely to the programming decisions being made. Instruments used for identification should vary depending on the programming to be provided. The next several chapters present a range of examples that illustrate in greater detail each aspect of the processes we have just outlined. Of course, it's important to remember that the methods and systems of "identification" referenced in our examples are not the only methods of identification even for a single program. Just because our examples may present the use of achievement test data to form flexible cluster groups does not mean this is the best or only way to locate students for such a service. It is up to the professional judgment and expertise of teachers and administrators in any given setting to apply our general principles to their own unique setting, their local educational priorities, and their understanding of the students whose learning needs they seek to address.

Total School Cluster Grouping
Illustrative Example

4

Chapters 4–7 serve as illustrative examples of many of the ideas and methods posed so far. Because our main philosophy is that identification is only effective if it is for a special program, the following chapters present example programs or purposes, along with how a school might identify students in need of those particular programs.

Ability grouping in general is one of the most researched and discussed topics both within the gifted education literature and in the world of general education research. Throughout the book we have made several references to the Total School Cluster Grouping Program (TSCG)—a program developed by Marcia Gentry and colleagues (Gentry & Mann, 2009; Gentry & Owen, 1999) to implement flexible achievement grouping in the elementary grades. Most of the information regarding the background of the program comes from the book *Total School Cluster Grouping and Differentiation* (Gentry & Mann, 2009). Even though TSCG deals exclusively with elementary grades, this chapter will include references and discussion regarding how a similar program might work at the middle and high school levels.

Before we discuss the identification of students for placement within a TSCG model, we first need to explain why such a model is necessary and what need it fills within a school setting (i.e., a needs assessment).

After all, school programming should respond to students' academic and affective learning needs. To do this, we need to look at the makeup of the average classroom in the United States. In the K–12 setting, this process could be accomplished by, for example, a school principal reviewing state achievement test scores. To show what might be learned, instead of looking at school-level data (as a K–12 practitioner would), we will look at national data and averages. Although much attention is paid to average student scores over time on assessments such as the National Assessment of Educational Progress (NAEP) or the NWEA MAP, the standard deviations of such scores often are not considered. The standard deviation is a measure of variability—the degree to which a group of scores is clustered around the mean—and smaller standard deviations indicate consistent or similar scores across a group of test takers, while larger standard deviations indicate scores that tend to be very different from each other and from the average level of performance. When examined for a single grade level within a single school, the standard deviation indicates the degree of diversity in achievement in that setting.

For example, the National Center for Educational Statistics provides NAEP data for the last few decades regarding the average achievement of students in fourth-, eighth-, and 12th-grade math and reading. The same datasets also provide the standard deviations for these scores. For example, in 2011, the average NAEP Scale Score for Reading for eighth-grade students was 265. This raw score aligns with the bottom of the NAEP "proficient" category for grade 8 and indicated that the average eighth grader in 2011 possessed skills and abilities such as the ability to "Recognize the motivation of the narrator in a literary essay" via a multiple-choice question and could "Use information from an article to provide and support an opinion" in a constructed response question (this interpretive information is provided in the NAEP 2011 eighth-grade report card; see http://nces.ed.gov/nationsreportcard/itemmaps and select 8th grade from the menu options). Teachers and stakeholders can understand and use this information about what the average student can do as a guide for their instructional decisions. However, in addition to what the average student knows, what is equally important is the range of what students know. For the score of 265 from 2011, the standard deviation was 34 points. Based on how the normal distribution works, this means that roughly two thirds of eighth-grade students received scores between 231 and 299 (the mean score of 265 +/- 34). Because these are NAEP scores, which are sampled such that they are representative of all students in the country, this information can be interpreted as saying that two thirds of all of the eighth graders in the country scored between 231 and 299.

On its face this may not appear to have much meaning—it doesn't answer the "so what?" question. However, the NAEP item map reveals that this score range is quite large when it comes to what students know and can do. An individual teacher or principal seeing these data should think "Wow, that's a pretty wide range for one person to teach." Students with a score of 231 are at the very bottom of the eighth-grade NAEP (they are below minimal proficiency for an eighth grader, or far below grade-level expectations). Such students can "Recognize an implicit main idea of a story" in a multiple-choice question but cannot yet use that information to support an opinion. In fact, the students with scores of 231 are actually closer to the average score of a fourth grader (221) than they are to the performance of the average eighth grader (265). At the other end are students who scored near 299—one standard deviation above the mean. Students at this level can "Explain a cross-text connection between a poem and a fable" in a constructed response question, or "Evaluate how a subheading relates to [a] passage and provide text support" in a constructed response question—the evaluation level of Bloom's taxonomy. Comparable data for 12th-grade students are not available for 2011, but in 1998 their average NAEP Reading score was 290 (eighth graders averaged 263—similar to now). *This means that across the United States in 2011, the average heterogeneously grouped eighth-grade classroom included students who scored close to that of the average fourth grader as well as others who scored higher than the average 12th grader.* To be sure, this range of diversity is not present in all eighth-grade classrooms, but it is an average—there are classrooms that have a narrower range of student achievement and readiness, as well as classrooms that have a wider range.

An important point to consider further is that everything discussed so far describes *two thirds* of eighth-grade students (the score range of 231–299). This means that it only applies to about 20 of the 30 students in the average classroom. The students who remain are those five or so students who are below 231 and five or so who are above 299! This translates to eighth graders who are nearly nonreaders all the way to those who are closer to college-level readers—all in one classroom. Again, these are averages, which assume that students are randomly placed into classrooms and schools (which of course is not the case). In actuality, there are schools that have very little variability (i.e., that are very homogenous) in their eighth-grade classrooms (all 30 students score near 265), but there are also those with far wider ranges. Understanding where your particular school falls in this regard is crucial to your ability to make appropriate decisions about programming!

Our reason for presenting this example is to show that the "typical" classroom (if there is any such thing) is likely to be a very diverse place, with students who demonstrate a wide range of proficiency. To return to the beginning of this rather lengthy example, if we examine score variation in standard deviations within a single grade level, this could serve as the initial indicator of need that we discussed in the introduction to the example chapters. As we have demonstrated above, the average eighth-grade classroom likely contains readers from nearly the full K–12 range, as measured by grade-level standards. This diversity in grade-level student performance is a perfect impetus for the adoption of a program like TSCG.

The TSCG Program

The purpose of Total School Cluster Grouping is to narrow the range of achievement levels of the students within every classroom at a given grade level so that each teacher can more effectively meet the needs of his or her students. It therefore can serve as a program to meet the needs of all students—including those in need of advanced academic programming. A key characteristic of TSCG is that the identification or placement of students into cluster classrooms is ongoing—occurring at least yearly and across multiple subject areas. It is also different from traditional homogenous grouping in that a range of student achievement levels in a given classroom still exists. However, this range is not as wide as would be found in the typical classroom to which students have been assigned at random. The overall philosophy of TSCG is based on the idea that a narrower range of student achievement levels will help teachers more effectively differentiate their curriculum and instruction for students' learning levels. This, in turn, yields improved learning outcomes for all students (including gifted or advanced students). Student achievement status is reevaluated at least yearly in TSCG, and students move in and out of the five clusters based on need. The five clusters in the TSCG model include high achieving, above-average achieving, average achieving, low-average achieving, and low achieving. It's important to note that these groups are intended to be very flexible; students are reassessed frequently in order to assure that *all students* are being challenged, while at the same time learning to work with others of similar *and* differing achievement levels. It is important that all students learn to work with those who are different from them, both academically and in other ways, and TSCG provides for this. Research has supported that teachers do feel more comfortable and effective differentiating in cluster-grouped classes (Gentry & Owen, 1999), and a variety of studies have demonstrated achievement growth for gifted students and nongifted students alike when TSCG is implemented (Brulles, Peters, & Saunders, 2012; Brulles, Saunders, & Cohn, 2010).

Total School Cluster Grouping is not simply a structural model in which students are moved around as the sole intervention. Instead, TSCG requires that teachers differentiate in all classrooms regardless of the current achievement levels of their students. For this reason, TSCG could be seen as a mandatory Tier I to Tier II intervention for all schools. If Tier I is to reach a large portion of students (up to 80% in an RtI model; Pereles, Omdal, & Baldwin, 2009), then systems and procedures need to be in place to aid this goal. If every classroom is completely heterogeneous, as discussed earlier, and includes students who are several years below grade level as well as several years above, there is little chance that even the best teacher would be able to differentiate effectively enough to enable the students at all ability levels to learn (Firmender, Reis, & Sweeny, 2012). Schools, and even individual grade levels within a single school, are very diverse places with regard to what students currently know and are able to do. Something like TSCG must be in place if a school is planning to implement RtI. Otherwise it is likely that in a heterogeneously grouped classroom some students will be left behind and others will remain unchallenged. Such a system also would result in Tier II interventions being overpopulated by students who could have their needs met most effectively in the regular classroom, and potentially would "water down" the level of challenge provided in advanced programming for students who really do need and can benefit from it. Because of the TSCG emphasis on providing conditions that allow for successful differentiation, quality assessment data are key both for student placement in clusters (identification) and for differentiation following student placement into clusters.

Because of the total school emphasis of TSCG, the program may be viewed as a Tier I RtI intervention for all students (i.e., with most students being served in the "regular"/clustered classroom), as well as possibly a Tier II intervention for students identified as in need of advanced academic intervention or remediation. In this fashion, the cluster or clusters with the highest performing students could also include additional challenge activities as one aspect of the Tier II intervention. Although students still would remain in the clustered general education classroom, the Tier II students would be clustered together within this classroom for targeted support and more intensive intervention.

The Content Area

Total School Cluster Grouping offers a particular form of cluster grouping targeted toward the elementary level. The reason for this is that most middle school or junior high models already have a structure in place to allow for flexible, leveled classrooms based on students' demonstrated levels of achievement and need. The content areas within which students are clustered in the primary and elementary grades are not set in stone. However, the majority of schools that have implemented TSCG have done so for math and reading. In the upper elementary grades, especially at larger schools with wider ranges of achievement, it also is feasible to cluster students for science and social studies instruction. What should dictate the content areas in which clusters are needed is the standard deviation or relative diversity within each content area. If the fifth-grade science lesson is supposed to challenge those students who have minimal science mastery, as well as those who are ready for high-school-level science, then clustering across classrooms based on science readiness is necessary in order for this to be possible.

The Need

Much of the identification or needs-assessment process for TSCG has been detailed in other sources (e.g., Gentry & Mann, 2009). We present similar information as well as some expanded suggestions here. The Gentry and Mann (2009) approach to cluster grouping uses student achievement, as measured by standardized achievement tests, and teacher input to place students into classrooms using five identification categories. Both of these data sources offer information on student need and therefore both are used as methods of *inclusion*. As we discussed in Chapter 3, when dealing with programs or interventions that are unlikely to result in high risks of negative outcomes should an inappropriate placement be made, identification systems should default toward inclusion. TSCG has the same philosophy.

The Gentry and Mann (2009) TSCG model suggests that the five different clusters should be determined based on local norm percentiles on achievement tests, or by a teacher recommendation if considering a placement other than what test scores would suggest (i.e., if the recommendation is for inclusion in a higher cluster). Both sources of information are local and in the present tense. They are not based on national norms or even district-level comparisons. What this means is that if 10 schools in a given district implement TSCG, a given cluster (say, above-average) could look very different from school to school and would contain students with very different levels of mastery in different school settings. In School A, the above-average cluster could involve students who are working on Common Core State Standards grade-level content, whereas at School B, this same cluster could involve students working on below-grade-level content (despite being called "above-average"). The level of the cluster depends on the overall achievement level of the students within a given school. Thus data related to current levels of student mastery (achievement) and relative to other learners within each school (local norms) are critical to the effective implementation of the TSCG model.

Identification or program placement in TSCG takes the form of class lists that incorporate from three to four achievement levels in any one classroom: no single classroom receives all of the high or low students lest that room be perceived as the "smart" or "weak" room. Further, the highest achieving students (highest single cluster) are all clustered together within a single classroom. Schools with very high numbers of students in a given grade level can create additional classrooms containing clusters of high-achieving students. The highest achieving cluster allows the highest students to work on more challenging tasks together. This "gifted" cluster may also receive additional interventions beyond TSCG; such additional interventions are akin to a Tier II intervention. Such clustering also facilitates budgetary and reporting requirements for schools subject to a gifted mandate or that receive targeted funding for gifted education programming and services. Of course, if the program goes especially well, additional classes may need to include groups of the high-achieving students, but no teachers should be required to have these students in their classes unless they are *willing and able* to meet the academic and affective needs of these learners. It's also important that the students in the lowest performing clusters not receive the lowest performing or least experienced teachers. In fact, students at both extremes of the distribution will need the most-skilled teachers if they are to make appropriate progress.

Imagine that a given school or district has noticed an especially wide range of achievement levels at a given grade level—a needs assessment similar to what was presented earlier with NAEP scores. A concerned administrator has noticed this high level of variability in performance on standardized achievement tests and wants to do something to better target instruction to students' needs. How would he and his staff create a TSCG identification plan?

Identification/Creation of Clusters

TSCG identification uses two data sources: teacher identification of classroom achievement and achievement test results. Gentry and Mann (2009) emphasized that teacher recommendations need to take place *before* teachers see student achievement test data because teachers might change their recommendations based on the test scores. However, teacher recommendations provide a second, sometimes different, source of data; not just a rubber stamp endorsing the results of the achievement tests. If recommendations end up being based on achievement test scores, then that goal has not been achieved. In addition, for the teacher recommendations to be most effective, teachers need to have a good understanding of the TSCG model. This can be accomplished through a traditional professional development session or through the online modules that are available at http://www.purdue.edu/geri. Training is critical—the key to obtaining useful recommendations is for teachers to know why they are recommending students. For more information on effective use of nominations, see McBee et al., in press.

Total School Cluster Grouping Placement Survey

Page 1

1. Below is your current class roster. In order to facilitate student class placement for the coming academic year, we would like to get your thoughts on which Cluster Level would best meet each student's academic needs. Do not worry about being perfect in your ratings as the cluster placements are flexible and this process will be repeated a year from now. Please compare each student to his or her age / grade-level peers and then suggest he or she be placed in one of the following five clusters:

   High Achieving
   Above-Average Achieving
   Average Achieving
   Low-Average Achieving
   Low Achieving

	High Achieving	Above-Average Achieving	Average Achieving	Low-Average Achieving	Low Achieving
Matthew Anderson	○	○	○	○	○
Kylie Abel	○	○	○	○	○
Michael Bennett	○	○	○	○	○
Ben Carson	○	○	○	○	○
Carter Casey	○	○	○	○	○
Amy DeWitt	○	○	○	○	○
Devon Franklin	○	○	○	○	○
Virginia Porter	○	○	○	○	○

Figure 4.1. TSCG placement survey.

Teacher Recommendations

The teacher recommendation phase is straightforward. At the end of a given academic year (often in April or May), teachers identify the achievement cluster level of each of their students, using definitions for each of the five categories (see Gentry & Mann, 2009, for these definitions) and working in consultation with other colleagues at their grade level. This can be done in the form of a bubble sheet where each student's classroom achievement level is noted, in an online survey where each student's name is presented along with an option for placement in each of the five categories (see Figure 4.1), or using paper data cards placed in each teacher's mailbox. Whatever method is chosen should be the easiest and least work-intensive for teachers. If the process is too complicated or cumbersome, some students could end up not being rated, or teachers may rush through the rating process, which increases the probability of making inappropriate recommendations.

If the teacher recommendation data are collected via an online survey, the data can simply be printed with student identification categories. Because most such survey systems can export into Excel or another database format, these data also could be imported into a school's data management system. Regardless of how the data are collected, they need to be organized in such a way that faculty and administrators are able to examine these draft placement recommendations that are based only on teacher recommendations.

Achievement Test Data

Many schools administer summative achievement tests in the late spring in order to gauge student achievement over the preceding year. Unfortunately, summer learning loss has been well documented (Cooper, Nye, Charlton, Lindsay, & Greathouse, 1996), with some students losing or forgetting a substantial amount of content from the prior year over the summer break. What's especially unfortunate is that summer learning loss is much more of an issue for students from low-income families (Cooper et al., 1996) and for students with lower achievement levels. Because of this, TSCG placement decisions should be based on the most recent testing information possible. Ideally, placements would be made immediately following testing. However, because it is too late to place students in classes beginning in the late spring of a given year, prior year spring achievement data often are the best and most feasible to use for TSCG placement beginning in the fall semester. While students are taking their spring achievement tests, their teacher can complete their cluster recommendations for the following year. The timeline for this process would be as follows:

1. In the late spring, students take achievement tests, which will be used as one data source in cluster placement.
2. At the same time, as students are taking achievement tests in the spring, current grade-level teachers complete a "recommended cluster level" form on each of their students.
3. Just before school lets out for the summer, the teachers who did the ratings (grade-level teams) review the draft cluster slates based on their recommendations and make any necessary changes.
4. Once achievement data are available, individual student cluster placement (based on achievement data) is then compared to

cluster placements based on teacher recommendation data. These two slates are then reconciled, by the same staff members who originally did the ratings, to determine a final placement for each student.

5. In the late summer before students return for the start of the semester, grade-level teams of teachers for the upcoming year review the draft slates to see whether any students are in inappropriate placements (this may be based on new information, if available), or if there are certain students who should not be clustered together. Changes can also be made at this time in response to parent requests.

Ideally, a school's student data management system could be modified to include "cluster placement" and "teacher recommendation" categories. This way an administrator or data staff member could simply look up those students for whom the recommended cluster placement based on test score and teacher recommendation differ. This process would eliminate the need to review two very long slates (one based on achievement data and one on teacher data) for all students, and instead would focus extra attention on decisions for students for whom the two slates do not agree about a proper cluster placement.

Gentry and Mann (2009) suggested using a local norm of high scores in both math and reading (90th+ percentile scores in both) to determine placement in the highest cluster. Although this works for elementary levels where math and reading are often taught by the same teacher, we believe a different system should be used at the secondary level. Instead of basing placement on a norm-referenced basis (even a local one), we suggest criterion-referenced evaluation should also be considered. In other words, mastery of content also is relevant at the secondary level, rather than considering only how well students fare in comparison to their classmates. Instead of simply breaking up the students of a certain grade level into groups (e.g., 50th–75th percentile, 75th–90th percentile, and 90th and above), we endorse the creation of clusters based on class content as aligned to Common Core State Standards or state content standards. Not all content is created equal—some content might be easier to teach to a very wide range of students at the same time, while other content is very difficult to teach to a diverse group. To illustrate this point we will use the

2011 MATHEMATICS STATUS NORMS (RIT VALUES)			
Grade	Beginning-of-Year Mean	Middle-of-Year Mean	End-of-Year Mean
K	143.7	150.7	159.1
1	162.8	172.4	179.0
2	178.2	185.5	191.3
3	192.1	198.5	203.1
4	203.8	208.7	212.5
5	212.9	217.8	221.0
6	219.6	222.8	225.6
7	225.6	228.2	230.5
8	230.2	232.8	234.5
9	233.8	234.9	236.0
10	234.2	235.5	236.6
11	236.0	237.2	238.3

Figure 4.2. 2011 math test norm score ranges for the MAP. From *2011 Normative Data*, p. 2, by Northwest Evaluation Association, 2011, Portland, OR: Author. Copyright 2011 by Northwest Evaluation Association. Reprinted with permission.

NWEA MAP. Figure 4.2 presents the math test norm score ranges for the MAP in 2011.

The MAP is a vertically scaled score test, which means that the same numerical scores are comparable regardless of the students' grade level. These norms (NWEA, 2011a) were developed based on a sample of 20,000 students drawn from the pool of roughly five million students who took the NWEA MAP test in 2011. For example, the grade 3 data were based on a sample of 20,294 students (NWEA, 2011b). As such, the scores serve as an indicator of average performance for the students tested. It's important to note that, unlike the NAEP discussed earlier, the NWEA MAP test does not represent the full U.S. population of students because districts and schools choose to use MAP on a voluntary basis. As with the NAEP data, the MAP RIT score standard deviation is a critical consideration when evaluating student mastery. For third-grade math scores in 2011, the standard deviation was just over 14 points. Just as we discussed with the NAEP scores, this means that roughly two thirds of third-grade students in 2012 scored between 189 and 217 (the mean of 203 +/- 14) and the final third scored outside that range (both above and below) in math. If we look at the mean score plus or minus two standard deviations, we can encapsulate nearly all (just more than 95%) students. This score range comes out to 175–231. Before we discuss the implications this has for cluster placement in TSCG, let's first examine what this means about the students at a hypothetical school that just happens to mirror the MAP average scores for 2011 in math. The score range of 175–231 (representing 95% of students) means that the average third-grade classroom is made up of students who score below the performance expected for an average first grader and above the average for seventh graders. This "typical" classroom then includes students performing across roughly seven grade levels (from first-grade level material through seventh-grade level material). That's the full range of students that the third-grade teachers in this particular hypothetical school are charged with educating. This range itself can be regarded as one measure of student need in mathematics.

This range of 175–231 is substantial and represents wide variability in what third-grade students know and are able to do when it comes to math. It would be extremely difficult for a single teacher to effectively challenge every student across such a wide range (assuming 25 to 30 students in a class). The goal of TSCG then is to narrow this range so that each teacher has a classroom composition that is more manageable in terms of effective teaching. What is nice about the TSCG model is that the "narrowing" process is not prescribed. In other words, depending on the actual range of student performance, the number of classrooms at a given grade level, the number of students in each classroom, and a host of other factors, clusters may be structured differently in response to these needs. When these numbers are applied to this example school (five grade-level classrooms serving 125 third-grade students), a structure starts to take shape. Table 4.1 breaks down the range of math scores into the five clusters.

Table 4.1 breaks the range of student achievement into groups using the standard deviation. For example, the average cluster students include those from one half a standard deviation on each side of the mean. Similarly, each other cluster also includes a half-standard deviation of current math achievement. This is a simple way to make clusters, but as was mentioned earlier, there might be a reason to have some clusters larger or smaller. For example, students at the upper ranges may be getting into novel content for which they have little prior experience (such as algebraic thinking). Because of this, an administrator could believe that the range for this group should be a little narrower than for the other clusters. This might result in the above-average cluster going up to 225 (instead of 217). This

TABLE 4.1

Cluster Grouping Breakdown by Achievement Level

	Total
High Achieving (217–231+)	14
Above-Average (210–217)	20
Average = 203 (196–210)	55
Low-Average (189–196)	20
Low (-175–189)	14
Special Education	5
Total	125*

Note. This total should add up to 128. It doesn't because some special education students did not take the test because of a documented disability(ies), while still others are receiving special education services while also being counted in one of the other clusters (including high achieving/gifted).

would mean the high-achieving cluster would start with those students above 225. Considering actual content in the creation of cluster levels is preferable to using only statistical methods such as percentiles or standard deviations. Although percentiles or standard deviations are a great way to create initial cluster cut scores, content, as well as other factors, should be considered to make sure the groups will function smoothly and can be differentiated instructionally.

Cluster levels should never be translated directly into the makeup of individual classrooms—having one class made up of only below-average students and no others would be a bad idea. Table 4.2 presents what the cluster classrooms might look like based solely on test scores. As mentioned earlier, teacher recommendations and considerations also are taken into account. For example, the three students in the low-average cluster of Classroom 1 could easily have been placed in Classroom 2 or Classroom 4 with similar-achieving peers. However, there are students in these three groups who do not get along, and this could cause behavior problems if these learners were placed together. This was noted by classroom teachers in the teacher recommendation and placement phase, and based on this information, a change was made to the initial slate of cluster placements. In a similar fashion, there are two English language learners who are receiving some support for language acquisition but who also have average to above-average skills in math. Because of this particular need, they are clustered together in order to facilitate an itinerant bilingual educator

TABLE 4.2

Student Cluster Assignment by Classroom—
Based on Achievement Test Only

		Classroom				
	Total	**1**	**2**	**3**	**4**	**5**
High Achieving (217–231+)	14	14[1]				
Above-Average (210–217)	20		7	6	0	7
Average = 203 (196–210)	55	8	14	14	11	8
Low-Average (189–196)	20	3	4	0	5	8
Low (-175–189)	14	0	0	5	9	0
Special Education	5	1[1]				4[2]
Total	123	25	25	25	25	23

Note. Special education category does not count toward the total as these students are already counted in their respective achievement category.

[1]Twice-exceptional child who is learning disabled and gifted
[2]Students with a disability who are also average achieving

when needed in Classroom 5, while at the same time allowing these two students to receive math instruction at an appropriate level.

Once the draft slate (Table 4.2) is created based on test scores and other relevant factors (such as behavior issues), teacher ratings and recommendations are considered by comparing two draft slates—one based on test scores and the other based on teacher recommendations. Because both test scores and teacher recommendations adopt the perspective of inclusion (as TSCG is a low-risk program), the identification system for TSCG should err on the side of a higher placement. However, there will be cases where a cluster teacher for the upcoming year doesn't believe a certain student would be well suited for a particular placement. Although placement decisions (the teacher slate) are based on the previous year's teachers, the upcoming year's teachers should still be involved to create buy-in and to proactively address any issues that might come up. These subjective decisions can be made on an individual basis at the early fall semester grade-level team meetings. This should be done keeping in mind that even after initial placements have been made, students still can be moved mid-year as needs dictate. Table 4.3 presents a revised slate after upcoming year teacher suggestions are considered.

Note that the students and the cluster levels into which they fall have changed. This doesn't mean their scores have changed; rather, they have been moved in response to teacher recommendations or other instruc-

TABLE 4.3

Student Cluster Assignment by Classroom—
Achievement Test and Teacher Recommendations

		Classroom				
	Total	**1**	**2**	**3**	**4**	**5**
High Achieving (217–231+)	17	14[1]	3			
Above-Average (210–217)	17		7	4	0	6
Average = 203 (196–210)	55	8	14	9	16	8[2]
Low-Average (189–196)	20	3	4	5	0	8
Low (-175–189)	14	0	0	7	7	0
Special Education	5	1[1]				4[2]
Total	123	25	28	25	23	22

Note. Special education category does not count toward the total as these students are already counted in their respective achievement category.

[1]Twice-exceptional child who is learning disabled and gifted
[2]Students with a disability who are also average achieving

tionally relevant factors. For example, in Table 4.3, we assume that two above-average students from Classroom 3 and one from Classroom 5 were recommended for the gifted cluster. Ideally these students would have been placed in Classroom 1, but assume that a parent requested a particular teacher (a common occurrence), and to accommodate this request, these students were placed in Classroom 2. Gentry and Mann (2009) recommended that individual schools decide how they want to handle parent requests. In cases where students could really benefit from Tier II material as provided in Classroom 1 for the other high-achieving students, they could simply be moved across the hall for specified instructional periods. A final important note is that all of the clusters as defined by MAP scores are subject to standard error. For the national MAP score data, this error is around three points. This means that any student score needs to be considered within the range established by the standard error (+/- 3 points). This is especially relevant because if a parent or teacher challenges a classroom placement that is on the border (i.e., that is within the standard error), the change should be made to move to the student to the higher cluster. If, in the future, this student's scores do not improve, this may be an indication that a lower placement would be better suited for his or her needs. Ideally, such situations will be relatively uncommon and can be dealt with on an individual basis.

Multiple Content Areas

So far this example of cluster grouping has focused on a single content area: mathematics. For some schools or districts, as in the example, one particular content area might possess more variability in student readiness than in the other areas—thus necessitating the clustering based solely on a single content area. Perhaps the school used as the example above had a wide range of math scores for its third graders, but a much narrower range of reading scores. Alternatively, perhaps the students with the highest math scores are also those with the highest reading scores. For this reason, students are only clustered for math, and scores in reading are not considered (beyond the minimum reading level demanded by the math content instruction). However, it's also possible that a school's scores in one area vary just as widely as they do in others, necessitating consideration of additional information.

Full-time clusters can be made based on teacher recommendations plus a single achievement test score (such as math) as detailed above or can include multiple achievement test scores. In one variation, a certain classroom might include all of the students who scored high on both math and reading achievement test scores, whereas a different room would have those who scored high only in math and still another for those who scored high only in reading. Again, there is no one single way to cluster. The overarching goal is simply to narrow the range of student achievement levels that any one teacher needs to address.

The timeline for the process of identification, including solicitation of scores in multiple content areas, does not change regardless of the specific clustering pattern a given school chooses to implement. Gentry and Mann (2009) recommended that when using math and reading scores, students in the high-achieving cluster should be those who receive scores at the 90th percentile or above in both math *and* reading. Students who are placed in the above-average cluster are those who receive math and reading scores at or above the 75th percentile or those who receive either math *or* reading scores above the 90th percentile. As mentioned earlier, these criteria are not set in stone, and some schools may choose to group by either or both criteria, or even to have multiple types of clustering, depending on the size of the school and its local needs. Slight changes in order also can be made to yield a better set of instructional levels for a given classroom and teacher. Following the criteria for using more than one content area is no different for a single content area. A table similar to Table 4.3 will be the end result, except that the high-achieving cluster will be high achieving in both math and reading (or whatever two content areas are in need of clustering).

Conclusion

Although this chapter presented TSCG as an example of how to identify students for a particular program, TSCG is unique in that it offers a schoolwide approach to classroom organization. If students are placed in classrooms at random and thus completely heterogeneously, then every teacher has an exceptionally wide range of students to teach. With increasing emphasis on student growth, including for purposes of teacher evaluation, we believe this is an unreasonable expectation with a class of 30+ students. For this reason, we see TSCG as a kind of universal total school model that could serve as the Tier I in which most students have their needs met within the clusters. Additional programming can then be made available (albeit for a much smaller group than is typical) for those who still need additional challenge or support. If such a system is not in place to address the needs of the vast majority of students, far larger numbers of students will need to be placed in Tier II programming at both the remedial and advanced academic ends of the RtI spectrum.

Acceleration
Illustrative Example

5

Despite the fact that student ability varies widely within grade-level classrooms, even within gifted magnet school settings (Firmender et al., 2012), the U.S. educational system overwhelmingly uses age as the primary factor when matching students with curriculum. Parents, teachers, and schools assume that if a student is a certain age, then this tells us what he or she needs to learn. In reality, some elementary students already have mastered around half the curriculum at their grade level when they enter school; Reis, Gentry, and Maxfield (1998) found that 40%–50% of grade-level instruction could be eliminated without affecting academically gifted elementary students' standardized test scores. When forced to repeat material, children and adults alike become frustrated, bored, and unengaged. We can't help but wonder what kind of negative psychological and motivational consequences happen as a result of being retaught content for several years. This repetition wastes valuable time that could be spent in learning new material.

Academic acceleration in its many forms is without question the most effective means of ameliorating these concerns. Acceleration (especially of the whole-grade variety) also is one of the least consistently utilized strategies, among those approaches the field of gifted education knows are effective, for meeting the needs of academically advanced learners. Despite its rarity, a wide range of literature supports the efficacy of acceleration when used appropriately; much of this literature is presented or discussed in the influential two-volume report, *A Nation Deceived: How Schools Hold Back America's Brightest Students* (Colangelo et al., 2004) as well as in a recent meta-analysis (Steenbergen-Hu & Moon, 2011). The bottom line is that when implemented correctly, acceleration, whether partial- or full-grade, works very effectively to increase student learning without undesirable social or emotional consequences.

Two key reasons behind schools' reluctance to accelerate students are fears about students' social and emotional development or readiness to be placed with older learners and fears that "if we let one student do this, then everyone will want it." As is the case with gifted identification (Pfeiffer & McClain, 2012), wide variation in policies guiding acceleration, or even a lack of policy altogether, leads to wide variation in the implementation of acceleration from one school setting to the next. Fortunately, these issues can be addressed using the free publication entitled *Guidelines for Developing an Acceleration Policy* (http://www.accelerationinstitute.org/ resources/policy_guidelines/Acceleration%20Guidelines.pdf), which was coauthored by the Institute for Research on Acceleration Policy, the National Association for Gifted Children, and the Council of State Directors of Programs for the Gifted (2009). This document is designed to walk school personnel through the process of developing policy regarding student acceleration, and it includes sample language from state policy. Perhaps the most common policy when it comes to deciding who to accelerate involves use of the Iowa Acceleration Scale (Assouline, Colangelo, Lupkowski-Shoplik, Lipscomb, & Forstadt, 2009) which we discuss below.

In the sections that follow, we begin by describing the many varieties of acceleration that teachers and schools can offer to *improve the match between student needs and learning opportunities* as part of advanced academics. We specifically examine whole-grade acceleration and partial acceleration (i.e., acceleration in one or more content areas; also called subject-based acceleration), as these broad categories meet the needs of different subsets of learners. We briefly summarize some of the relevant research that supports acceleration, and we conclude with information detailing the considerations that should inform decisions about acceleration. Specifically, we focus on how teachers and schools can use the Iowa Acceleration Scale and other related sources of data to make informed, defensible decisions about student placement.

Multiple Approaches to Acceleration

Colangelo and colleagues (2004) summarized 18 related forms that acceleration may take, which Southern and Jones (2004) categorized as full-grade or partial-grade (i.e., subject-based) approaches. Full-grade approaches may include early entrance to kindergarten, first grade, middle school, high school, or college; grade skipping; and continuous-progress or self-paced instructional models, both of which allow for individuals to progress through the curriculum at a rate faster than that of their age-level peers.

Partial-grade approaches to acceleration include subject-based acceleration (i.e., a student moving to a higher grade classroom for math only), as well as multiage classrooms that are combined across grade levels; curriculum compacting or telescoped curriculum; and individualized tutoring or mentoring. Credit through extracurricular or correspondence programs, concurrent or dual enrollment in college and high school, and credit by examination are subject-based approaches that may lead to early graduation; thus, these also may lead to full-grade acceleration. Advanced Placement programming is a widely practiced approach at the high school level that involves both accelerated and enriched coursework as well as credit by examination.

Full-Grade Acceleration

As its name suggests, in whole-grade or full-grade acceleration, a student moves from the end of one grade level (most commonly) into a placement one or more years above the normal grade-to-grade progression. For example, a student completing first grade may be moved directly into third grade, without ever sitting through a school year in the second-grade classroom. This same student could also move straight to fourth grade or higher depending on the documented need. Whole-grade acceleration commonly is referred to as "skipping a grade," as this is exactly what it involves (Assouline et al., 2009). Grade skipping is what many people instinctively think of when the topic of acceleration comes up in casual conversation. It's important to note that skipping a grade does not mean skipping the content in that grade level; in fact, students are skipped precisely because they have already mastered the content being skipped, or because the content missed is relatively minor and can be covered through the normal review activities in the new classroom placement.

Even though parents and teachers alike often perceive a risk of adverse social or emotional consequences if they allow whole-grade acceleration, this is usually not an issue; in fact, students accelerated by a grade level often find greater friendship and more social acceptance among their new peers than they had experienced in the same-age setting. This finding holds true both in the year following the grade skip, and for students' retrospective recollections of acceleration over the decades that follow. The Iowa Acceleration Scale (see next section) makes very conservative recommendations due to the small yet real potential for harm that may result from inappropriate accelerated grade-level placement. Because acceleration is a case where potential for risk is high, educators should default to conservative decisions when it comes to placement and programming. This conservatism is somewhat unique to acceleration, as few other advanced academic programs carry a similar level of risk. Of course, current practice involving age-based programming and instruction may be harmful to the student's motivation and achievement, but this concern is rarely considered. Often, other less drastic forms of acceleration will be appropriate even when grade skipping does not appear to be the best approach, and Assouline and colleagues (2009) presented a variety of case studies showing how such situations might work out; it is vital that fear or lack of knowledge not prevent grade skipping when evidence suggests it is appropriate.

Subject-Based Acceleration

Multiage classrooms are a combination in which (for example) the second-grade and third-grade teachers collaboratively teach a classroom of second- and third-grade learners. Children in second grade who are ready for third-grade content in a particular subject area are placed in the third-grade group within their same classroom for instruction in that subject. In this way, the programming appears similar to within-class cluster grouping or partial-grade acceleration. Another nuance possible within this approach is bridging, in which one or both of the teachers remain with a classroom group of their students as they move up a grade level the following year. The third-grade teacher (to continue the example) might move with all of the students into a combined third-/fourth-grade classroom the following year with a new fourth-grade teacher, while the second-grade teacher moves to a combined first-/second-grade classroom with a collaborating first-grade teacher. During the second year, the teacher who bridged with the students is familiar with the capabilities and learning needs of students from the previous year, and therefore instruction at the new grade level can build more effectively upon the previous year's learning.

Curriculum compacting (also described as telescoped curriculum) involves pretesting students for mastery of learning objectives, then eliminating instruction in those areas that students already have mastered. The instructional time saved then is used to provide acceleration and/or enrichment options. Curriculum compacting (Reis, Burns, & Renzulli, 1991) in particular appears exceptionally well-suited to address student complaints of boredom, which emerge when students are forced to sit through instruction in content they already have mastered. The nuances of how to use curriculum compacting are too lengthy to present here, but Reis and her colleagues (1991) have authored a guide to curriculum compacting that details the strategy and some of the research that supports its use. Importantly, there was no difference in above-level test scores between students who had up to half of their grade-level instruction eliminated by curriculum compacting and control group students who received the regular grade-level instruction. *When implemented properly, student learning was not harmed when half of their traditional, grade-level content was eliminated and not taught.* What does it mean to be implemented properly? It means that the content was only compacted or eliminated for those students who had already demonstrated mastery. It's that simple.

Individualized tutoring or mentoring offers another effective approach for students who may be ready for subject-specific acceleration but who are unwilling or unable to accelerate their classroom placement. Tutoring and mentoring also offer a solution for learners whose interests lie outside the traditional academic subject areas or in narrow academic fields—such as hydrogeology or entomology—in which school personnel are untrained. Although tutoring and mentoring programs are widespread in schools, such programs almost always are targeted toward mastery of basic skills or for students judged at risk of dropping out. Thus, the responsibility for securing appropriate tutoring or mentoring for the academically advanced learner most often will rest with the learner's parents. For an overview of an ideal mentoring program at the secondary level, see Palmer's (2009) article in *Teaching for High Potential*.

Credit through extracurricular or correspondence programs, concurrent or dual enrollment in college and high school, and credit by examination are acceleration options that allow learners to receive credit for their additional work or expertise in a topic. Rather than skipping the learner over a year or more of repetitive content, as whole-grade or subject-specific acceleration do, these options allow the older student to receive credit as if he or she had sat through the course (credit by exam), or to receive credit by actually completing the more advanced coursework (dual enrollment or correspondence). AP courses have characteristics of both credit-by-exam and dual-enrollment options.

For high school learners, Advanced Placement and dual enrollment (taking courses in high school and college at the same time) both offer the potential for completing college early. AP courses are college-level courses taught in the high school setting by highly qualified high school teachers. Students take a subject-specific exam, developed by the College Board, following completion of the course. Exams are scored at the national level by panels of experts whose independent ratings of each examinee's performance must agree. Exam scores of 3, 4, or 5 on a 5-point scale indicate mastery of the course content, and are granted varying amounts of credit by different universities. At many institutions, a score of 5 allows the student to receive college credit for a full year of freshman-level coursework in the subject.

In dual enrollment, the student has completed all of the content-area coursework offered by his or her high school prior to 12th grade. The student then is allowed to enroll in appropriate coursework at a university or community college, often one close to the location of the high school, while remaining in one or more high school classes that are still meeting the student's needs or the school's graduation requirements. Dual enrollment can be especially effective in the content areas of math and science; in both areas, high school faculty may not have the specialized content expertise to teach courses at or above the level of Advanced Placement coursework. Particularly in the sciences, the expense of laboratory facilities needed for higher level courses may be prohibitive. Often, dual enrollment coursework is offered at no cost to eligible students.

Both Advanced Placement and dual enrollment programming are à la carte rather than full programs per se. If either were a coherent, stand-alone program, they would feature standardized offerings across learners and would have established feeder programs to guide students toward the advanced programming in a consistent, coherent manner. Because these offerings are not organized systematically at the program level, the burden of matching student needs to appropriate coursework may fall upon parents, individual teachers, or even the student him- or herself (see the self-enrollment discussion in Chapter 3), much as it does in the case of whole-grade and some other forms of acceleration.

Considerations in the Acceleration Decision

Student Selection

Returning briefly to the discussion from Chapter 3, we believe identification systems should default toward inclusion in selecting students for programs or interventions whose risk of negative outcomes is relatively low if an inappropriate placement is made. From the AP teachers' point of view, overly inclusive enrollment can result in watered-down instruction that fails to adequately prepare participating learners to succeed on the accompanying AP exam. From the student's point of view, the risk is that they might have learned more in a less advanced class (where one exists).

We suggest that if schools desire to increase enrollment in their AP coursework or other advanced learning options, then development of an appropriate feeder network of rigorous coursework at the lower grade levels is needed. The potential negative outcomes of inappropriate placement decisions should be considered not only at the level of the individual student, but also at the school level; the potential for diluting advanced instruction should be viewed as one potential negative outcome at the school level. Recent research at the University of Virginia (Callahan et al., 2013) found that providing intensive interventions for students, teachers, and guidance counselors was shown to lead to improved retention rates in AP coursework and to more effective instruction of low-income and minority students. Awareness of these varied factors can help districts and schools develop relevant programming and professional development to ensure that their Advanced Placement coursework is provided in the most effective manner possible.

School Profile Considerations

As with the other interventions discussed in this book, it is important to consider the overall learning characteristics of a given school setting and how these may inform the use of different forms of acceleration. As states adopt the Common Core State Standards as their learning objectives, these may offer one consistent means of determining what mastery of grade-level material looks like across school settings. However, what grade-level instruction looks like within the school is ultimately the more important consideration when a student is being considered for any gifted or advanced academic programming including partial or full-day placement into a higher grade level setting within the school. Placement at the same or different grade level but in a different school setting (e.g., a magnet school or content-focused charter school) will need to consider the fit of the new environment, as well as additional considerations such as the feasibility and logistics of transportation to the new location.

Policy Considerations

The National Association for Gifted Children's (NAGC & CSDPG, 2011) biannual *State of the States Report* is a national survey of gifted education policy and practices. Included in the results for the 2010–2011 year were data on state-level acceleration policy. Twenty-three states had no state-level policy regarding acceleration, while 12 of the 45 responding states and territories left it to the local education agency (LEA) to make any such policy. In a similar fashion, seven states specifically allow early entrance to kindergarten while 10 states expressly prohibit it. This item in particular serves as an example of the effects of misperception regarding the potential benefits and drawbacks of acceleration. Perhaps the most encouraging finding regarding acceleration options was that 27 states reported that either the LEA or the state would pay for any dual-enrollment/college-level courses once a student had exhausted other local options. Unfortunately, overall the vast majority of policy regarding acceleration options is left up to the individual school district, resulting in a large degree of inconsistency across locations.

Relatively few districts have policies in place guiding the implementation of all of the varied forms of acceleration. Rather, some subtypes of acceleration (such as dual enrollment) may have specific guiding policies, while others may be left to the discretion of the principal (such as whole-grade acceleration) or of the individual teacher (such as curriculum compacting). In North Carolina, for example, in late 2012, the State Board of Education adopted a state-level policy on Credit by Demonstrated Mastery (see Item 13 at http://sbepolicy.dpi.state.nc.us/policies/GCS-M-001.asp?acr=GCS&cat=M&pol=001) that will allow academically advanced learners in grades 6–12 to test out of course content that they already have mastered. The policy provides that both the student's performance on a state-level or locally developed content area exam and a product or artifact will be evaluated by a local (district) committee, following specific implementation guidelines that will be developed at the state level. This policy is a positive step for advanced learners in North Carolina schools, yet despite this progress there is not currently a statewide policy governing the use of whole-grade acceleration or a description of the circumstances under which schools must allow a student to demonstrate proficiency for advancement.

A few states and districts have adopted the Iowa Acceleration Scale (Assouline et al., 2009; see description later in this chapter) as the process of choice for informing decisions about whole-grade acceleration. For other types of accelerated placement, or in locales that have not developed policies, the school or parents may wish to advocate for the development of formal policies to guide acceleration decisions; some guidance in this process is available in the literature (Colangelo et al., 2010). In the states where a written gifted education plan is required of districts (i.e., in 32 of 45 states reporting), a policy on acceleration may be a required component of that plan.

Having a policy is important. In the absence of specific policies, the decision often comes down to "no" simply because this is perceived to be easier than having to treat one student in a way that is different from his or her classmates, or out of fear of setting a precedent that others will seek to exploit. However, individualized treatment based on student need is precisely what makes education most effective for the academically advanced learner, and indeed for all individuals who differ from the hypothetical "average student."

Research on Academic Acceleration

Fact: Acceleration Does Not Harm Students

Research consistently has shown that acceleration does not harm students in the great majority of instances, and no evidence suggests that the decision to accelerate, when made appropriately (i.e., using Iowa Acceleration Scale guidelines) was harmful. Lee and her colleagues (Lee, Olszewski-Kubilius, & Thomson, 2012) found no differences in social competence among academically gifted students who had participated in whole-grade acceleration and those who had not. Additionally, the accelerated students had significantly higher self-reported interpersonal ability scores than students in the same study who had not been accelerated. In another study, Lee, Olszewski-Kubilius, and Peternel (2010) found that gifted minority students who were given access to accelerated content in mathematics viewed the opportunity as a challenge that was exciting, and these students felt that it was good preparation for future study in high school and college.

Long-Term Benefits of Accelerated Placement

Students who skip one or more grades go on to show greater positive long-term outcomes than equally able learners whose education was not accelerated. In a recent review and synthesis of 38 studies published between 1984 and 2008, Steenbergen-Hu and Moon (2011) found overall that accelerated students outperformed students who were not accelerated on measures including standardized tests, college grades, degrees obtained, status of university attended, and career prestige. Although certainly suggestive, it must be pointed out that researchers have not been able to show conclusively that acceleration *caused* these different outcomes, although this seems the most logical explanation.

Whole-grade acceleration has lasting effects on overall career productivity in the STEM fields. Among students identified as highly talented in mathematics, recent longitudinal evidence (Park, Lubinski, & Benbow, 2012) established that students who skipped a grade were more likely to obtain advanced (graduate) degrees in STEM fields. They also had produced more, earlier, and more highly cited publications by age 50 than a matched group of students who had not skipped a grade.

Practical Considerations

When to accelerate—and when not to do so (identification decisions)—are important practical considerations. In the discussion that follows, we focus predominantly on whole-grade acceleration because this is the option that tends to be opposed most vehemently by gatekeepers who are unfamiliar with the research supporting acceleration. The same general issues and approaches also are relevant in advocating for other forms of accelerated placement that may be appropriate in a given setting with a given learner. Within the framework we have suggested in Figure 3.5 in Chapter 3, single-subject acceleration and other forms of accelerated placement short of whole-grade acceleration would fall most closely under Tier II's "extra challenge," whereas whole-grade acceleration falls under the rubric of Tier III's "intense interventions."

When to Accelerate?

The most sensible time to implement whole-grade acceleration would appear to be at a natural transition point in the student's education. For example, when transitioning from one school building to another, as from fifth to sixth grade, it may make sense to skip either fifth or sixth grade, as opposed to skipping fourth grade and remaining in the same building with one's former classmates. However, Assouline and her colleagues (2009) suggested that this in fact may not be the most appropriate timing. Because teachers and schools often conduct transitional activities during the students' last year in a given school building, the preferred timing actually is to skip prior to the final year in the building. These authors suggested that, for example, it would be better to skip a student attending a K–5 elementary school from third grade into fifth grade, rather than accelerating from fourth grade at the elementary school into a sixth-grade placement in the middle school building. Skipping from the end of one grade level into the beginning of the following year's grade is generally preferable to skipping during midyear, unless the school is organized in such a manner that a midyear skip would produce a smoother transition for the student.

Grade skipping also makes more sense during the early years (grades K–7) than it does during high school, because in high school other appropriate options (such as AP coursework for college credit or dual enrollment) are more often available that might better challenge a student. Assouline and colleagues (2009) suggested that skipping during the very early elementary years may have the least disruptive effect on the child's social life, because strong peer relationships are only beginning to develop at this stage.

Early entrance to kindergarten can be very appropriate for some learners, but often strict state policies may prohibit this, or policies (as referenced earlier) may make it so difficult or expensive that it rarely happens in practice. Over the past several years, as full-day kindergarten and high-stakes testing have become more common, many states have changed the kindergarten entry age to ensure that students are at least 5 years old when they enter kindergarten. In fact, a review of current state policies reveals that nearly every state that defines the kindergarten entry age requires students to be 5 years old by September 1 (or earlier). (Several states, such as California, are in the process of changing their entry ages to September 1 or earlier as of the writing of this book; by 2015–2016 this process will be complete.)

Some states (such as Iowa and California) have policies that explicitly prohibit students younger than 5 from enrolling in kindergarten. In fact, in Iowa, the attorney general has ruled that it is illegal to admit children that are younger than 5 (as of September 15) into kindergarten, and has stated further that school districts have no discretion to admit such children. In Maryland, a parent/guardian may request early entrance into kindergarten for children who turn 5 years of age between September 2 and October 15 of that year (State of Maryland, Education Article, §7-101, COMAR 13A.08.01.02, Age for School Attendance). In Ohio,

> a parent may request early admission to kindergarten if the child turns age 5 after the district's kindergarten entrance date (August 1/Sept. 30) and before January 1. The Ohio Department of Education recommends that districts follow their Academic Acceleration Policy for Advanced Learners in making decisions about early admission. (Ohio Department of Education, 2013)

Interestingly, the differences across the states in terms of kindergarten entry ages result in the inadvertent early entry of students who begin their educational career in one state and move to a state with an earlier cut-off date.

When Not to Skip

The authors of the Iowa Acceleration Scale suggest that there are four a priori conditions that would indicate that whole-grade acceleration should not be implemented even if other data suggest it would be appropriate. First, acceleration should not be considered when the student has a sibling in the grade level to which he or she would be skipped, as this may create conflict within the family. Further, students whose tested ability is less than one standard deviation above the mean, as measured by an IQ test score, should not be accelerated. Also, the student should not be accelerated by grade skipping *if he or she does not want to be*. As we referenced in Chapter 3, this is an important and often-overlooked consideration. Lastly, if the student is strongly involved in athletics and these interests might be harmed by being a year younger (and therefore, likely, smaller) than other students, whole-grade acceleration should be avoided. These considerations are in place because of the higher potential risk of an inappropriate acceleration decision.

When all other data indicate that the student would be a good candidate for whole-grade acceleration but one of these four conditions is present, then other forms of subject-specific acceleration should be used instead. Its authors note that the Iowa Acceleration Scale should still be completed in these instances, as it can be used to identify and advocate for other appropriate forms of acceleration even when whole-grade acceleration does not appear to be an appropriate option.

How to Accelerate: The Iowa Acceleration Scale

The Iowa Acceleration Scale (IAS; Assouline et al., 2009) was developed as a systematic way to guide schools, parents, and students through the decision-making process for whole-grade acceleration. The IAS manual explains who should be a part of the child study team convened to consider the decision to accelerate a student and provides case studies depicting students who should and should not be grade skipped, based on the use of the scale. The case studies are particularly helpful in conveying to the reader how the scale should be used, and indeed, the authors recommend that anyone using the measure should read the full text of the 146-page IAS manual before applying it to the students in their care.

The IAS is made up of a series of questions that evaluate the child's readiness for acceleration using a variety of indicators. Scale questions are divided into 10 sections, and responses in five subscale areas are assigned a point value. The 10 sections address the child's background and school history, including prior professional evaluations for disabilities or disorders; critical items (such as when not to skip); indicators of ability, aptitude, and achievement as measured via standardized assessments; school and academic factors; developmental considerations; interpersonal skills; and the child's attitude and parental support related to acceleration. In this sense, the IAS has been developed systematically to collect multiple measures that help predict whether or not a child will be successful in an accelerated placement.

Point values from five subscale areas drawn from these 10 sections are summed to yield a total score that is used to indicate the appropriateness of grade skipping for the student. The highest possible sum is 80 points, and scores in the range of 60–80 receive the recommendation of "Excellent candidate for whole-grade acceleration. Acceleration is recommended." A total score in the range of 46–59 indicates "Good candidate for whole-grade acceleration. Acceleration is recommended," while scores in the range of 35–45 indicate a marginal candidate for whole-grade acceleration. Total scores at or below 34 points suggest that whole-grade acceleration is not recommended. Although the IAS provides guidelines and recommendations, this process is and should be individualized. As is demonstrated by the existence of the four deal-breakers with regard to acceleration, the scores on the IAS need to be considered within the context of the individual student.

As we discussed in Chapter 3, a formal and strictly followed identification process is most necessary when the consequences of an incorrect decision are potentially serious (in that they pose a high risk). Due to the potential for harm if the acceleration decision proves unsuccessful, the IAS sets conservative criteria for the decision to accelerate. In other words, it errs on the side of caution and is more likely to fail to recommend acceleration for a student who would benefit from it than it is to recommend acceleration for a student who would fail to benefit from it. This is not to say that acceleration is dangerous or has been shown to yield negative outcomes. Rather, taking a child back who no longer wants to be accelerated can be complicated and logistically time consuming. For these reasons, acceleration should be undertaken with a more conservative eye than is needed for many other programming options for academically advanced learners.

Illustrative Example: Adela's Case

Adela is a kindergarten student with advanced reading ability (test results show a grade level equivalent of 2.3 in reading) and comprehension in reading and mathematics at the first-grade level. Her birthday in late spring makes her older than more than half of her kindergarten classmates. Her kindergarten teacher at the beginning of the school year had resisted suggestions to accelerate Adela's placement or to compact her curriculum. Among other indicators, Adela was becoming bored when repeatedly subjected to instruction in the sounds each letter makes, because she was already reading chapter books independently.

It is now midway through the spring, and Adela has been single-subject accelerated in reading and mathematics to the first-grade classroom across the hall for the past 10 weeks. She is performing successfully at the first-grade level and seems to be getting along well socially with the first graders. Her kindergarten teacher still does not favor acceleration, and has administered a teacher-developed math test from the end of second grade to demonstrate her contention that Adela is not ready for whole-grade acceleration the following fall. Standardized testing is not used in kindergarten at this school, but her parents had Adela independently tested on an academic aptitude test just before entering school and she achieved overall scores in the 98th percentile. These scores also qualified Adela as gifted under her school district's criteria, although formal services to accompany this designation do not begin until third grade. She took an achievement test with the first graders, scoring in the 99th percentile for reading-related areas and 90th percentile in mathematics. The principal also recently agreed to let Adela take the school's standardized second-grade achievement test, which the school uses to screen students in preparation for further testing to establish giftedness (note the traditional focus on testing for giftedness even after a clear need has been established). Adela scored in the 55th percentile overall on this measure, with subscale scores somewhat higher in reading and somewhat lower in mathematics.

At Adela's parents' request, the principal has convened a child study team meeting to consider formally their request for whole-grade acceleration for Adela the following fall, in which she would move into second grade (rather than first) if accelerated. Study team members include Adela's parents, her kindergarten teacher, her first-grade teacher, the school counselor, and the principal. The second-grade teacher into whose class Adela may move has a scheduling conflict and is unable to attend the meeting, but has sent notification that she will follow the team's decision.

On the Iowa Acceleration Scale response form, the team indicates that Adela has been accelerated in reading and math, and has demonstrated talent in reading and writing. She has had no prior professional evaluations that might suggest a need for disability-related services. Considering the four critical items on the IAS, Adela has aptitude test scores between two and three standard deviations above the mean so she does not fall under the "less than one standard deviation above" critical criterion. She has no siblings in the same grade or in the grade to which she would be accelerated, as her brother is two grades ahead of her in school. Adela is excited about the possibility of skipping a grade, and has indicated how much happier she has been in school since she has been allowed to go with the first graders for part of the day.

Adela's scores are entered on the IAS worksheet, using the above-level achievement test as a measure of aptitude (see IAS manual for explanation) and the first-grade achievement test as a measure of achievement. The total score for Academic Ability, Aptitude, and Achievement adds to 14 of a possible 16 points for this section. Following the instructions, a score here of 10 or above indicates that the student may be a good candidate for whole-grade acceleration. Based on this evaluation, the team is instructed to move on to complete the IAS sections that follow.

Section VII of the IAS asks about School and Academic Factors. For the grade under consideration (i.e., second), a placement within the same school building receives a score of 4. Because her brother is two or more grade levels above her current grade, she receives a score of 2 for this area. She has excellent attendance, so receives all 3 points for this area. Her positive attitude, completion of nearly all assignments, and enthusiasm for new academic challenges yield 5 of the possible 7 points in Motivation and Attitude Toward

Learning. She has not participated in extracurricular activities due to their lack of availability at kindergarten in her school, so receives 0 points in this area of the scale, but receives the full 2 points for Academic Self-Concept due to having a positive and realistic view of her own abilities. Thus, her total score for School and Academic Factors is 16 of a possible 22 points for this section.

Section VIII considers developmental factors. Adela is among the oldest in her kindergarten classroom, so receives 3 points here. She is of average stature compared to her classmates, for 2 points, and is about as coordinated as they are (2 more points), for a total of 7 of the possible 9 points for this section.

Section IX of the IAS covers interpersonal skills. Completing the appropriate responses about Adela's emotional development, behavior, out-of-school extracurricular activities, and relationships with peers and teachers yields a score of 12 of the possible 16 points for this section.

Section X addresses the child's attitude and available support. Adela is enthusiastic about the possibility of moving into a full-time second-grade classroom in the fall (4 points), and her parents are strongly supportive and committed to working with her school to meet Adela's academic needs (3 points). The school demonstrates ambivalent support for acceleration, due to the mixed attitudes of different staff members (1 point), and as a consequence, limited planning for Adela's acceleration has taken place (1 point). These yield an overall score for Section X of 9 of a possible 11 points.

Summing the scores Adela obtained on each section yields a total score of 58. This is at the upper end of the range labeled "Good candidate for whole-grade acceleration. Acceleration is recommended" but just below the range labeled "Excellent candidate for acceleration." Although recommended by the IAS, Adela's kindergarten teacher remained opposed to the decision to accelerate; she was able to indicate her disapproval on the line of the IAS form provided for each team member to indicate his or her opinion of the scale's recommendation. Despite the one teacher's misgivings, the principal felt that the support of the other teachers (particularly the second-grade teacher) and guidance counselor, as well as the IAS results were sufficient to justify placing Adela into the second grade the following year. The second-grade teacher, taking into account the kindergarten teacher's concerns, took special care to take note of Adela's development over the course of the second grade. As should be clear, the class and teacher into which a student will move is an important stakeholder to have on board in the process.

The kindergarten teacher's concerns in this case centered primarily on her perception of the potential social and emotional consequences for Adela of being younger than her classmates, and of the potential harm to Adela's self-concept that she felt would result when Adela was no longer working at the top of her class. However, as Assouline and colleagues noted (2009), students who participate in appropriate whole-grade acceleration tend to remain at or near the top of their class in the new, accelerated placement. Today Adela has completed elementary school, and academically she has remained near the top of her class since being accelerated to second grade from kindergarten. She enjoys good relationships with her peers and teachers, and if asked, will tell you that she is proud of having been able to skip a grade.

As mentioned previously, the IAS is designed to make rather conservative recommendations regarding the appropriateness of whole-grade acceleration, so not all cases will lead to a decision to accelerate. We encourage the reader to carefully peruse the several examples of decisions both in favor of and against whole-grade acceleration that are presented as case studies in the Iowa Acceleration Scale manual.

Special Considerations for Acceleration and Early Entry to Kindergarten
(adapted from Feldhusen, Proctor, and Black, 1986)

1. The decision to accelerate a child into a higher grade level should be based on comprehensive psychological evaluation of the child's intellectual functioning, current academic skill levels, and social-emotional adjustment by a trained psychologist.

2. Intellectually, the child should have mental development well above the mean of students who are currently enrolled in that grade and should have high cognitive ability, ideally two standard deviations above the mean.

3. Academically, the child should demonstrate skill levels that are stronger than those of the typical-aged students in most or all subject areas. A child who is advanced in only one academic area should not be grade accelerated.

4. Ideally, the accelerated child should exhibit academic skills that are substantially above the mean for the grade level to which he or she is being accelerated.

5. Socially and emotionally, the child should be reasonably well-adjusted, mature, and motivated.

6. Physically, the child should be in good health.

7. The parents must be in favor of grade advancement, but the child should also independently express the desire to accelerate.

8. The receiving teacher (and school) should have positive attitudes toward the acceleration and be willing to help the child adjust to the new situation.

9. Public school teachers might confuse a very bright child's misbehavior in reaction to inappropriate instruction with immaturity. Therefore, judgments about the child's maturity should include input from parents and the psychologist.

10. When possible, grade advancement should occur at natural transition points such as the beginning of a new school year.

11. The receiving teacher should be made aware of any special needs and weaknesses or likely gaps in knowledge or skill that may occur as a result of the grade skip.

12. All cases of grade advancement should be arranged *on a trial basis*, which typically lasts 6 weeks. During the trial period, counseling services should be available to the child or teacher as needed. The child should be allowed to request to be returned to the original grade if he or she is unhappy with the move. The child should understand that he or she is not a failure if it does not go well or if he or she chooses to return to the earlier grade.

Conclusion

Acceleration is a vital option for students whose learning needs are above and beyond the needs that can be met in the regular general education or gifted education classroom placement. Although research strongly supports acceleration in its various forms, widespread but largely misinformed opinions prevent the use of appropriate acceleration options in many settings. Whole-grade acceleration (grade skipping) in particular constitutes a Tier III or "intense intervention" according to the framework we suggest in Chapter 3, while the other forms of acceleration may be more widely used within the less-intensive Tier II category of this organizational schema.

By considering all of the sources and types of information together and in a systematic fashion, the Iowa Acceleration Scale can assist the child study team in arriving at an acceleration recommendation (whether positive or negative) that is relatively free from personal biases either toward or against acceleration, is consistent with the research on what makes acceleration effective, and is in the best interests of the student. Using this tool will help in providing appropriate acceleration strategies that can assume a central role in efforts to match student needs with appropriately advanced academic services and learning opportunities.

But What About Enrichment?

6

The 2010–2011 National Association for Gifted Children and Council of State Directors of Programs for the Gifted's *State of the States* report listed resource rooms as the most common form of gifted education programing for the elementary grades. Resource rooms were also the fourth most common form of programming in middle school. Although what actually happens in resource rooms is not specified, it's likely that much of the content involves enriching the standard academic curricula and/or providing enrichment beyond material covered in the regular classroom. Whereas acceleration involves moving through the normal curriculum at a faster pace, enrichment involves going beyond the curriculum either through increased depth of curricular topics or via the addition of nonstandard curricular topics. Done correctly, enrichment can play an important role in a program of advanced academics. Implemented poorly, enrichment can dredge up the same tired arguments against gifted education that the approach we promote in this book seeks to counter.

In Chapter 2, we made some statements about the relative merits of acceleration versus enrichment that advocates of enrichment may deem unfair. One reason we were critical of enrichment as a form of gifted programming is simply because the data on the positive benefits of acceleration are so compelling, and yet acceleration is so rare. We hope that all advocates for children can agree that acceleration should be far more common in schools. But that doesn't mean that there is no place for enrichment. Indeed, enrichment-type interventions can play an important role in responding to students' advanced academic needs, assuming the selected enrichment activities are well tailored to that need.

Enrichment programs typically are easier to set up within schools because they do not require the same degree of planning and coordination across grade levels that acceleration programs often require. However, just because an enrichment program *can* be set up with little planning does not mean that it *should* be set up that way. Nearly any program can be implemented badly, but that doesn't mean a given type of programming should never be implemented. Quality enrichment programs require as much thought and planning as would be required for an effective acceleration program. Because it is possible to set up an enrichment program with little more consideration than (a) determining how to create the instructional time (e.g., pull-out resource time, compacting, telescoping) and (b) deciding what to do with this found instructional time, the unfortunate truth is that many enrichment programs in our experience seemingly have been created with little consideration of the important components we have discussed throughout this book (such as the connection to student need).

For example, a prominent colleague of ours has a very bright son in elementary school. The boy is fascinated with math, science, and engineering, and has exhibited very high academic performance in these areas, but he has demonstrated fewer strengths in the areas of language and social studies. Because of this, the school has focused on his areas of weakness, devoting little attention to his areas of strength or interest. However, his school has created a LEGO League team in which students build and program autonomous robots using the LEGO Mindstorms™ system. As such this LEGO League team is a component of his school's gifted and talented education program. In order to qualify for the LEGO League, students must meet basic criteria on academic ability (in other words, IQ) and must have high scores across the board on academic achievement. Unfortunately, the boy's reading score was not quite high enough for him to be identified as gifted, and therefore he was not allowed to join the LEGO League team—an enrichment program that does not appear to require highly advanced reading skill. This is not to say that reading is not involved—just that a student is unlikely to need a reading score placing him or her at the 99th percentile in order to need, benefit from, and be successful in a LEGO League program.

The LEGO League example illustrates one of the most common problems with enrichment programs. Enrichment programs are frequently only tenuously connected with the assessment tools used to admit students (see discussion in Chapter 8 on common pitfalls). This lack of correspondence is problematic on two fronts. First, it severs the tight linkage between academic need and the service or intervention. When this happens, the question becomes, "If we are not going to provide the program to students based on need, then on what basis will we provide it?" Returning to the previous example, do good readers need the LEGO League[4] or do they need more advanced reading instruction and more challenging texts to read? At the same time, which students actually do need and could benefit from LEGO League? When this link is severed, the assessment process begins to look needlessly exclusionary—it begins to provide programming to students based on seemingly random criteria that often may be perceived as privileging some students over others, a system for exclusion with no defensible justification other than decreasing the number of students eligible for the program. Assigning advanced readers to the LEGO League program—and acknowledging that some of these students will be interested in and enjoy the enrichment—does little or nothing to address the academic need that these students possess in *reading*. As we have said multiple times, the mismatch between need and program is the problem, not the student's level of need, the school, or the program itself. Furthermore, privileging the population of students with high reading scores needlessly excludes other students whose demonstrated interest, ability, and prior accomplishment in scientific, engineering, and mathematical areas suggests that the LEGO League program activities may be an appropriate match to their area of academic need. To summarize, one frequently occurring problem with enrichment programs might be termed the *identification problem*: How do we ensure that our means for selecting students for the program is accurately targeting that portion of the student body with relevant need? This issue is one we have addressed repeatedly throughout this book, and we will return to it again now: We believe that the enrichment program should be designed *first*, and the means for identifying students whose academic need can be addressed by the program

---

4   For readers of this chapter who may not be familiar with LEGOs, we note that the basic assembly directions usually are wholly picture-based because the toys are marketed in many different countries; some reading is involved in the LEGO League competition activities.

should come *second*. Traditional gifted education programming inverts the order of these steps.

A second common problem with enrichment programs may at first sound absurd. Many enrichment programs are designed to be much more engaging, interesting, and respectful of students as autonomous learners than the standard curricula. Enrichment programs are sometimes created to counter the stifling "drill and practice" focus on basic skill acquisition—to allow bright kids to flex their brains on engaging content. As a result, they often involve free-form creativity and self-directed learning alongside a passionate teacher who has volunteered for the program. Furthermore, they emphasize higher order thinking skills such as evaluation and synthesis, rather than the lower order skills of knowledge and comprehension that are dominant in the traditional curriculum. The ascendance of standardized testing in schools as a result of increased accountability demands has only further cemented the general education curriculum into lower order skills, a natural consequence of the fact that these skills are relatively easy to measure (Gentry, 2006). This, of course, is not a problem with enrichment itself, but rather with the common occurrence that enrichment is restricted to students identified for gifted and talented programs; this restriction leaves all other students with little access to critical thinking, creativity, or other higher order skills.

Every student should be entitled to an enriched curriculum. Most students would prefer to be engaged, interested, and respected as intelligent and autonomous learners in their educational experiences. As far as we know, no students enjoy endless drill and practice. Although on occasion all students will need drill and practice that is focused on basic knowledge and comprehension (although some students need it less often than others), the opportunity to engage in higher order thinking should not be limited to gifted students or to those whose academic needs are not met by the traditional curriculum. Restricting these "fun" educational experiences to (what typically amounts to) high-IQ students is simply unfair, and it is not in alignment with the structures and procedures we have discussed throughout this book regarding advanced academics. Frankly, in spite of the good intentions of the people who have designed such programs, it is simply a public relations disaster for gifted education when it appears that high-IQ children (who are often from already privileged backgrounds: see Peters & Gentry, 2012) are being rewarded with fun activities during school, as Lohman (2006) wrote, to "congratulate them on their choice of parents or some other happenstance of nurture or nature" (p. 7).

Some gifted education textbooks (e.g., Davis et al., 2011) describe the justification for enrichment programming as something like the following: Gifted students excel at abstract and higher order thinking skills. Therefore, educationally appropriate instruction for the gifted should emphasize these skills. Although it is true that gifted students do excel at synthesis and evaluation, they also excel in the basic areas of knowledge and comprehension! *An emphasis on higher order cognition alone does not result in a particular educational unit being suitable only for gifted students.* It is simply not the case that only gifted students should have access to the upper reaches of the cognitive domain. A cynic might even observe that depriving the nongifted from opportunities to develop and exercise these forms of higher thinking serves only to increase the higher order thinking gap that exists between students identified as gifted and other student populations. In fact, shouldn't we provide explicit instruction in higher order thinking skills to the students who do *not* already exhibit those skills? Aren't the nongifted students the ones who are more likely to need explicit training to develop their higher order thinking skills? Restated briefly, the second problem with enrichment programs as they are commonly implemented is that many kids who have not been identified as gifted likely could do and could benefit from those very same activities if given the opportunity. All students deserve an engaging curriculum that provides numerous opportunities to exercise higher order cognition.

Furthermore, it is now much more generally understood that the *content* of thinking (i.e., basic knowledge and comprehension) cannot be separated from the *process* of thinking. In other words, it is simply not possible to teach people how to think without their possessing rich interconnected schema and some automated basic skills in the domain. You can't teach someone to think before they have something to think about (Anderson & Krathwohl, 2001). This was not nearly as well-understood 20–30 years ago when much of the original work on academic enrichment was underway. As a consequence, many times enrichment programming tries to stimulate high-level cognition in content domains in which children possess almost no knowledge. We all recognize this when we see it. We call it "fluff"— instruction that is bereft of rigor, in which the (typically) effortful and difficult climb up the learning curve toward a mastery of basic knowledge, skills, and conceptual understanding is replaced by a shortcut to the "fun stuff"—the creative and the evaluative. Unfortunately, there is no shortcut to the development of competence, and when the fundamentals are discarded, the operation of higher level cognition results in little long-term learning. So yes, when given a choice between this type of enrichment—which offers little lasting value to students while emboldening critics of advanced academic programming—and acceleration, then absolutely, we prefer acceleration.

It does not follow, however, that all enrichment programs suffer from these two basic flaws. In fact, enrichment programming can play a vital role in alleviating and addressing academic need when it is thoughtfully designed to conform to a few sensible principles—the same principles we've presented throughout this book. The remainder of this chapter will describe their application to enrichment programs. Here again are the steps we introduced in Chapter 2:

1. design or identify the program we want to offer;
2. think locally and in the present tense about student need;
3. identify those who have a need for and would benefit from the program we want to offer; and
4. regularly review student progress.

The first step may be the most critical when it comes to enrichment. The program needs to be designed to address a specific area of academic need, generally one that has been neglected or overlooked. For instance, perhaps there are a cadre of students in the school who have very high achievement in mathematics and science. Many of these students, due to their outside reading and other learning activities, know on the first day of school most or all of the science content that will be taught that year. Furthermore, they are also recognized as "math people" who not only have high achievement in math, but do so with little apparent effort, requiring only minimal practice in order to master the mathematics content of their lessons. The school decides that these students can and should be learning more about math, science, and the application of these domains, so they begin to design an enrichment program. Furthermore, let's assume that these students are in upper elementary school.

The school selects the concept of "signal to noise" as the organizing principle for the enrichment program, recognizing that this idea is central to many aspects of physical science, medicine, engineering, and even social science. The school puts together a curriculum for the program that focuses on basic applied statistics (an area that could readily be connected to the Common Core State Standards if someone was inclined to do so, although carefully drawing these connections is outside the scope of this book). Mathematical topics include ideas such as mean, median, mode, variance, and standard deviation. Understanding of these topics will require that the students learn about mathematical operations such as squaring and square roots, understand formulas in which letters represent unknown quantities, read and make plots and graphs, as well as perform other fundamental mathematical operations. Students would also need to learn about random variables and statistical distributions. The overarching concept of signal to noise in diverse areas such as astronomy, medicine, and psychology would be explored through applications and project-based learning. Practical questions in those disciplines involving questions of signal to noise may include items such as the following: For astronomy, "How can we determine whether a distant star possesses a planetary system?" For medicine, "Do these MRI scans of the brain and spinal cord suggest that the patient may have multiple sclerosis?" For psychology, "Does talk therapy reduce symptoms in depressed patients?" For economics, "Does change in government policy cause the unemployment rate to change?"

How is such a program defensible as advanced academics? First, not all students can do it (or even would want to try). As a general rule, if all students could do it, should do it, and would want to do it (we attribute this thought to researcher Harry Passow, although we have been unable to locate the original source of the idea), then it is not an advanced academics program. This could/should/would rule of thumb also has the nice side effect of making any student exclusion much more defensible. The prerequisites for the program include mastery of grade-level math and science content. This, in turn, enables the presentation of concepts that are above grade level. The program is not "fluff" because it requires students to understand and comprehend advanced mathematical concepts and operations, which require considerable instruction, practice, and effort for mastery. Second, it is advanced academics because it addresses need, at both the student and school levels. These criteria make the program itself defensible. From a programmatic point of view, the topic is effective due to its breadth. There is no area of science or technology in which the concept of signal to noise does not play a pivotal role or to which it could not be extended, based on student interest. Thus, students are afforded considerable latitude for self-directed exploration of the basic concepts, with some perhaps choosing to focus on applications in physics, others in economics, and others in biology.

The Process

The next question, then, regards developing the process for selecting students for the program. The general principles of defensible identification discussed at length in Chapter 3 apply here. The concept of potential risk again becomes salient; we review risk in the context of acceleration below before explaining why there is less risk inherent to enrichment programming.

For acceleration programs, the potential for risk is relatively high, with more risk being involved for more radical forms of acceleration. This is because in many cases there is no easy way for a student who drops out of an accelerated program to go back and obtain instruction in the grade-level content that was missed because of the acceleration. Affective or motivational damage in backing out of an accelerated placement could also present additional risk. Also, there may be considerable organizational and bureaucratic headaches involved in "undoing" a student's accelerated placement. For example, if a student has skipped a grade but is failing to thrive, it may be very difficult to move him back to his original placement in the middle of the year without significant disruption. In such a case, there may be difficulties in finding the student space in his previous classroom; determining where the "holes" might be in the student's grade-level content knowledge, and determining how those holes can be filled; evaluating the student's performance in the new setting when much of the work has been missed; and, of course, the social upheaval involved. For those reasons, acceleration programs typically have high potential risk. Therefore, when designing the identification process for selecting students for those programs, it makes sense to be more accepting of false negatives than false positives. Of course, placement errors are inevitable, but, in this context, failing to accelerate a capable student may be less dire than accelerating a student who proves to be incapable of it.

Enrichment programming typically has a much lower potential for risk than acceleration does. The risk to the student in enrichment usually occurs because students are generally either exempted from instructional time and content or have progressed through that content more rapidly (via compacting or telescoping) in order to make time for the enrichment program in the busy school day. The primary risk to the student is that he spends his time inefficiently—in other words, the hours he spends learning the mathematics underlying the concept of signal to noise would have been better spent engaging in further practice of grade-level math or science content. If this proves to be the case, then it is usually minimally disruptive (from an administrative standpoint) to discontinue the student's participation in the enrichment program or to restructure it in such a way as to make it more effective. From the student's perspective, the risk of undoing a placement is also relatively small because it may simply involve being in a different group or classroom during the time scheduled for the enrichment programming. Because enrichment programs typically have low potential risk, their identification procedures should be biased toward false positives—they should be more focused on inclusion than on exclusion. Again, errors will happen, but when they do, it is better to err on the side of enrolling students who aren't quite up to the task, rather than erring in the other direction by failing to enroll qualified students. After all, if a student can't handle the content, it's no tragedy to return him or her to the original coursework, because it typically is being offered at the same time and possibly even within the same classroom as the advanced academic programming.

If the assessment systems for identifying students involve multiple assessments, the desired directionality of placement error (e.g., toward false positives or false negatives) should directly inform the method for combining the scores. Obviously the ideal situation would be no placement errors at all, but because this is extremely unlikely (see details in the discussion in Chapter 9), a consideration of relative risk may indicate that one type of error is less desirable than the other (see also discussion in Chapter 3). As detailed in Chapter 9, "or" combination rules result in a bias toward false positives and lead to larger overall variability in the ability profiles of the identified students, whereas "and" combination rules result in a bias toward false negatives and a smaller variations in ability. The "mean" or "average" combination rule balances the risk of false positives and false negatives and, under many circumstances, results in the lowest overall error rate (McBee et al., in press). Because of this, it seems to us that "or" systems would be most appropriate to identify students for enrichment programming unless there are clear skills that must be mastered prior to placement in the program. If this is the case, then perhaps a combination "and/or" system would be preferred—all students must posses the prerequisite knowledge and skills, but beyond that, any one of multiple pathways could be used to "identify" students for participation. If it's determined that students entering the program need math skills that are two grade levels above average and at-grade-level reading scores to succeed in the program, then both of these can be required in an "and" system of identification. Beyond that, students could be entered based on the extreme nature of their scores (i.e., all students at the 80th percentile in science are automatically in), or students could write an essay explaining their interest. These multiple pathways will allow more students to be involved, assuming the program has sufficient but not unlimited space available.

Another issue to consider in low-risk enrichment program scenarios is whether formal assessment procedures are needed at all. As we discussed at length in Chapter 3, the need for assessment increases in step with the potential risk of harm in the case of an incorrect placement. Enrichment programs deemed to have low potential for risk may be able to rely much more strongly on student self-selection than on the insistence that students meet minimum cutoffs on a series of tests. This is particularly the case when teachers understand the importance of not reducing the rigor or difficulty of the instruction in order to accommodate the less-prepared students. When assessment is necessary, it may be sufficient to determine only whether students have mastered the prerequisite skills necessary for program success. Returning to the example of the signal to noise enrichment curriculum, given the mathematical content of the intervention, students who have not mastered basic concepts such as fractions, square roots, and unknown quantities will simply have no hope of understanding the first day's lesson, because it assumes some prior mastery of these concepts. Therefore, should assessment be needed, it is often better to measure highly proximal (i.e., directly relevant to the *particular* enrichment program to be offered) achievement, such as mastery of these specific mathematical skills and content, rather than more distal constructs like the student's general intelligence or grades in unrelated subjects. Notice how different this process is from the traditional "identify the gifted and then serve them" system common in gifted education?

A final consideration with respect to the identification of students for enrichment programming is to consider what instructional time in the regular curriculum will be sacrificed, if any, to make time for enrichment. In some cases, enrichment can be offered after school, on weekends, or in lieu of nonacademic school time. However, in some states with gifted education mandates (such as Wisconsin), gifted programming must take place during the school day. Schools also need to be sensitive to the likelihood that out-of-school programming may disenfranchise some students, such as those whose families are unable to provide transportation if the student remains after school for extracurricular activities. In most cases involving in-school programming, enrichment time is "bought" via curriculum compacting—often in a related subject, but not always. We have encountered examples in which students miss reading instruction time to participate in mathematics enrichment. Of course, decisions about how to buy the time needed for the enrichment program must be part of the school's overall instructional planning process. When time is culled from related subjects—for instance, if students attend the signal to noise class instead of the ordinary grade-level mathematics class—then there is essentially a complete correspondence between the skills the student needs to succeed in the advanced academic program and the skills that would be developed during the student's regular instructional time that has been eliminated or reduced. This is the ideal situation. There is no harm to the students who are missing the standard grade-level content because they already have demonstrated mastery.

In cases where nonrelated instructional time will be used for the enrichment program, the identification process must now serve two purposes—to find those students who can succeed in the enrichment program, *and* to ensure the selection of those who can afford to reduce their regular instructional time in the to-be compacted subject. If students are to miss reading class in favor of the signal to noise program, we now must not only assess students for the prerequisite math and science knowledge, but must also assess their reading skill to make sure they will not miss important skill development in their reading content-area instruction. This necessitates at minimum a two-criteria system and requires that those assessments be combined via the "and" combination rule, as only those students with both sets of skills should be allowed to participate. The unfortunate side effect of buying time from unrelated subjects is that we are now likely to miss some students with significant academic need in math and science simply because they aren't sufficiently advanced readers to justify a reduction in their regular instructional time in reading or language arts.

Conclusion

To summarize, enrichment can play a vital role in advanced academics. Although anecdotal evidence suggests enrichment is sometimes practiced without due diligence or is chosen solely because of its perceived administrative and bureaucratic convenience, we believe that carefully designed enrichment programs can play a powerful role in challenging students in need of advanced academics.

When Addressing Underrepresentation IS the Goal
Illustrative Example

So far, all of the illustrative examples we have presented have been based on programs that a particular school might want to provide (such as implementing cluster grouping, providing opportunities for acceleration, etc.) based on some kind of observed need. However, as has been noted many times (i.e., Yoon & Gentry, 2009), gifted education programs have experienced low rates of participation by students of some racial and ethnic minority groups and especially by students from low-income families. This differential representation in itself can be considered a need for equity that all schools should seek to address—just as offering a STEM enrichment program might address a need for more advanced science and math instruction. However, this is not such an easy problem to solve. If, for example, different specialized criteria are used to identify students from low-income families, then it is possible a school will inadvertently identify students who are actually unlikely to be successful in the programs educators want to provide (Lohman, 2006). In fact, this very issue was referenced as "mismatch" with regard to affirmative action programs at the university level (Sander & Taylor, 2012), and has been noted by others in the field of gifted education for some time (Lohman, 2005a). The criteria used to locate students for admission or identification to a special program often are chosen (or should be chosen) because they are predictive of success in that program, or similarly because they identify a need for a program. This means that if educators modify the criteria to be more inclusive (by simply lowing entrance requirements, for example), they could lose the predictive power that is the rationale for the identification system in the first place! The issue that remains is, how do we foster and develop the skills of all students (including those from underrepresented groups), while also making sure we aren't encouraging inappropriate program placements just for the sake of making participation rates look better? If educators place students into advanced programs for which the students are not ready and do not have the prerequisite skills, all they have done is set students up for failure. The situation in K–12 settings is somewhat different than in higher education (e.g., law school admissions), in that in higher education there are far more highly qualified applicants (i.e., those who could succeed in law school programming) than there are slots available for new law school students. In K–12 education, not all students will be capable of succeeding in advanced academic programming, provided the programming is appropriate. If all students can succeed in it, by definition it is general education; although when compared to other schools' programming it may be advanced, it is not advanced academics in that setting!

The entire issue of underrepresentation is too complex to be addressed in a single chapter. Instead, we provide here an example of what a program might look like that has as its stated purpose (or need) the goal of increasing the achievement of underrepresented students—specifically those who are in need of additional challenge—in a particular content area.

Earlier in this book, we discussed observed needs such as the following:

> Mr. Allen teaches math at Middle Ground Middle School and has noticed that for the last several years that more and more eighth-grade students are in need of algebra (needs assessment). Because of this he plans to offer an additional section of the course (program).

In this case, the issue being noticed was a need for more challenging math. Many of the same methods and procedures we have described in earlier example chapters can just as easily be applied to a system where the following is the observed need:

Principal McIntosh, in reviewing test scores for the past several years at Bayview Elementary, has noticed that almost no students from low-income families are enrolling in AP or other advanced math courses once they get to high school. He suspects that this is due at least partially to the fact that these students have significantly lower test scores than would be needed to get into or succeed in these advanced courses.

This is not an uncommon occurrence. In fact, Wyner, Bridgeland, and DiIulio (2009) in their *Achievement Trap* report found that nationally, students from low-income families are less likely to achieve in the top quarter in math in first grade than their higher income peers. Even for those who do achieve highly in first grade, students from low-income families are less likely to remain high achieving by high school in comparison with their peers from higher income families. A recent study by the Fordham Foundation similarly found that only 57.3% of *all* high-achieving students in third-grade math remained high achieving by eighth grade (Xiang, Dahlin, Cronin, Theaker, & Durant, 2011). This percentage is likely to be much worse for low-income students. Xiang and colleagues (2011) also found that high-achieving math students grew at about the same rates as lower achieving math students. This means that gaps in mathematics achievement are unlikely to close over time, and students who might be considered "high-average" achievers are unlikely to break into the ranks of advanced programming.

This same underrepresentation issue has led to what Plucker, Burroughs, and Song (2010) have termed the *excellence gap* between low-income and high-income students. This gap represents the difference between representation rates of students from poverty in the ranks of advanced achievers and those students who are from higher income families. In the eighth grade National Assessment of Educational Progress (NAEP) scores for 2007, 10% of students from high-income families scored at advanced levels in math. This is compared to only 1.7% of students from low-income families. Although this represents an increase in percentages for both groups since the previous administration of this assessment, the increase has not been proportional; there is now an even wider excellence gap than existed in any prior year since 1996. With students from low-income families trending toward becoming an increasingly larger proportion of K–12 students in the United States, this clearly is a need that deserves attention in the form of appropriate programming.

What is perhaps even more shocking than these national excellence gaps are some gaps that exist within individual school districts. At the time of this writing, one metropolitan school district in Wisconsin demonstrated excellence gaps at third grade of 18% versus 43% (low-income high achievement rate vs. higher income rate), with some individual schools showing excellence gaps as high as 15% versus 70%. These gaps represent a perfect example of an observed need for which a school might provide a targeted program. What these gaps indicate is that there are students currently rated as "proficient" and who come from low-income families who could perhaps do more if they received some kind of intervention. The goal here isn't simply to relabel or reclassify kids into "advanced" categories, but rather to better match their needs with instruction both now and for the future, with the end goal that these students will be ready and able to pursue college programs and careers that require advanced skills.

The difference between this and previous chapters is that here the thing we are identifying students for (the "need") is filled by a specialized program designed to move students from low-income families into the ranks of advanced math learners. The long-term goal for such programming would be to foster more students taking advanced math courses, who subsequently would also be more likely to pursue math-related fields in postsecondary education. Now that the need or initial impetus for a program has been established, an appropriate intervention or program can be created. As was clear from the Xiang et al. (2011) report, students in a given achievement category are not likely to move up in category over their K–12 careers unless there is some kind of accelerated programming or intervention provided to help them do so. The low-income students who are the highest achievers compared to other low-income students (but not when compared to all age-level peers) are unlikely to break into the "advanced" ranks of achievement unless a program is designed and implemented specifically for this purpose.

The Alternatives

Before we present the program and identification system based on the perspective put forward in this book, we should first consider the two most widely offered suggestions for increasing the diversity of identified gifted and talented populations. Although they make some sense, each idea has flaws that prevent it from being as effective as we might wish.

Using Different Tests

One prominent idea for locating more low-income and racial/ethnic minority students was proposed by Naglieri and Ford (2003). It involves changing the tests typically used in gifted and talented student identification to those that are more culturally neutral and therefore show smaller differences between subgroups of students. This method presumes two things:

1. that traditional academic achievement and aptitude tests are flawed and biased against low-income and minority students (thus explaining their underrepresentation), and

2. that students from traditionally underrepresented populations already have the necessary skills to benefit from a gifted program if issues related to culture and unfair testing practices were no longer acting as a barrier.

These ideas are based on lower observed scores on traditional academic tests as well as lower representation rates in gifted programming for students from low-income, African American, Native American, and Hispanic families (see Yoon & Gentry, 2009). As a counterpoint, McBee (2006) provided evidence that minority and low-income students were filtered much more strongly by the nomination stage of Georgia's two-stage identification procedure than by the psychometric testing stage—so the tests themselves might be less of a problem than schools' determination of who is allowed to take them. Other studies have concurred that when systematic screening of students' test scores is implemented, participation by traditionally underrepresented groups in gifted programming increases noticeably. Although systematic screening is not a complete solution to the complex issue of underrepresentation, it is clear that it should be included in efforts to increase access to advanced academic programming.

Using Tests Differently

A second method, proposed by Lohman (2005a) but often discussed in mainstream measurement and assessment textbooks (see e.g., Anastasi & Urbina, 1997) involves using local and/or group-specific norms based on traditional achievement and aptitude tests in order to locate those students with high potential relative to their peers (this conceives of identification in terms that are local and in the present tense). The idea is that if a researcher or administrator wants to know which students have the most *potential*, that question is always relative to some group (i.e., the most potential compared to whom?). If the administrator compares students from wealthy families to those from poor families, the poor families will appear as if they have less academic potential—but this is not a valid comparison. In fact, every country in the industrialized world shows lower average test scores for students from poverty as compared to students from wealthier families (Carnoy & Rothstein, 2013). The higher income family can and often will provide their children with far more opportunities to learn and likely even additional years of education (e.g., through summer academic programs and preschool), making these children's potential more likely to manifest itself in achievement. The solution then, when looking for academic potential or aptitude, is to compare students to others who have had similar previous life experiences. This will yield data concerning who has learned the most or is the most capable of new learning within a given set of educational and life experiences.

Peters and Gentry (2012) showed that such a process of using group-specific, local norms will increase the representation rates of under-represented subgroups just as affirmative action programs result in greater rates of first-year college entrants (Sander & Taylor, 2012). Unfortunately, there is a significant barrier to just using group-specific norms for gifted and talented student identification. Simply placing students into programming *does not mean that the identified students have the necessary skills to be successful in or benefit from the program they were identified for*. Instead, it just means the students have higher levels of mastery when compared to a similar peer group. This statement says nothing about their match with the programing to be provided. As we have stated throughout this book, there is no justification for a *generic* gifted identification system or a *generic* advanced academic program, because advanced academic programs as we have described them are always tailored to the local context.

The goal is locating students in need of *specific* programming. Any identification system needs to be based on what programming will be provided for those who are identified. For example, giving a math exam written in English to an ELL student with low English language proficiency will result in scores that are unduly biased by language effects—the test does not set out to assess language mastery, but it does so anyway (because the questions are in English), resulting in nonvalid inferences regarding the relationship between her test scores and her math knowledge. To alleviate this problem, the student could be given the math test in her native language. This would yield more valid information regarding her *math* skills. However, math knowledge is not all that is needed to be successful in a math class. These two things are not the same. If we placed this student in an advanced math classroom where instruction takes place in high-level academic English, she is not likely to succeed. The same problem holds true for group-specific norms. Group-specific norms can yield a measure of relative potential compared to others who have had similar prior educational experiences. The issue is that this measure of potential says nothing about students' mastery of the prerequisite skills necessary for success in a particular program. The identified student might be the strongest math student from a non-English language background in the state—but this doesn't mean she has the skills to benefit from the programming the school wants to provide. As we have stated throughout this book, the content of the resulting programming must be considered when making identification decisions.

Why Both Methods Fail

In 2011, the NAEP test was administered to a representative sample of fourth-grade students across the United States. The average score for students who were eligible for free lunch at school was 238, while the average score for students not eligible for free meals was 252. If either of the two methods outlined above were implemented, it's likely that more students from the underrepresented population of students eligible for free or reduced meals would be identified. If the goal is simply to say that we have successfully "identified" more students, then either of the two methods described above will work. However, simply identifying them would not change their current level of math mastery or achievement even if they are then placed in an academically advanced mathematics program.

If we suppose that the program for which the students were being identified involved advanced math instruction akin to content at the 260 score level, then identifying students scoring at the 240 level (advanced relative to their peer-group average but not advanced enough to be ready for the program) will likely set them up for failure. This is similar to what happens if we implement group-specific norms without any modification to the resulting programming. The students may well be advanced compared to their peers, but the advanced academic programming in this case is still beyond what they currently need/their current level of readiness. They either need a differentiated program or some kind of supplementary support in order to be successful in the existing program.

As stated earlier, this same type of score disparity due to poverty has been observed for every country in the industrialized world (Carnoy & Rothstein, 2013). In fact, the Program for International Student Assessment (PISA) in 2009 showed smaller advantaged-disadvantaged student test score gaps for the United States than in many other industrialized countries (Carnoy & Rothstein, 2013)—in the U.S., we simply have proportionally more disadvantaged students than do most of our peer nations, which in turn brings down our average test score. These score differences could be explained by supposing massive rates of test bias against low-income families—an unlikely scenario, but one that would support the solution of simply using a different test—or they could indicate real differences in what certain students know and are able to do, differences whose most likely explanation lies in the different home and preschool learning opportunities that are associated with differences in household income.

It is worth mentioning that observed subgroup score differences can, but do not necessarily, represent an issue with the test itself. For example, the NAEP scores referenced above show score differences between students from high- and low-income families. This *could* indicate a test is working perfectly and that a certain subgroup actually does have a lower level of the thing being measured—just as women, on average, are shorter than men. For example, African American students have received lower observed achievement test scores for a very long time (see Jairrels, 2009, for a summary of current thinking). Some have argued this is caused by test bias (Naglieri & Ford, 2003). Again, observed score differences between subgroups could be an indication of test bias, but they also could indicate that students from African American families, for one reason or another, come to school with lower levels of academic preparation. Part of this may be explained by the fact that African American students are far more likely to come from poverty than their Caucasian peers—in 2009, 26% of African Americans lived below the poverty line, as compared to 13% of Caucasians (U.S. Census Bureau, 2012). If being from poverty means you receive less education or a lesser quality education early in life, then the test is not biased; it's just measuring what it's supposed to measure. Observed score differences are necessary but not sufficient to establish test bias. Those more interested in this topic should consult Peters (2012), Lohman (2006), the NACG (2008) position paper on assessment (included in Appendix C), and especially the chapter by Camilli (2006).

The Program

To recap, there are two goals of interest in this particular identification: (a) to locate additional underrepresented students, and (b) to locate students who both need and are able to be successful in their resulting programming. There is a simple rule that must be followed in order for any kind of identification system to accomplish goals such as these: *Any differentiated identification system must be paired with differentiated services.*

This has important implications for programming when diversity is one of the needs that the advanced programming seeks to foster. If we implement a differentiated identification system, whether it uses group-specific norms, multiple pathways, a nonverbal ability test, or anything in which we use new (different or nontraditional) methods to locate students, we cannot expect the newly identified students to do equally as well in the original program as those identified via more traditional methods. After all, the program wasn't made for their needs. An example follows to clarify what we mean.

Consider briefly, as an illustrative example, a university that once required all starting students to have a 24 on their ACTs in order to be admitted. Now, in order to admit a greater number of students, they have lowered their required score to 20. More students will be identified, including proportionally more students from low-income and minority families. However, these students, *because of their lower scores*, will be a poorer match with existing programming. Modifications need to be made to the programming (e.g., by implementing remedial coursework), and/or support

structures need to be put in place (e.g., tutoring), or else the newly admitted students will fail at a higher rate than those admitted with higher
scores. If these new students already had possessed the prerequisite skills,
they would have been identified via traditional methods (i.e., by the original score requirement). The fact that differentiated identification criteria
were required to "find" these additional learners suggests that they are in
some way different from their higher scoring peers and therefore need
some kind of differentiated programming or additional support if placed
into the standard programming (i.e., the regular coursework at the university in question). We will return to this point later in this chapter.

To offer a second and more extensive example, we will seek to identify elementary students for the Mentoring Mathematical Minds (M³)
program from the National Research Center on the Gifted and Talented
(Gavin et al., 2007). The M³ curriculum is based on National Council of
Teachers of Mathematics standards and was developed as part of a federal
Javits Grant. The M³ curriculum includes 12 units, four each for grades 3,
4, and 5. The units represent a blend of both enrichment and acceleration,
with each unit's content being advanced by roughly 1–2 years compared to
typical grade-level content. This content includes numbers and operations,
geometry and measurement, data analysis and probability, and algebra. The
acceleration of the content is key because the goal of the program is to
help low-income students who have high relative potential to catch up
to their higher income peers so that they subsequently can enter and perform successfully among the ranks of advanced math students in the usual
advanced academic program setting.

The purpose in offering this program is to create more high-achieving math students from low-income families. To accomplish this goal, the
focus will be on those students who meet traditional or expanded identification criteria relative to their individual peer group (in other words,
using low-income group-specific norms) who also fall below the advanced
threshold of traditional achievement tests or fall just below the threshold
of gifted.

To further illustrate the M³ example, we have selected one urban school
from Wisconsin to use as a case study. In this study, we use data from the
math section of the Wisconsin Knowledge and Concepts Examination
(WKCE)—a fairly typical, low-ceiling, state-level achievement test. One
third-grade level of data were disaggregated for students who are and are
not eligible for the federal free or reduced price lunch program, and all

	Enrolled at Test Time	No Score	Min Perf	Basic	Proficient	Advanced
Economically Disadvantaged	19	5.3%	26.3%	15.8%	26.3%	26.3%
Not Economically Disadvantaged or No Data	63	0.0%	3.2%	6.3%	25.4%	65.1%

Figure 7.1. Economic differences in achievement at Stevens Elementary (Wisconsin Information Network for Successful Schools, n.d.).

students were classified into one of five achievement categories (one being no data available). This school, which we will call Stevens Elementary, has a relatively small population of low-income students compared to the rest of the district (which is closer to 50%; see Figure 7.1 for a complete break-down of the economic differences in achievement at this school). However, it is often these schools that have the wider excellence gaps. In this school, the gaps are close to 40% (close to but below the average for the district). To proceed, we focus on how to find those low-income students who, with support, could be successful in the M^3 program and could develop their math potential into math achievement. For this example, we are also assuming that many higher income and already some low-income students would be identified for the program based on traditional criteria.

In a school like Stevens, it is likely that little attention is paid to students from either income who fall into the upper end of the proficient category or into the advanced category; after all, they are already proficient. We have explained previously why this thinking should be reconsidered, but that is not our current focus. Our goal in this example is to find some additional math potential in the low-income student population and to give those students a chance to demonstrate any math abilities they might already possess. Table 7.1 presents the cut scores and proficiency ranges for the Wisconsin Knowledge and Concepts Examination test in Math for 2010.

Stevens Elementary would not offer the M^3 program for low-income students alone, for two reasons: (a) there aren't likely to be enough of these

TABLE 7.1

Wisconsin Knowledge and Concepts Examination
Proficiency Score Categories in Mathematics for 2010

Grade	Score Range			
	Minimal	Basic	Proficient	Advanced
3	220–391	392–406	407–451	452–630
4	240–420	421–437	438–483	484–650
5	270–444	445–462	463–504	505–680
6	310–463	464–484	485–531	532–700
7	330–479	480–503	504–554	555–710
8	350–482	483–512	513–572	573–730
10	410–515	516–540	541–594	595–750

Note. From *Wisconsin Knowledge and Concepts Examination: Fall 2010 WKCE Technical Report*, p. 262, by the Wisconsin Department of Public Instruction, 2011. Copyright 2011 Wisconsin Department of Public Instruction. Reprinted with permission.

students to constitute a full class or program, and (b) some level of cognitive heterogeneity is a good thing. Although being "advanced" on the WKCE is unlikely to translate to an identification as gifted (because the category of advanced includes a wide range of scores), it is still clear that this school has a large number of high achievers, especially from higher income groups. The question is, "Are they having their needs met by whatever program is currently provided?"

In this example of a "modified" identification system, we will follow a similar path as outlined by Peters and Gentry (2012) but with one critical addition. In this system, the top 10% of all students were identified as in need of a particular program, followed by the addition of the top 10% of students from low-income families whose scores were high relative to their income-level peers. Many students overlapped both of these categories, but this approach also found many new students of potential. In this fashion, no fewer high-income students were identified; rather, Peters and Gentry (2012) augmented the pool of students to include more from low-income families. These additional students—those who are not in the top 10% overall but who are in the top 10% when compared to a closer peer group—will never be a large number of students (because of the substantial overlap between the two top 10% groups), but they will represent those with the greatest math potential relative to their peers. At Stevens, there are roughly five low-income students each in the proficient and advanced categories (25% of the low-income students). If we assume that one scored high enough to be identified using traditional means (90th percentile), this leaves nine possible candidates for our program (10 in the proficient and advanced categories, minus the one who was already identified). We will also assume that about 10 high-income students were already identified using the same process (there are about 36 high-income students scoring advanced, so we have assumed that 10 scored high enough to be identified). Further, we will assume that because there are so many advanced students at this school, there already are some programming or curricular systems in place to challenge students who are somewhat above grade level. This is where the other 26 or so high-income students who fall in the advanced category would be served.

When Peters and Gentry (2012) used this method in reading, the result was an approximate increase of 25% for the identified low-income student population. So far, this is nothing more than applying a group-specific norm with an underrepresented group as a means of inclusion. It's important to note that this practice will increase the size of the identified population—something that can be unpopular. The only alternative to this increase in size is to use group-specific norms for both low- and high-income students that will de-identify some students. We do not recommend this for political reasons, and it is additionally problematic because it will result in students who do likely have prerequisite skills not being identified.

Table 7.1 tells us that the cut score between proficient and advanced in math on the third-grade WKCE is at 451–452. The cut score between basic and proficient is at 406–407. Based on these ranges, we can get an idea of the level of prerequisite skills in the students of interest. Here are the example students that our group-specific norm process has identified, as well as their respective math WKCE scores—Table 7.2 includes the nine students referenced earlier, not including the one who would have already been identified.

If we were to stop at this point and identify all nine additional students listed above and place them in the program, they would likely not be successful in our program because, by definition, they do not have the prerequisite skills (this assumes WKCE scores are a close approximation of each student's "true" score, a simplification we have made here for purposes of illustration).

For these moderately advanced learners to be successful, supplementary support needs to be provided. Any new students we identify are

TABLE 7.2

Students' Math WKCE Scores

Student	Math WKCE Score
Katie	448
Emily	440
Maria	457
Jennifer	451
Jeffrey	440
Lacey	499
Michael	445
Javier	455
Alex	449

behind—that is why they scored below the traditional cut score. They have not mastered as much math content as their higher income peers. Still, we want them to be ready for the same advanced math later on in school as their higher income peers. This means we will need to provide accelerated learning and additional support in order for these learners to be successful in the advanced M³ content.

Ignoring for the moment the fact that the standard error of measurement for these WKCE math scores is around 50 points (see Chapter 3 for a discussion of standard error of measurement), these students do not have the prerequisite skills for a program in which successful students show prior mastery as evidenced by a minimum WKCE score of 460 or higher. This is why if we just used group-specific norms and then placed these students in the program, they would feel lost—they are outside their Zone of Proximal Development (Vygotsky, 1978) and do not have the necessary skills to benefit from the content of the advanced academic programming.

There are two potential solutions to this problem of mismatch: (a) provide additional tutoring or scaffolding in some way in order to help these students catch up faster than their higher achieving peers, or (b) provide a second tier of gifted programming that is better targeted toward their needs. Given the relatively small number of students who would need additional support at this school, additional scaffolding could be as simple as the lower performing students arriving 15 minutes earlier to go over some introductory material before the rest of the class arrives. The second option might look like a gifted/high-achieving M³ program as one level of service, for those students who have scored at least a 460, as well as a second section of high-achieving students who are still in need of advanced content, but who are not ready for the standard (M^3) advanced academic program. The more advanced group might start with later/more advanced units than the second section would. Such dual classes would be more administratively feasible in a larger school that has more students in need. Because a second section could be subject to the same differential representation that we are trying to address with this intervention, our opinion is that the former option is preferable. If possible, including all students in the standard program is ideal *as long as additional support is provided so that mismatch does not occur.*

This might seem a little backward. After all, if these students don't have the prerequisite skills and scores to benefit from the gifted program, then why should we go through all of this work? This takes us back to the original need for this program—to increase the numbers of advanced math students from low-income families. If a school district has decided that this is an important goal, then such action is appropriate.

Continuing the Example

We turn now to the implementation of the actual identification system and program using the school and data presented earlier. For this example, we will assume that the M^3 curricula already are being implemented as an advanced-academic program for some number of the (primarily higher income) students who have scored at the advanced in math (in the 500+ range), with some low-income students placed having obtained the minimum score of 460. This 460 represents the cut score at the 90th percentile of a general all-student local norm comparison. This group already includes one low-income student, for a current program size of around 11 students. This is somewhat small—a principal or administrator might argue that a program for only 11 students is too expensive. There is also an issue of underrepresentation. The school has about 25% low-income students, and yet only about 10% of these learners are represented in the identified pool using traditional measures. This adds two additional reasons for finding more students, not including the initial desire to increase student achievement!

Returning to the pool of other potential students to include in this program, we could simply lower the overall cut score for identification into the program—say moving from the 90th percentile to the 80th. This might increase the program from 11 to 25, including five additional low-income students (see Figure 7.1). However, the problem of underrepresentation remains, and we've now included a majority of students in the program who do not have the prerequisite skills to be successful (the 460+ score). This cannot be a viable solution.

Implementing a group-specific norm at the 90th percentile for students from low-income families will increase the population identified from 11 to 13 by adding two more low-income students (10% of 19 students). This is progress because now the program is more balanced in terms of enrollment by low-income students (closer to proportional representation). These two additional students would need extra support in order to be successful, but for two students that shouldn't be too challenging—it would take the form of tutoring or coming in early, as described earlier. Still, with this change, the program remains relatively small, and we haven't done much to increase the overall ranks of high-achieving math students from poverty. That said, this method is a viable option, particularly for those schools that have slightly larger populations of low-income students than our example school does.

More drastic measures could be taken. An even more inclusive identification criterion could be used for the low-income group of students, accompanied by intense scaffolding so that they could succeed. Taking the top 25% of students from the low-income group would yield a total identified population of 16 (25% of 19 students). Some of these learners would require quite a lot of support in order to be successful in a program that is over their heads, but this still is not an unreasonable number. They could also be admitted on a trial basis to see if the exposure to the advanced content helps them to demonstrate more advanced abilities than the WKCE initially reflected. This kind of trial basis is a useful tool for students who are on the cusp of program readiness. The teacher's preparation time saved due to still having a relatively small class size (at 16) is made up for by the fact that additional support will be required for those students who do not currently possess traditional levels of prerequisite skills. Keep in mind that such drastic changes to identification criteria are only rationalized by the fact that the goal of this program is developing the math talents of students from low-income families.

Conclusion

There is no simple solution to issues of underrepresentation. On one hand, it might seem simple to just let more kids in by lowering cut score requirements for all students, but this has the potential to decrease the rigor of the program as a whole because the teacher may be unable to provide additional support for so many new and unprepared students. Additionally, such an action could be setting these kids up for failure by putting them in a program for which they are not ready.

The primary concern whenever a gifted coordinator or administrator seeks to locate more underrepresented students should be the match between potential students' current levels of demonstrated mastery and the level of content to be covered in the program into which these students might be placed. If that mismatch is great—as was discussed above—then either supplementary support will be needed, different levels of programming need to be provided, or the students simply should not be identified for the program.

Common Pitfalls in
Identification

8

This chapter is a little different from the others, for in it, we critique usual practices in gifted education to better differentiate our advanced academics approach from the status quo. To understand how we propose to structure the identification of students in need of advanced academic programming, it is important first to understand the variety of practices currently in use and the various ways in which these current approaches may be limited. For those who are interested in what practices are common regarding gifted education programming and identification policy, we recommend the National Association for Gifted Children's biannual *State of the States Report* (NAGC & CSDPG, 2011); many of the pitfalls we identify stem from the practices described therein.

Problems may arise at various points in the gifted identification process, and we've referenced many of the same problems throughout the book. Therefore, in this chapter, we address in greater detail a variety of common pitfalls in the procedures commonly used during attempts to identify students with gifts and talents. Below we address five common areas for mistakes and dispel some commonly held misconceptions related to the gifted identification process. These criticisms have all served as the basis for our focus on advanced academics and the methods we have outlined throughout the book.

Pitfall #1: Choosing the Test
Based on Convenience

One of the practices implemented across a wide range of schools is the use of a single specific test for identification purposes, simply because it's what the school already has or already uses for other reasons. Often, this takes the form of a state-mandated achievement test that is given to all students at certain grade levels and is based on a state's general content or curriculum standards. In some instances, these tests can be very useful as one tool in making identification decisions. These tests often are very closely tied to the content that is actually taught in the school curriculum (which cannot be said of IQ tests), although in many cases this is because the curriculum follows the test and not the other way around.

It is likely that existing measures are used because of their low additional cost and time requirements. This is convenient; existing measures do not require the purchase of additional tests or additional time to administer them. As we discussed in Chapter 2, the decision of which students are identified and what content areas and skills should be included in gifted and talented programming should depend first on the philosophical and cultural values of the local school or district, and only following this decision should practical considerations such as cost or time efficiency enter into the process. When schools default to using their state tests or other existing measures without first having the necessary underlying philosophical and cultural conversations, the identification practices that result yield a specific and very limited range of skills and content areas, which may or may not be those areas for which the school wants to provide advanced academic programming.

Defaulting to existing measures for identification purposes also poses both practical and theoretical problems. On a purely practical level, most state achievement tests are plagued by a limited range of topics being assessed and by great variation across settings in terms of what "high performance" actually means (Matthews, 2006). Standards for performance categories such as "Level IV," "Advanced," or "Exceeds Expectations" vary over time within, as well as across, states, and the difficulty level of test items also may change over time. Many states have recently moved up their expectations for grade-level proficiency after having lowered them significantly following the passage of the No Child Left Behind Act in 2002. For example, North Carolina redefined the meaning of "at or above grade level" for its reading end-of-grade tests, causing the percentage of students deemed to be at grade level for reading to drop from 85.5% overall in 2006–2007 to 55.6% overall in 2007–2008.

Complicating the use of these tests for identifying high levels of achievement is that they typically are designed to measure performance most accurately near the average level of performance—also known as grade-level performance. Although most tests will yield relatively inaccurate (or unreliable) scores at the upper and lower end of the score distribution, most tests also suffer from an even more severe problem called a *ceiling effect*. Ceiling effects occur when the test has insufficient range to measure high levels of ability as students approach the test's maximum score (see McBee, 2010b). Ceiling effects make it very difficult to assess high-performing students accurately using these measures (Matthews, 2007). What happens when a ceiling effect is present is that scores tend to "pile up" at the high end of the score distribution. This frequently takes the form of some number of students (more than the top 1% that would be expected) having scores at the 99th percentile on a given test. The problem arises because these students now all appear as if they have an identical level of knowledge in the given content area, something that is highly unlikely. What is more likely is that the test does not have a sufficient range to differentiate within these students' high relative level of achievement. As far as the test can tell, these students are all the same. This limited range of knowledge and information makes matching programming with student need a far more difficult task than it would be without these ceiling effects.

Imagine if a group of average college students were all given a single-digit multiplication test; most would score very well. Unfortunately, this high average observed score would not tell us what each student really knows about math. Because teachers or administrators have no way of knowing the students' true levels of knowledge (because of a low ceiling), they are now prevented from making informed placement or instructional decisions. Such a process would place nearly all of the college students in question into the same class, one teaching (for example) two-digit multiplication! Moving to an example in the K–12 setting, imagine 100 fifth-grade students have taken a standardized achievement test. This test was designed for fifth-grade students but covers a grade equivalent range from about third grade to seventh grade. One of the students is actually performing at the 10th-grade level (the kind of student the school's identification system is looking for). However, because of the test ceiling, he or

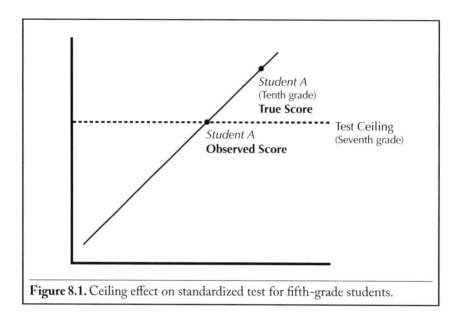

Figure 8.1. Ceiling effect on standardized test for fifth-grade students.

she can score no higher than a seventh grader would perform on the same fifth-grade content, because that's as high as the ceiling goes (see Figure 8.1). We would not know how an actual seventh-grade student would perform on this measure, because when developed it only was tested on fifth-grade students!

The solution to this problem is to use tests that have wider ranges (higher ceilings and possibly also lower floors). If this isn't possible, another approach is for those students who reach close to the maximum score on the test to be reevaluated using additional measures in order to obtain a clearer picture of their current level of understanding. An administrator could take all fifth-grade students who scored at the 99th percentile and give them an above-level test (one meant for eighth graders), and this test would yield a clearer picture of what those students know. Only with results from measures on which the student may express his or her true level of understanding can appropriate programming or instruction be implemented. This is essentially what happens with above-level testing, as in the Talent Search model (Matthews, 2007). Students who already have demonstrated high scores from grade-level tests are given above grade-level tests in order to obtain a more accurate measure of their current understanding.

An additional practical problem can arise when a state achievement test is used, often in those states where gifted identification is mandated by law. In many such cases, identification must take place K–12, or, in some states, in grades 3–8. Even if state achievement tests were of a high quality and provided an appropriate measure of the construct of interest, most states only implement them in certain grade levels in order to comply with relevant federal requirements (e.g., No Child Left Behind). This would leave schools or districts out of compliance because they would have no data from grade levels where students were not already being tested. This same problem could occur when schools, in an effort to decrease the time and money spent on testing, decide to identify students only at certain grades. For example, some schools only identify using aptitude tests in second and fifth grades. By design, this means that students who are not identified in these years cannot be identified as gifted. It also means that the school may be in violation of state statutes if there is a law to identify and serve throughout grades K–12.

Pitfall #2: Failing to Connect Identification With Programming

By far, the most significant fault in choosing a test before first identifying a need to be addressed or program to be provided is the lack of connection between the assessment(s) and the program itself. If not closely matched with the content of the program, the test will not effectively identify the students whose needs the program was designed to meet! In sum, stakeholders must first decide what programs are to be served and identified for, prior to choosing which assessment measures or other identification tools will be used. Too often, this process is completed the other way around, and the resulting gifted programming does not do a very effective job of linking services to students' needs. We concur with Feldhusen, Asher, and Hoover (1984), who 30 years ago wrote, "it would be desirable to place less emphasis on labeling students as gifted and to place major emphasis on devising programs to meet the needs of youth who have special talent and abilities" (p. 150).

Being identified as gifted does not mean a child necessarily exhibits superior performance in every subject. Although some students do show profiles of high ability across many or all of the major academic content areas, far more learners are academically advanced in one or two content areas but are closer to average (or maybe even below average) in the other domains. These differences have important implications for the process of matching students with appropriately advanced academic learning experiences. Differences in individual profiles of ability also suggest that identification needs to happen at a point close in time to the provision of the program; the common practice of identifying students once in early elementary school and assuming on this basis that gifted services are required for the remainder of the students' public education is questionable at best.

A similar problem is when a mismatch occurs between the services or programs identified students will receive and the measures or procedures used to locate or qualify students for those programs. Such a mismatch can occur for a wide variety of reasons. Perhaps the most general example occurs when a number of students are identified as gifted/not gifted and then all identified students are provided the same programming. For example, a policy might allow for students to be identified if they score in the 85th percentile or above on an achievement test in either math or language arts. Although the ability to be identified in one area without necessarily being identified in the other might seem in line with a focus on domain-specific giftedness, if the identified students are all placed into a single generic gifted program, one that often emphasizes only language arts or verbal talents, then there will be a large disconnect between what some students need and what they are receiving. Most often, these types of generic gifted programs are highly verbal places that would not serve well those students who do not have advanced language arts or vocabulary but who do show a need for advanced math instruction. Occasionally, mismatch also can go in the other direction, as when students identified through their performance on a verbal subscale are placed into a program setting that only emphasizes mathematics. Although learners with high general ability would still likely accrue some benefit from this type of placement, in comparison to placement in an undifferentiated general education setting, there have been few if any systematic studies addressing these situations. One would not expect these mismatched systems to be as effective for all learners, as a system would be in which identification and programming were more closely connected.

The same problem occurs when students are assumed to need the same services in multiple successive years even though a testing or identification program was only conducted in one year (based on the premise that constructs such as IQ are generally stable over time). It is far too common that the gifted identification process only occurs systematically at certain grade levels. For example, as presented earlier, a given school might identify students in second grade and again in fifth grade. Unfortunately, just because a student is found to have a need for advanced content or programming in second grade does not mean that same student necessarily needs advanced programming in third or fourth grade. The student's need may have changed, the programming could have changed, the teacher will be different, and the regular classroom-level content could have changed. All of these variables influence whether or not a child is gifted—if gifted is interpreted to mean a need for a service that is not already being provided. When wide gaps exist between the date of the identification and the date of the service, the information gained from that identification becomes stale, especially at younger ages, as test scores of young students tend to be unstable over time. This doesn't mean a child with a 145 IQ in second grade will no longer be smart by fourth grade, but it does mean that that child's current level of need may be different—different enough that the program is no longer a good match. He or she may have advanced more quickly than expected or become part of a cohort of highly advanced learners, or alternatively, may have become overwhelmed and in response slowed to a more average pace and degree of educational need.

Children change so rapidly as they develop, especially in the early years, that updated assessment information is critical to assure the best possible match between need and service. We cannot stress enough how important the match between methods of identification and resulting program placement really is. If stakeholders determine that a program needs some kind of identification policy (i.e., because the program could cause harm if provided to the wrong students), then school officials must be sure that the program is appropriate for each individual placed into it. If language arts achievement test scores from 3 years ago are being used to identify students for a science-focused enrichment program, there will be a serious mismatch that leads to an ineffective educational intervention.

Because we long have known that test scores are less reliable at younger ages (McCall, Appelbaum, & Hogarty, 1973), in some settings (e.g., North Carolina) systematic gifted identification efforts do not take place before the end of second grade. However, we also know that scores are more likely to fall over time for students traditionally underrepresented in gifted programming, especially among those from low-income households (Wyner et al., 2009), which suggests that early identification is preferable for these learners. Both of these trends support that assessment for placement in advanced academic programming should take place on a regular and ongoing basis. In fact, the 2010 Gifted Programming Standards from the National Association for Gifted Children support this stance. As "Standard 2: Assessment" states in part, "All students in grades PK–12 have equal access to a comprehensive assessment system . . . Educators establish comprehensive, cohesive, and ongoing procedures for identifying and serving students with gifts and talents" (NAGC, 2010a, p. 9). Some kind of ongoing, systematic, and universal identification system is important for compliance with these NAGC standards, with Response to Intervention frameworks, and with many state laws.

Corollary: Even children identified as gifted within a specific content area can be quite different from one another. A similar problem can result when all students who are identified under any single content area are then perceived and served as if their needs were identical, simply because they all were identified within a single content area. To continue with the example from earlier, suppose a school identified students as gifted and talented in math if they scored at or above the 85th percentile on the math section of the state achievement test. This is a step in the right direction from the other earlier example—at least now the content area of the test and program are the same. Still, students who score in the 85th percentile are likely to have very different needs in terms of the advanced content they are able to master or need in order to be challenged, in comparison to students scoring at the 99th percentile on the same measure. If students were identified in this manner as sixth graders, many may be ready for mathematics at the seventh-grade level, some at the high school level, and maybe even a few at the college level—but now we are placing them all in the same program. Of course, there would not be a large number at the extreme (i.e., capable of college-level mathematics), but for those who are, their learning needs likely are not addressed in a program based on seventh- or eighth-grade content. Although instructional differentiation certainly would be possible within a general gifted mathematics classroom, this example suggests the problems inherent in the assumption that all students who are identified as gifted and talented within a single content area are the same or have the same instructional needs. This problem also exists at even more extreme levels of need for advanced academics. Even if only those students who score at or above the 95th percentile are identified, this group still will include some individuals with much higher levels of knowledge than the test score adequately describes (ceiling effects). In IQ testing, a score of 130 is roughly the 97th percentile. However, while most people who score at this level are likely to be very close to 130 (say from 130–145), few will score at the 160 level. Such students may have very different learning needs from those whose score is closer to 130, but it would be hard to determine just what these might be on the basis of IQ tests alone because they do not measure what children know and are ready to learn relative to K–12 content.

Even once students are formally identified, the need for up-to-date information about their current level of knowledge and instructional needs remains. As mentioned earlier, a student who has his or her IQ tested at a 145 is very able (relative to his or her age peers). However, that score does not tell teachers exactly what this student needs as far as instruction or services. Even when students meet identification criteria, sometimes additional information is needed to actually know what content that student has mastered and what he or she still needs to learn. This connection between assessment results and instructional needs has long been recognized as a weak point of current procedures in gifted identification practice (Stanley, 1978). The fact that a child has been identified as gifted often yields very little diagnostic information regarding what educational services he or she needs and yet, schools somehow consider this to be the most important information. Following formal identification, curriculum-based assessment offers an effective tool for identifying specific instructional needs within a given academic content area. However, these measures do not negate the need for ongoing universal assessment.

In talent search testing (Lee, Matthews, & Olszewski-Kubilius, 2008; Matthews, 2007), two seventh-grade students who score at the 99th percentile on a grade-level assessment would take a test designed for 11th to 12th graders. One might score in the same range as the average eighth grader, while the other may score at the higher end of the range for 11th graders; these two students would benefit from very different instructional environments, whereas the seventh-grade test would have shown them both as needing the same instruction due to its limited range. Gifted education researchers have known for decades (thanks to the pioneering work of Julian Stanley) that above-level testing is extremely effective in showing us the relative abilities of these high-scoring students (Stanley, 1990). Unfortunately, this awareness is not often reflected in gifted identification policies.

Luckily for schools, many states are now moving to types of computer adaptive testing as their main state-level achievement test. The Measures of Academic Progress from the Northwest Evaluation Association and the Smarter Balanced Assessment System are two examples of achievement tests that have virtually no ceiling. Because both tests are computer based and adaptive in response to a student's answer to a previous question, the idea of grade-level tests almost disappears. The third-grade student who has always scored at the 99th percentile on his third-grade test now has the room to score as high as he can—maybe at the eighth-grade level for math. Adaptive tests have a much higher ceiling than traditional assessments, which allows for a much closer match between need and programming.

Pitfall #3: Validity Problems in Identification

Perhaps the most important issue in gifted and talented identification is the degree to which the assessment tool or tools actually measure what they are supposed to be measuring, and whether we can make the inferences that we would like from the assessment—whether or not a student needs and would benefit from a program we seek to offer. Unfortunately, the issues involved here often require expertise beyond the level of the teacher or school administrator. Even the most concerned teacher in the world can't make psychoeducational measurement more accurate. However, this same teacher can work to make sure that the skills or content areas in which he or she wants to provide programming for students are represented in the procedures or tools to be used for student identification.

Nonverbal Measures Are Not a Panacea

A classic example of where identification goes wrong deals with nonverbal ability tests. Many gifted and talented identification policies rely on such tests in an effort to make their systems more culturally neutral or unbiased. The problem is that if students obtain high scores on such tests and are then placed in traditional academically focused gifted programming, which often involves a high emphasis on verbal skills, this clearly is a mismatch and these students will not be well served. Just as a test of math ability would not be used to identify verbal talent, nonverbal measures should not be used to identify talent in areas where verbal skills are important—such as in most K–12 academic subject areas. In such areas, verbal ability is actually part of the construct of interest, and therefore should not be removed from the requisite assessment (as is the case in nonverbal measures). Although nonverbal-format testing has been recommended widely in the gifted education literature, often for its perceived ability to increase the representation of English language learners and other cultural and linguistically diverse groups who traditionally have been underrepresented in gifted education settings, most of the evidence in support of using nonverbal testing for this purpose is either anecdotal or has been seriously debated (Lohman et al., 2008; Matthews & Kirsch, 2011). Lohman (2005b) has explained convincingly how, in fact, overreliance on nonverbal testing actually would fail to identify the most able learners from all ethnic groups. Even among English language learners, the group with whom one might expect language-reduced testing to be most efficacious, these measures may not be any more effective than traditional IQ testing for gifted identification purposes (Matthews & Kirsch, 2011).

Without delving into the controversy over the Naglieri Nonverbal Ability Test (NNAT; Lohman, 2005c; Naglieri & Ford, 2005), there also are several less controversial nonverbal ability tests commonly used in gifted and talented identification. Tests such as the fourth edition of the Test of Nonverbal Intelligence (TONI-4; Brown, Sherbenou, & Johnsen, 2010), the Universal Nonverbal Intelligence Test (UNIT; Bracken & McCallum, 1998), and others potentially could all be used to identify students for certain programs—just as the NNAT could. The validity issue comes in when we start to consider two questions: For which programs are these tests valid measures of student need or readiness? And, to what degree are the students these measures identify able to achieve success in the related program? These should be the primary questions with any identification tool, as opposed to theoretical discussion of which tests are "good" versus "bad."

As Lohman (2005b, 2005c, 2006) and Lohman and Lakin (2008) have argued, nonverbal measures actually are less likely to identify students who will be successful in traditional, *academic* gifted and talented programs than traditional measures are. To identify students using nonverbal identification and then place them into very verbally loaded programs is educationally unsound. This problem is a textbook example of a mismatch between what the identification test measures and the content of the programs that are provided to students so identified. If a nonverbal ability measure is used (often in a well-meaning attempt to decrease cultural bias or to better evaluate English language learners, as noted previously), then a program must be designed in conjunction with that test. This is not an impossible feat, as the Paradise Valley district in Arizona does just that.

An Aside: What Might Programming Based on Nonverbal Identification Look Like?

Using the NNAT2 (Naglieri, 2003), the Paradise Valley School District evaluates all of its sixth grade English language learners from Title I schools. If these students meet certain NNAT2 cutoff criteria, then they are placed in the Nonverbal Honors Core program for seventh and eighth grade. This program is taught by teachers with both gifted and ELL certifications. The curriculum is heavily project-based, with a developmental emphasis on language; specific program components are designed to prepare students for future success in traditional language-based academic areas.

In such a situation, there is a close connection between the assessment tool and the program. If the students who were identified were instead placed in traditional honors or accelerated academic programming with a heavy emphasis on already-developed advanced English language skills, then there is little chance they would be successful. The Paradise Valley program offers one example of what a strong match between identification and curriculum might look like, but, of course, it is not the only way to accomplish these goals.

One of the easiest ways to assure a strong connection between assessment/identification tool and program is to review the stated purpose of the tool itself. In fact, one of the first items listed for test developers in the *Code of Fair Testing Practices in Education* relates to this very issue: "Provide evidence of what the test measures, the recommended uses, the intended test takers, and the strengths and limitations of the test, including the level of precision of the test scores" (JCT, 2004, p.4). Test developers are often very explicit in what their instruments have been designed and researched to do, and this offers one of the easiest ways to see if an instrument will indeed assess level of need for a given program. Test users (schools) shouldn't simply look for which test states it can be used for gifted identification. Instead, what should be of interest is to what degree a test measures high levels of mastery for a given content area. For example, the Otis-Lennon School Ability Test (8th edition) states as its purpose that it is "designed to measure those verbal, quantitative, and figural reasoning skills that are most closely related to scholastic achievement" (Pearson Education, 2003, p. 1). This means the test measures academic readiness in verbal, quantitative, and figural areas. If we wanted to know more specifically what scores on this test predict, we could look further to see what the relationship is between scores and academic achievement in math. This is the kind of connection that is critical to evaluate before implementing any identification tools.

Pitfall #4: Tests Don't Identify the Gifted; People Do

Tests and other assessment tools do *not* make decisions. They are just tools that provide stakeholders with important information on which to base their decisions. As such, test users and administrators need to understand the purpose of specific tests and what they have been developed to do, or what kind of information they have been designed to yield. Only with this information can valid decisions be made.

Know Guidelines for Fair and Ethical Testing Practices

The *Code of Fair Testing Practices in Education* (JCT, 2004) outlines a wide range of things a test user (school or professional) should evaluate before adopting a test or assessment for any purpose. The following is taken directly from the "Test User" section and is similar to what was listed above for test developers:

> Test users should select tests that meet the intended purpose and that are appropriate for the intended test takers. [Test users should] define the purpose for testing, the content and skills to be tested, and the intended test takers. Select and use the most appropriate test based on a thorough review of available information. (p. 5)

Tests typically are designed and researched to yield specific information on a certain group for a certain purpose. This information and the test's purpose often are described at the front of the test manual, and these are also an initial component of all Buros *Mental Measurement Yearbook* (MMY) test reviews. Measures that do not have reviews published in the MMY should be considered suspect, unless they are too recently published to have been reviewed, as this comprehensive publication reviews all published measures that meet its test quality standards. Informed test consumers can use this information to select measurement tools that are designed for the purpose or content area that their available programs are meant to serve.

Another valuable resource (currently in revision) is the *Standards for Educational and Psychological Testing* (AERA, APA, & NCME, 1999). This resource has chapters on ethical standards in testing, including specific details about best practices for avoiding bias in the testing of culturally and linguistically diverse individuals.

In some cases, the issues presented are relatively obvious to even the casual observer: Using a math test to identify students for a language arts program would make little sense. However, often it is not that simple. Even a test that has not been designed specifically for gifted and talented identification purposes could still be used to yield information on the current needs of students, which could in turn be used for matching student needs with appropriate programming.

Know About Other Sources of Bias and Reduced Validity

Bias is a complex issue within the larger realm of psychoeducational assessment. In relation to testing or assessment, bias refers to a situation "when deficiencies in a test itself or the manner in which it is used result in different *meanings* [emphasis added] for scores earned by members of different identifiable subgroups" (AERA, APA, & NCME, 1999, p. 74). In other words, a biased assessment is one that *functions* differently across subgroups in the population that the test is intended to measure, such as racial groups or genders (JCT, 2004). This is not the same as producing differences in average scores for different subgroups, nor is it something that can be easily or directly observed. The classic example of African American students receiving lower average scores than Caucasian students could, but does not necessarily, indicate bias. Bias is only indicated if tests produce different scores across subgroups for individuals with exactly the same amount of the construct being measured by the test. So if Caucasian students and African American students with the exact same underlying math achievement receive systematically different scores on the test, the test is racially biased. Possible subgroups within whom bias may exist might include race or ethnicity, ELL status, gender, and socioeconomic status.

Current best practice addresses this aspect of bias by examining something known as measurement invariance, which provides a mathematical way of comparing performance across different groups conditional on the underlying true level of the construct being measured. We encourage the reader who would like to learn more about this topic to refer to recent publications by Peters (2012) and by Peters and Gentry (2010) that illustrate these methods within the field of gifted education, or to the seminal work by Vandenberg and Lance (2000).

Bias is a specific form of poor validity, but the concept of validity goes beyond bias. For example, imagine a science test for which the items are supposed to be read to the students by a proctor. If these instructions are ignored and students have to read the items themselves, some students will miss questions only because they were unable to read the items and solutions effectively. In that condition, the validity of the test is reduced because the test now measures reading ability (the irrelevant construct) in addition to the construct the test is designed to measure (science). Another obvious situation might be when a test's overall (or composite) score is used to identify students to receive gifted and talented programming in a subarea measured by the test, such as language arts or mathematics. This would be a validity-reducing use of the test in question because, as Lohman (2009, p. 984) showed, using only the composite score would fail to identify approximately 40% of the highest scoring learners on the reading subscale. If the gifted programming were in mathematics, then the same proportion of learners who should have been identified for this program would not have been, because their abilities were missed due to having used the test's composite score. These biases still would exist, even if the test's technical manual provided evidence that the composite score has no biases against specific subgroups.

The *Code of Fair Testing Practices* (JCT, 2004) offers the following guidance with regard to test development:

Obtain and provide evidence on the performance of test takers
of diverse subgroups, making significant efforts to obtain sample
sizes that are adequate for subgroup analyses. Evaluate the evidence to ensure that differences in performance are related to the
skills being assessed (p. 4)

Many tests and assessments fall short on these criteria. For whatever
reason, test manuals sometimes fail to present evidence confirming that
extraneous factors such as race, gender, ethnicity, or SES have no influence on test scores. This presents a serious dilemma for the end user (i.e.,
the teacher or administrator) because he or she is left on his or her own
to decide whether the measure in question is appropriate for his or her
purposes. An instrument might otherwise appear potentially useful, but in
the absence of information that would allow the user to evaluate whether
or not it works equally well for members of diverse populations, it probably should not be used. For whatever reason, instruments specifically
designed for gifted education seem to be more plagued by this deficiency
than are psychoeducational assessments as a whole. Schools and districts
could collect and analyze their own information about a given measure,
and this information would be even more relevant to their needs than any
evidence provided by the test's publisher (because the publisher's perspective is based only on the norming sample with whom the measure was
standardized, and a local sample always will be the most directly relevant).
Unfortunately, this is a time- and labor-intensive process, and schools
rarely if ever possess the financial and human resources needed to accomplish this task in any systematic fashion. On a case-by-case basis, developing research partnerships with local university personnel can offer one
way to gather evidence about the appropriateness of a given measure; such
collaborative research can have beneficial outcomes for all involved (e.g.,
Matthews & Kirsch, 2011).

Be Suspicious of Homemade Measures

Producing measures of psychological and educational constructs that
exhibit adequate validity for a given purpose and that produce scores with
adequate reliability is difficult and technically demanding, requires substantial expertise and training, and typically involves extensive rounds of
trial and instrument revision. All too often, gifted identification practices

rely upon measures that have not been evaluated systematically or that have been copied and pasted piecemeal from other sources. This seems to be a particularly pervasive problem when using behavior rating scales, although in recent years the number of commercially available rating scales that include some evidence of reliability and validity has grown. In some settings, multigenerational photocopies suggest that no one can recall the original source of a given measure; it's just "what we've always used." Unfortunately, this is by no means a recent problem; more than a quarter century ago, Feldhusen and his colleagues (1984) recommended that "program directors should be cautioned not to attempt to develop their own rating scales unless they have had substantial training in psychometrics" (p. 149). In addition to the cost of published measures, high personnel turnover and the correspondingly short institutional memory that accompanies such turnover also can lead to this state of affairs.

School staff responsible for the choice of identification measures should be aware of copyright considerations, and also of the potential legal consequences the district may face if the measures it uses for identification cannot be demonstrated to have sufficient evidence of reliability, validity, and lack of racial and gender bias. These potential legal considerations alone should be sufficiently persuasive to convince a district to allocate the resources necessary to purchase or develop adequate identification measures. Collaboration with university researchers, as well as offering to pilot new measures for a test publisher, can help reduce costs while assuring the adequacy of measures in use.

A larger problem with homemade assessments is the lack of information regarding their quality. There's simply no way to confirm that homegrown tests actually measure what they are supposed to measure, or if the questions are clearly worded or even written at an appropriate reading level. Instrument development is a very complex process and in the absence of due diligence in this area, an attempt to make identification more accurate can actually have the opposite effect. We have personally seen such measures that contain many obviously bad items such as double-barreled questions (two questions in one), questions that do not appear to have any connection to theory, and even questions pasted together from several different published rating scales. None of this is appropriate, nor will it lead to more accurate decision making.

Be Aware That All Test Scores Include Some Amount of Error

As previously discussed, all test scores have measurement error and are imperfect indicators of what they are designed to measure. Therefore, hypothetically, a test given to the same student over and over (assuming no additional learning related to the test items occurs between the two administrations) will yield slightly different scores *even though nothing else changes.* This natural variation in test scores, due to measurement error, yields an uncertainty range around the tests scores called the standard error of measurement.

Measurement error has two main implications for gifted and talented identification. The first is that a different group of students can be identified each time a process is implemented, even if the exact same procedures were used. This fact, combined with the issue that students change, learn, and develop as time goes on, means that the group of students who might be identified in third grade likely will differ from the group identified using the same procedures in fifth grade. This is one reason why we argue repeatedly that it is vital to regard giftedness not as a permanent, categorical definition, but instead as a current need for differentiated educational services. This is also why we argue against using set test scores or especially stringent testing criteria for identification. Identification, in the end, is a subjective decision that must be based on available data, but must also be made by consideration of a person rather than strictly by a number.

A second implication of measurement error is that even if a hard cutoff score is used in the identification process, procedures should be developed to take into account the existence of measurement error. Because error estimates differ slightly from one measure to the next, we suggest that at a minimum, identification procedures should describe the circumstances under which the standard error of measurement may be taken into account in qualifying students to receive programming. Such a description might read like this:

> A score of 1XX+ indicates that the student is in need of gifted program services. The school psychologist who administered the individual IQ test shall indicate that the student qualifies for services with a lower score, within the bounds of the particular test's standard error of measurement, by checking the appropriate box on the identification form and indicating "eligible for services" on the form's final line.

Of course, measurement error results in more qualified students not being identified (false negatives); it also causes unqualified students to be identified (false positives). There have been relatively few investigations of the impact on gifted identification of the influence of measurement error and repeated measures, but we would encourage the interested reader to refer to McBee et al. (in press), as well as to the excellent article by Lohman and Korb (2006) and chapter by Lohman (2009).

Don't Invoke Too Few Measures (or Too Many!)

There are other issues that should be considered in relation to the number of measures used in any identification plan that relies upon testing, and these also have to do with measurement error. Common practice in gifted and talented identification over most of its history has been to rely on a single measure as an indicator of giftedness and talent. This is a very effective process for those learners who do qualify, as it is extremely unlikely that a student would score highly on an achievement or aptitude test in the absence of high-level ability. However, as a way to determine who should *not* qualify for services or who might not need services now but may need them later, this process is much less effective.

Some sources of error in using a single measure are readily apparent. For example, when only one assessment is used on a single occasion, a given student might be ill that day, might not have eaten breakfast, might not have gotten enough sleep, or might have done any number of activities the day before or that morning that would prevent her from demonstrating the maximum performance that is an assumption of any standardized testing situation. Achievement and aptitude tests all assume that the student is giving 100% on the assessment. If this is not the case, which might be due to any of the reasons mentioned above, then the measurement error goes up and the accuracy of the assessment results goes down.

Unfortunately, just making sure students are well-fed and well-rested will not fully solve this problem, although it certainly could help. Simply adding more measures may seem like an easy solution to this problem, but here too, there are some potential pitfalls that must be considered— many of which we address in Chapter 9. There seems to be an assumption in gifted and talented student identification that says educators must use multiple measures in identification, which also are called multiple criteria (Krisel & Cowan, 1997; McBee, 2006). As should be clear, using more than one measure is almost always preferable in educational assessment than just assuming that any single test yielded perfect results. However, the practice of using multiple measures needs to be implemented with caution.

In the 1980s and 1990s, arranging multiple measures into identification matrices (e.g., Baldwin, 1984) became a prominent part of recommendations for moving away from single-measure identification practices. Today, matrices remain widely used in gifted identification practice. Unfortunately, as with behavior rating scales used for gifted identification, many identification matrices have been developed locally by personnel who have little experience or formal training in psychometrics. In our experience, gifted identification matrices tend to have little or no justification for the specific measures included or for the relative weight assigned to each component. When we have tried walking composite student profiles though a number of these identification matrices, this process often revealed that a single score (most often IQ) made the difference between whether or not a given student was identified to receive gifted programming services, regardless of his or her other non-IQ attributes! Although this may sound cynical, gifted identification matrices in some instances appear to be merely a tool serving to disguise the use of a single-score criterion. Just as with behavior rating scales, much thought must be put into the design of an identification matrix in order to allow for the combination of measures to match with gifted education theory. How much to weight each instrument and even what instruments should be used is not a simple decision. In general, we greatly prefer the "mean" combination rule (Chapter 9) over the use of identification matrices.

Pitfall #5: Generic Identification Followed by Multiple Programs

If a school makes the decision that a student can be identified in a number of different areas, then programming must be matched to those different areas in order to have a logical match between students' needs and the service provided. After all, if programs or services will not be offered, then why waste time and money on identification? In practice, as the number of areas that require programming grows, scheduling and staffing considerations also multiply. Because of this, it would seem that small or medium-sized schools and districts likely would be unable to offer a wide variety of services without resorting to magnet schools, online course delivery, or some other manner of consolidating demand across a wider geographic area.

We suggest that in response, it may help to reframe one's conceptualization of what gifted or advanced academics programming is. All children need to be placed in a classroom with a teacher, regardless of whether the teacher is certified or otherwise trained in meeting the needs of advanced learners. In many states, in fact, no additional specific training is required for teachers to work with high-ability learners because this matter is left to state and local control. The evidence supporting the beneficial outcomes of university-based teacher training in gifted education is relatively strong (Hansen & Feldhusen, 1994), and we support requirements for teacher training in gifted education as well as greater pay for teachers who have completed additional, rigorous training in this or other relevant areas of education.

Because all students must be placed in a classroom, and because in most settings (even those that require additional teacher training in gifted education) these teachers are not paid any differently than teachers without such specialized training (Shaunessy & Matthews, 2008), this presents the opportunity for all classrooms to be considered potential locations for specialized instruction to take place. One model that appears to be particularly promising in this regard is Total School Cluster Grouping (Gentry & MacDougall, 2009; Gentry & Owen, 1999), which we covered in Chapter 4.

To return to a broader view, we note that many gifted education systems focus on five general areas: general intellectual, specific academic, creativity, leadership, and visual and performing arts. This is by no means the case everywhere, but these categories seem to be relatively common. When these five areas are then implemented across grades K–12, the idea of appropriate educational programming becomes daunting. This is why we believe that before specific academically advanced programming can be implemented, schools need to understand what they already offer as part of the general education curriculum. In the traditional academic areas, this is often termed *curriculum mapping*. In the simplest sense, curriculum mapping is a means to understanding what is taught when and where. If we wish to identify students whose needs are not met within the general education curriculum, then it is important to first know what is provided in the general curriculum. This knowledge should include content as well

as depth and breadth of current offerings. Once decision makers systematically have made themselves aware of their school's current offerings, it
becomes much easier to determine what is missing in terms of advanced
academics. Awareness of available offerings and instructional strengths
(and weaknesses) of the curriculum can also be used to inform discussions
of what advanced academic programming might be most appropriate in
a given setting, to build upon the resources and personnel already present
in the system. This can lead to consideration and development of a locally
appropriate definition of advanced academics or giftedness, which leads
in turn to the selection of appropriate identification measures where such
are warranted. Thus, with awareness of the potential pitfalls kept clearly in
mind, an effective system of advanced academics can begin to be developed.

An Introduction to Combining Multiple Measures

9

Current best practice in gifted education, and indeed, many areas of evaluation, involves the combining of multiple pieces of data to arrive at a final decision. In traditional gifted education programs, this is often referred to as *multiple-criteria assessment*. For example, the state of Georgia's gifted education policy mandates that students be evaluated on aptitude, achievement, motivation, and creativity. Such a system is very different from what was common 30 years ago. Multiple criteria assessment stands in stark contrast to what many consider the "bad old days" of the field in which giftedness was defined only by a superior IQ score. The consideration of multiple criteria may indeed lead to better placement decisions being made, but there is considerable complexity to deal with—a point that has not yet been widely appreciated by the field. The complexity arises from the facts that the rich, multiassessment information is eventually used to make a binary placement decision and, moreover, that each assessment is imperfect, being contaminated with measurement error and having less than perfect validity. There are several ways that multiple sources of information can be combined, and the choice of how to do the combination can carry potentially serious consequences on the characteristics of the group of students identified for the program as well as type and frequency of placement errors.

Identification in general is one of the most complex and least under-stood sets of decisions that must be made when designing advanced academic programs. Here we will repeat a key theme from Chapters 3 and 4: The purpose of identification is not to discover which children are gifted or smart or special, but rather to discover which children have a need for and could potentially succeed in the particular intervention that has been designed—*this* year, in *this* school, relative to *this* curriculum, and in accordance with the values and needs of *this* community. With that key concept in mind, let us now briefly consider the parameters of the decisions that must be made.

Do We Even Need to Do Identification at All?

The issue of when identification is justified was discussed in Chapter 3. One factor that clearly justifies careful selection of students is when the intervention has high risk, implying that false positive placement decisions are significantly harmful to students and to the school. Another might be what we sometimes call *culture-sensitive programming*. Culture-sensitive programming means that the intervention only works to the extent that the enrolled students create and maintain an achievement-oriented and enthusiastically engaged culture around the program itself. Such cultures enable students to feel safe and supported in being themselves, taking risks, and pushing beyond comfort zones. Such cultures also tend to be highly fragile. The inclusion of even a small number of unengaged or actively disruptive students can destroy the culture of the program and lead to suboptimal experiences for all participating students. Students who are not both academically prepared and genuinely interested in the content are sometimes disruptive to the program culture. To maintain such cultures is a legitimate goal of identification, with the caveat that as long as removal criteria are articulated and enforced, it may be more just to remove disruptive students from the program than to not allow them in at all. After all, even students that you expect to be disruptive and disengaged could surprise you!

Quite apart from those issues, careful student selection is needed when academic need outstrips the available resources. Although denying special education services to disabled or cognitively impaired students due to lack of resources is not tolerated, the same cannot be said for services for high-achieving students. Schools might find themselves in situations in which 40 students exhibit sufficient academic need in language arts to warrant placement in an accelerated program, but resources only allow 25 students to be served. Obviously, in this case, the best solution is to obtain the additional resources needed to serve all needful students. As noted in an earlier chapter, all students need to be placed in a classroom, and teachers generally are not paid any more for teaching an accelerated or academically advanced class than they are for a regular class. If such resources cannot be found, perhaps the intervention can be redesigned with lower costs so that it could be made available to all of the students who need it. Presuming that none of those options are possible, the least ideal of the options is to attempt to provide those services to those students with the greatest need (thereby leaving some students in need unserved)—which generally requires formal student assessment.

A final situation may be called "panning for gold." Whereas the usual role of student assessment is to weed out unqualified students who are not likely to succeed in the program, another role of assessment can be to attempt to locate and enroll those students from the "low-interest, high-need" quadrant discussed in Chapter 3 who might enjoy and succeed in the program if they only had a chance, but who are unlikely to choose to enroll without some cajoling on the part of teachers or counselors. In this situation, evidence can suggest that a reluctant student has all of the tools needed to succeed in a more challenging academic environment, if only he chose to do the work.

If Identification Is Warranted, Will It Be Based on Data From Psychoeducational Assessments or From Performance-Based Assessments?

Decades of practice in gifted education have centralized the role of educational or psychological assessment in selecting students for programs, particularly regarding intelligence tests. It is almost reflexive for those of us accustomed to usual practice in gifted education to reach for our IQ tests as soon as we begin to think about identifying students, although nowadays perhaps we value measures of achievement and creativity equally. One theme of Chapter 3 was that selecting students for programs is fundamentally about making *predictions* about the future (albeit the immediate future)—who will thrive, whose needs will be met, and who will not do well if they are placed in the program. A core principle of educational and psychological measurement is that the best predictions are generated from observing performance on tasks as similar as possible to the target task. Once stakeholders have decided to use psychoeducational assessments, more questions must be addressed, including:

- Will we use a screening test or procedure to determine which students will receive the full battery of tests?
- How many and what constructs will be measured?
- Specifically, which assessments will we use?
- Will we rely on criterion- or norm-referenced tests?
- If norm-referenced, will we use national or local norms?
- How will we use the information to make placement decisions?

Although all of the points here are critical, the last is perhaps the most central. Even in situations in which a single assessment is to be used, the simplest scenario, deciding how to use the data can be difficult. The purpose of the advanced academic paradigm that we espouse in this book is to offer a defensible and ethical system for delivering rigorous and appropriately paced instruction for students who are currently exceeding the requirements of the typical curriculum. As such, one of the major flaws of the gifted education paradigm is the arbitrariness of the identification system—where, for instance, program entry might be limited to students scoring a 130 or above on an intelligence test, absent any evidence that this cut point is meaningful regarding the probability that our students can actually perform the tasks we've set out for them (the program). It is tremendously important that advanced academic programs do not fall into the same trap.

With a single assessment, two basic approaches can be used for selecting students. Either a cutoff can be imposed, such that all students scoring above it are selected for the program, or the highest-scoring *n* students are selected, where presumably *n* represents the number of students that can be served given the constraints of the program. We call the latter system *rank-ordering*. Each approach has its strengths and weaknesses.

Cutoffs

Cutoffs ensure that all qualifying students (i.e., students who have the need and/or the prerequisite skills necessary for success) are selected, implying that the program size may fluctuate from year to year. Some years, more students will exceed the cut score and some years fewer. The difficulty with a cutoff is determining where it should be set. The worst possible way to set the cutoff is to set it arbitrarily, such as the 90th (national) percentile on a norm-referenced test without evidentiary linkage to program success. A better method for setting the cutoff with respect to norm-referenced test results might be to first use a statistical model to predict program performance from the test score and then find a cutoff on the test corresponding to, perhaps, an 80% likelihood of adequate performance in the program. This is obviously superior to simply pulling a cutoff from thin air, but setting the cutoff at the 80% chance of success is still arbitrary (why not set it at 70% or 50% instead?). This approach would be superior to the former in that it at least acknowledges the predictive nature of the instrument. More importantly, the "chance of success" cutoff can and should be determined with respect to the relative risk of the program in order to provide administrators with finer control over the proportion of placement decisions they are likely have to undo for nonperforming students balanced against the number of students who would be able to succeed in spite of the odds if given the opportunity.

Rank Ordering

In rank ordering, the number of slots in the program is fixed. The number of qualified students granted the opportunity to enroll varies over time depending on the size of the talent pool for that particular session. This is the system used by selective college graduate programs, private employers, and many others. Occasionally, due to happy accident, it might be that the set of students admitted under rank ordering exactly corresponds with the set that would be admitted under a traditional cutoff system, but this will be quite rare. In rank ordering, school districts are relieved from the pressure of determining the cutoff but instead have the pressure of telling some qualified students that they do not get to participate in the program. Rank-ordered selection systems are no less arbitrary than the traditional cutoff alternative. The arbitrariness is instead linked to the number of seats.

Why have, for example, a 25-seat program rather than a 26-seat program? The size can be justified, perhaps, by appealing to rules regarding maximum class sizes or the physical constraints of a space, which help to alleviate the arbitrariness to some degree. To the extent that the number of seats or program slots is smaller than the number of students with unmet academic need, rank-ordered admission systems are nearly guaranteed to leave out some students who would benefit from the program. (Conversely, if the program size exceeds the needful student population, some students will be enrolled who will not benefit.) Rank-ordered admissions systems are therefore quite inflexible in the face of student needs that may fluctuate substantially from year to year. When the program is too small relative to student need, there may be clever ways to ameliorate some of the concern about false negatives to some extent, such as, for example, accepting the top 30 of 47 potential students into the program on a trial basis, and then further eliminating the five lowest performing students in the trial period. That type of hybrid approach may reduce the concern that the some of the students not in the top 25 to be ultimately served would have done well had they been admitted. Of course, it is still probable that some students would be missed even under a system like that if they fail to score as one of the top 30 who are then enrolled in the trial. The lower the predictive validity of the assessment used (in other words, the less accurately it predicts program performance), the worse that concern will be.

Norm-Referenced Versus Criterion-Referenced Tests

These are two general methods for understanding the meaning of a test score. A criterion-referenced test is one in which the score represents how well an individual performed relative only to the items/content on the test. Most tests that students take in schools are criterion-referenced tests—think of the state-level standardized tests mandated by No Child Left Behind. They are often scored on a percentage correct metric. So when your fourth grader tells you that she scored an 86 on her science test, you know that she answered 86% of the items correctly. Of course, not all items might have been worth the same number of points and there might have been extra credit, so the percentage correct interpretation may not hold exactly, but suffice it to say that the test score on a criterion-referenced test is a number that represents performance relative to the items on the test and little else. High-stakes professional licensing exams, such as physician board exams or the Airman Knowledge Test, are criterion-referenced.

Norm-referenced tests provide a relative metric for interpreting the score. The score on a norm-referenced test tells you how the student performed relative to the average performance of some group of students—the norm group. Generally, the norm group is selected in such a way as to be approximately representative of the intended population of test-takers. Scores on norm-referenced tests do not tell you how much a student knows or what he or she can or can't do; they only tell you how that student compares with other students. In fact, the person scoring number one in the country on a test of a certain skill could actually know very little of that skill—he or she just happens to know more than everyone else. Norm-referenced comparisons are firmly ensconced in the world of gifted education because the conception of giftedness has generally itself been norm-referenced from a conceptual standpoint. Where a criterion-referenced test of, for example, flying skills can determine who has or does not have the necessary skills to fly an airplane, a norm-referenced test would only tell you who is better at flying an airplane than the others who took a test. The person who was "better" could still be terrible—just less terrible than everyone else. So the identity of the norm group becomes crucial in interpreting the scores. For example, if the norm group consisted of ace combat pilots, even low scores might indicate sufficient skill to safely fly a Cessna during daytime VFR (visual flight rules) conditions.

From the point of view of a stakeholder seeking to select students for an advanced academics program, it is clear that a criterion-referenced test is much more closely aligned with our needs. Particularly if we have decided to use the cutoff approach rather than the rank-order approach, and even more so if we have identified specific prerequisite knowledge and skills needed for success in the program and now need to know the extent to which candidate students possess those skills. The dream scenario here is to use tests scored on an item response theory (IRT) metric, for on those tests, the score is *directly* linked to item performance, such that educators can, from a student's test score, determine the probability of the student getting a correct answer to each item and therefore identifying with great precision the student's level of skill development.

As most tests are not scored on an IRT metric, ordinary criterion-referenced scores may provide similar information with less granular detail. Criterion-referenced tests are particularly desirable when the content assessed by the test closely matches specific skills and knowledge deemed necessary for the program. More abstract indicators of program readiness, such as intelligence test results, are better considered from a norm-referenced point of view as the linkage from specific skills assessed by those tests to program performance are much less clear cut. For instance, we wouldn't be able to say that only students with a backward letter span (a task commonly found on IQ tests) of four or more characters—the information we could perhaps determine from criterion-referenced scoring—has a good chance of thriving in our program. It's just too hard to draw the connection between the skills on the assessment and the skills needed in the program. But we might know that our program, due to its rapid pacing, will pressure students' working memory resources, so therefore we might want to select students whose working memory is relatively advanced relative to other students, always keeping the point of comparison (i.e., the identity of the norm group) in mind.

Another issue to consider was addressed in Chapters 3 and 8 and deals with the selection of the norm group itself. Should each test-taker's score be compared against a national (or state, etc.) norm? Is such a comparison relevant? Do we care how well a student is doing compared to others across the country? Against national norms, the students in some schools are nearly all superior, while in others, most students may perform far beneath the national norm group. When cutoffs are inflexibly linked to national norms, as some state's gifted education policies require, the situation arises in which zero students are gifted in one school while nearly 100% of students in another school are gifted. In many, if not most, cases, the national norm group is not a particularly meaningful point of comparison when it comes to locating students who are in need of more-challenging programming. It is often more meaningful to compare students against local norms—the average performance of students in their class, school, or school district. Using local norm-referenced scores can provide deep insight into the lack of fit that some students experience between their curricular experience and their current level of preparation. As we have said before, there are numerous students in low-performing schools who are capable of doing much more advanced work than is typically delivered in their setting, even if those students might even be unprepared for the typical academic demands of a high-performing school. How the student might fare in a different setting is irrelevant.

Combination Rules

Once the previously mentioned details have been worked out, one must decide how to combine the scores provided by multiple assessments. There are three general methods from deriving a binary placement decision from these multiple criteria (McBee et al., in press). They are the "and" rule, the "or" rule, and the "mean" rule. Decision of how to use multiple data sources is very important. The "and" rule requires that students have some minimum score (above a cutoff) for every assessment given—although the cutoffs can vary across assessments. To be identified under an "and" rule here, the student would need math scores above some cutoff, and IQ above some cutoff, and so on. Missing even one of the cut scores would prohibit that student from program entry. The "or" rule is exactly the opposite. Under the "or" rule, a student is admitted to the program if he exceeds the cutoff on *any* of the assessments, regardless of how poorly he may have done on the others. The "mean" combination rule computes an average score across the assessments. Those average or mean scores are either rank-ordered, with the highest ranked *n* students selected for the program, or alternatively they are compared to a cutoff, with those whose scores exceed the cutoff selected. Of the three rules, only the "mean" rule can be used in a rank-ordered system. The "and" rule and the "or" rule only make sense with respect to the cutoffs on the individual assessments.

The "and" rule tends to result in an identified population of students who are very homogeneous with respect to their qualifications and prerequisite skills. One can be relatively[5] assured that all of the students possess a common minimal set of knowledge and skills. This can be very helpful from a programmatic perspective. The "and" rule also results in the smallest population of identified students. In an "and" rule, each additional assessment is like another hurdle that students must clear in order to make it into the program. The more hurdles are added, the fewer students will be able to clear them all. Therefore, the more measures are added to the assessment battery, the fewer students will qualify. The lower the correlation between assessments, the larger the impact the number of assessments has. For example, adding another math assessment to a battery that already contains a math assessment would result in a smaller reduction in the student population than would happen if a creativity test was added, because the two math tests measure similar skills and are likely to have substantially correlated scores.

---

5 "Relatively" due to the influence of measurement error.

The "or" rule, on the other hand, results in a population that is quite heterogeneous. Unlike the "and" rule, under an "or" rule, each additional assessment offers another pathway to admission. This implies that the identified population will increase in size as more assessments are added—because there are more pathways to admission. The increase in population size directly results from the correlation between the assessments, with low correlations causing a larger increase as additional assessments are added. The logic is parallel to the "and" rule condition, because if two assessments are highly correlated, it is unlikely that the student would have a qualifying score on the second if he or she did not qualify on the first.

As discussed in prior chapters, all assessments contain some degree of measurement error. Measurement error is random noise that causes scores to deviate from their true values. The relative composition of true score and measurement error in a set of test scores is called *reliability*. Tests with high reliability have only a small amount of measurement error, meaning that the scores they generate tend to be accurate measurements of each student's true scores. Conversely, tests with low reliability have a great deal of measurement error. They tend to be inconsistent and do not provide very accurate measurement of the child's true score. And of course, it is the true score that matters, because the student's true intelligence (or motivation, or math achievement, or whatever), not his or her error-contaminated measured score, is what influences how he or she will perform in our program.

Measurement error influences placement decisions differently depending on whether the "or" rule or "and" rule is used. Actually, the *maximum* performance under realistic conditions is that only about 84% of placement decisions are correct, and higher cutoffs result in worse performance[6]. Performance under the "and" rule or "or" rule will be similar on an absolute basis but will be biased in opposite directions. Identification errors under the "and" rule will tend toward false negatives, that is, omitting students that should be in the program. Because students must not miss even *one* cutoff in a multiassessment system under the "and" rule, all it takes is one unfortunate measurement error in the negative direction of sufficient size to prevent a truly qualified student from passing the multiple hurdles to identification. Identification errors under the "or" rule occur in the opposite direction; they tend toward false positives. By the same logic, all it takes is one *positive* measurement error to result in an unqualified student being identified. Errors across the two combination rules are not equally

---

6   This assumes a single-assessment system with reliability of 0.95 and a cutoff at the 90th percentile. See McBee et al. (in press) for details.

balanced in size. The magnitude of the false negatives that occur under the "and" rule are more severe than the false positives that result from the "or" rule. This is because we are generally seeking to identify students at the top ends of the distribution of scores, and a property known as *regression to the mean* causes measurement errors to preferentially occur in the negative direction, toward the mean of the score distribution.

The only score-combining method that can actually reduce the damaging influence of measurement error is the "mean" combination rule. We recommend that the mean be the default method of combining scores unless you have a very good reason to use the "and" or "or" rules, with one caveat. The mean rule reduces measurement error because the measurement errors tend to cancel out as more assessments are combined. For example, if scores from four assessments with mediocre reliabilities of 0.80 (implying that 20% of the score variance is measurement error) are combined using the mean rule, the mean of those scores has a reliability of 0.94. A test with a reliability of 0.80 would be capable of correct placement decisions only 68% of the time[7], whereas the average score of multiple administrations of tests with a reliability of .80, with its higher reliability of .94, would yield correct placement decisions about 84% of the time. Taking the mean of higher quality individual tests with higher reliability gives even better results. Another implication of the mean combination rule is that rates of the two placement errors, false positives and false negatives, are equal in the long run, making for more predictable program size and composition. Also, as we previously pointed out, the mean rule is the only multiple-criteria method we considered that can be rank-ordered. The "mean" rule is also the only rule in which weights can be applied to the assessments to allow them to have greater or lesser influence in the resulting decision. The problem with the "mean" rule occurs when the scores being combined are criterion-referenced. We previously described how criterion-referenced scores are tied directly to the content that the test measures. This interpretation is lost when one takes the "mean" of a set of scores, even if those scores were themselves criterion-referenced. In a mean combination rule, each possible mean score could have been obtained in many different ways.

---

7   Assuming that the cutoff is set to the 90th percentile. Higher cutoffs mean worse performance.

Weighting

If you are using the "mean" rule, you need not grant each measure the same weight in the placement decision. If you believe, for instance, that motivation is more predictive of performance in the program than IQ, you could give your motivation measure more weight. Details will be provided in the following example.

Screening Tests

In gifted education programs, it is common to require students to pass through a "nomination" stage (McBee, 2006) prior to receiving the full battery of assessments that determine program placement. These can take the form of teacher nominations, parent nominations, self-nominations, or even automatic nomination on the basis of prior test scores. Even though collecting a nomination from a teacher is not a formal test, it shares the same psychometric characteristics of tests. We presume that, in order to decide whom to nominate, teachers are making quantitative judgments about the various characteristics of the students, comparing them against some internal criteria, and nominating those students who meet or exceed them. Like all tests, teacher nominations have something akin to measurement error—how accurately can the teacher really judge the students' ability? This "measurement error" leads to false positives and false negatives at the nomination stage. Regardless of how the screening data are collected, whether by teachers' professional judgments, through grades, or through some formalized assessment, measurement error is a reality that leads to false positive and false negative placement errors.

The idea of a screener is that it allows you to reduce the number of students who must be subjected to the full battery of tests because only those who pass the screener are considered further, a process conserving the resources and time that would otherwise be spent in assessing a larger group of students (Matthews & Kirsch, 2011). False negatives are the overriding concern at the screening stage, as false positives will most likely be caught in the next phase. Too many false positives, though, reduces the usefulness of the screener.

Although screeners are attractive, they can be extremely harmful to the accuracy of placement decisions. Recent work presented by Peters and McBee (2012) at the National Association for Gifted Children conference (and hopefully in print by the time this book is published) showed that, when the screening tool uses the same cutoff as the following stage, the result is a truly huge number of false negatives. Under realistic conditions, as many as 80% of students who should be identified can be missed.

For screeners to be useful, they must have much lower cutoffs than the cutoffs in the formal identification stage. This means that, if you decide to solicit nominations from teachers regarding which students should be candidates for the program, they need to provide a list of the students they think are average to above average (corresponding to a low cutoff—closer to the top half to top quarter) rather than providing a list of students that they think could ultimately succeed in the program (a high "gifted" cutoff perhaps closer to the top 10%). The extremely harmful impact of badly designed screeners or "nomination stages" is not a fact that is yet widely appreciated by the field, but is something that requires immediate attention.

An Illustrative Example

It is easier to grasp the issues involved in multiple-criteria assessment through an example. Space prohibits us from providing examples of each of the many possible branches of the decision tree implied by the choices outlined in the previous section. We will focus on a single example that is designed to elicit some of the more complex situations that might arise when identifying students for program.

Imagine a school district that is planning to implement accelerated math curriculum, beginning with algebra for sixth graders. The program will be implemented at Karl Pearson Middle School, a large school serving a suburban and predominantly middle-class population. Many students in the school have historically earned near-perfect math scores on state assessments as well as high grades in math courses. Administrators have decided initially to devote one of the school's six math courses to a hybrid accelerated and enriched mathematics program, with openness to expanding the size of the program in subsequent years should circumstances warrant this.

After news of the program is disseminated to parents, it turns out that more than 40 students and their families are interested in participating in the program (and would self-enroll). As the program in its first year can accommodate only 25 students due to limitations on class size, some method is needed for selecting students (note there could also be students who need the program but do not self-identify: see Chapter 3). The school administrators realize that some needful students might not receive service under this model and plan to concurrently offer a mathematics enrichment program with a more open enrollment policy. After the details of the intervention have been created, a team of stakeholders meets to design the selection system. The team decides to rely on psychoeducational assessment rather than a tryout period for student selection.

To begin, the team attempts to identify knowledge, skills, and attitudes that will help students succeed—they try and decide which students have needs that are not being met by the current educational systems and therefore would benefit from the new program. Information about these qualities can help predict success or failure in the intervention. Their list looks something like this:

- *Motivation.* The workload will be heavy and the content abstract and challenging. Students will not be able to "coast by" on intrinsic ability as many are accustomed to doing in school. A certain degree of motivation will be required in order to keep up. This motivation may be intrinsic to the student or supplemented extrinsically via family involvement.
- *Interest.* Students with an intrinsic interest in the subject matter and an earnest desire for mastery of it will find it easier to put in the required work.
- *Specific knowledge.* As the usual prealgebra math curriculum will be dramatically compacted and/or eliminated, there will be no instructional time devoted to basic math knowledge such as inequalities, number lines, coordinate planes, proportional reasoning, etc. Students who enter the class without this background knowledge will have a difficult time following the instruction.
- *Intelligence.* One central aspect of intelligence is speed and ease of learning. As this class will proceed at a rapid pace and will feature much less review in instruction as well as greatly diminished repetition, students who learn quickly will have an easier time keeping up. However, the advantage provided by intelligence may be compensated by motivation. A highly motivated student may require more practice, but she will also engage in more practice outside of class.

- *Parental support.* Students who receive parental support in the form of structured homework time, high performance expectations, and emotional support are likely to do better than those whose parents do not provide these things.

The team decides not to consider parental support in the decision-making process because first, it would be very difficult to fairly assess, and second, it could create barriers to entry for low-income students. A tradeoff of bias with accuracy is identified about the issue of parent involvement. It is probably true that students with more involved parents will do better, all things being equal, compared to those students with poor family involvement. Therefore, if parental involvement is considered in the identification procedure, it may indeed result in more accurate predictions of student performance in the program. However, the team also recognizes that this criterion will place low-income students at an inherent disadvantage.

The team determines that the program to be offered does carry with it some degree of potential risk. Those students placed in the program without the prerequisite skills will miss their grade-level math instruction in favor of an advanced math program that they might be unable to follow. Furthermore, they could suffer damaged self-efficacy in the area of math. Those who truly do need the program but are not placed in it could also suffer stunted math learning. Because of this the team decides that a formal identification system is important and required both to protect students and the integrity/efficacy of the program. Evidence will be gathered in the areas of motivation, interest, knowledge, and intelligence.

First, what are the data sources that can provide relevant information?
- previous performance in math courses, as measured by grades and test scores;
- math teachers who have observed these students during previous instruction;
- the students themselves; and
- additional formalized assessments.

The team decides to gather the following evidence to support each of the areas to be considered:
- *Motivation.* Information from other math teachers regarding each interested student's demeanor in class and performance on homework. Teachers are questioned specifically regarding signs of

boredom or frustration with the pacing or peer ability. Grades in previous math courses are also considered evidence of motivation.

- *Interest.* Students who wish to be considered for the program are asked to write an essay describing their reasons for wanting to participate in the advanced math course, as well as the most interesting thing they have ever learned about mathematics.
- *Specific knowledge.* In order to determine whether students have the required knowledge base, the team will assess grades in previous math courses, scores on end-of-grade tests, and performance on an out-of-level math achievement test
- *Intelligence.* Due to budgetary constraints, individualized intelligence testing is deemed too expensive and impractical. The school therefore adopts the Cognitive Abilities Test (CogAT; Lohman & Hagen, 2001), a group-administered aptitude test with high reliability and validity in the area of math readiness.

The next task for the team is to decide how these pieces of evidence will be quantified. This can be among the most difficult decisions to make. There are many possibilities here:

- Grades in previous math courses come prequantified as they occur on a 0 to 100 scale.
- Student essays are read by multiple raters. Each rater scores the interest expressed in the essay on a three-point scale: not very interested (0 points), interested (1 point), extremely interested (2 points). The ratings are averaged across the raters to produce a final interest score for each student that can range from 0 to 2.
- Similarly, teacher interviewers on each student are coded: not very motivated in previous math instruction (0 points), somewhat motivated (1 point), extremely motivated (2 points). The ratings are averaged across the raters and teachers to produce a final motivation score for each student that can range from 0 to 2.
- Math test scores are expressed as percentile ranks, where the student performance is described relative to the average performance of a local norm group. Both the state achievement tests and any out-of-level math subtests provide percentile ranks.
- The CogAT provides a full-scale score that is on a common score metric, where 100 represents average performance and the standard deviation is 15. (It would also have been reasonable for the team to consider the CogAT quantitative battery alone).

The team now has six data points for each prospective student. The first problem to note is that the data all lie on different scales. Before going any further, it is helpful to transform each score for a common metric. The most universal metric for comparing quantitative scores is the z-score. This is a metric in which the average (or mean) is reset to zero and the standard deviation is set to one. Any intro statistics textbook will illustrate the method for transforming scores to z-scores, but the information that follows is a short illustration. For the purposes of this illustration, we'll use the students' interest scores (see Table 9.1).

In order to transform those scores to z-scores, it is first necessary to compute the mean and standard deviation of the scores. There are many ways to do this, but Microsoft Excel™ provides one simple way. First, the scores are entered into a spreadsheet (see Figure 9.1).

To calculate the mean score, enter the following into an empty cell (see Figure 9.2):

=average(B2:B8)

This will calculate the average of all the scores in cells B2 through B8. The average in this case is 1.21 (rounding is fine).

To calculate the standard deviation, enter the following into another cell (see Figure 9.3):

=stdev(B2:B8)

The standard deviation is approximately 0.39.
The formula for calculating z-scores is:

$$z = \frac{x - \bar{x}}{sd}$$

Where x is the original score, $\bar{x}$ is the mean of all student ratings, and sd is the standard deviation. To perform this calculation for the first student, type the following in cell C2:

=(B1-1.21) / 0.39

The result, 1.38 (rounded), represents Juan's interest rating transformed to a z-score (see Figure 9.4). This translates into his rating being 1.38 standard deviations above the average rating for his peers. To compute the z-scores for the remaining students, click on the result in cell C2. You will

TABLE 9.1

Student interest scores

Student	Average Interest Rating
Juan	1.75
Linda	0.75
Mary	1.25
Tyler	0.75
Christopher	1.5
Katey	1
Pablo	1.5

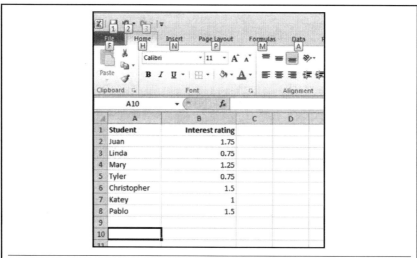

Figure 9.1. Interest scores entered into Microsoft Excel.

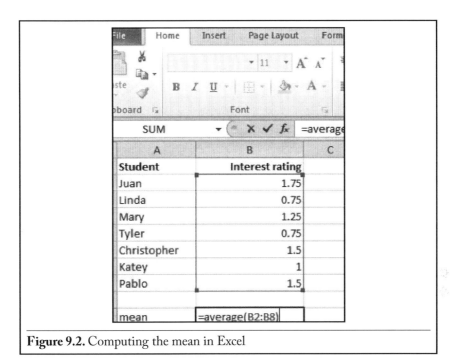

Figure 9.2. Computing the mean in Excel

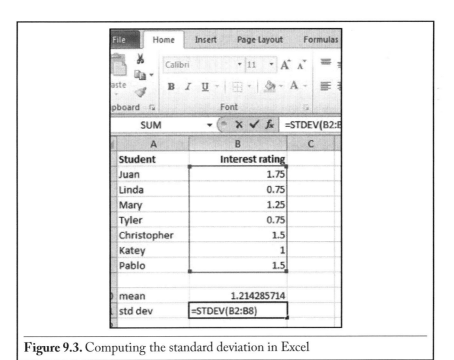

Figure 9.3. Computing the standard deviation in Excel

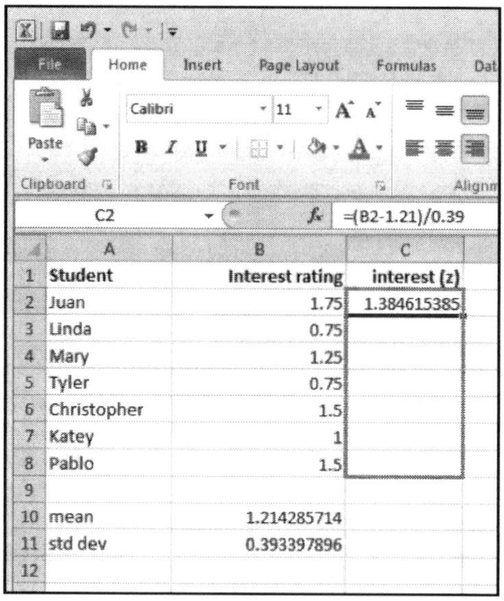

Figure 9.4. Computing the first z-score.

see in the lower right corner of the cell a small black square. Click on this square and drag the mouse until the cells adjacent to all the students are selected, then release the mouse button.

As a result, each student's interest rating will be transformed into a z-score (see Figure 9.5).

The same procedure should be used to transform the motivation, math grades, and IQ scores to z-scores. This will result in a single-scale metric for all assessment data. Note that the aptitude scores could be converted to z-scores using either the normative values (mean = 100, sd = 15) or the sample values, that is, the mean and standard deviation computed with respect to the 40 interested students. We recommend the second approach in order to maintain similarity to the procedure used for motivation, interest, and grades.

Most achievement test score reports provide percentile ranks. Percentile ranks are tricky. They should not be used directly because percentile ranks are a nonlinear scale. We recommend a two-stage procedure for percentile ranks. First, the percentile ranks should be converted to z-scores, computed with respect to the norm group. This can be accomplished by looking up values in a table based on the normal distribution or they can be cal-

	A	B	C	D
1	**Student**	**Interest rating**	**interest (z)**	
2	Juan	1.75	1.384615385	
3	Linda	0.75	-1.179487179	
4	Mary	1.25	0.102564103	
5	Tyler	0.75	-1.179487179	
6	Christopher	1.5	0.743589744	
7	Katey	1	-0.538461538	
8	Pablo	1.5	0.743589744	
9				
10	mean	1.214285714		
11	std dev	0.393397896		
12				
13				

Figure 9.5. The z-scores are computed.

culated directly in Excel. For example, to compute the normative z-score corresponding with a percentile rank of 92, enter the following in Excel:

=norm.inv((92/100, 0, 1)

92 is divided by 100 in order to convert it to a proportion. The value "0" is the mean of the reference distribution and the value "1" is the standard deviation of the reference distribution. Using this procedure assumes that the scores approximately follow a bell curve (i.e., a normal distribution), which is usually a reasonable assumption for these type of tests.

If we begin with a spreadsheet of percentile rank scores for each prospective student, we can either look up the corresponding z-scores in a table or we can use Excel to calculate them directly by entering the formula =norm.inv((B2/100),0,1) in cell B2 and then dragging it down in order to apply it to all students as previously illustrated. This will compute the normative z-score for all the students (see Figure 9.6).

We call these "normative" scores because they show how the students fare relative to the norm group of the test. We need to convert these z-scores to a final set of z-scores that illustrate how each student compares with the *other* students being considered for the program (local norm). In order to do that, we will compute the mean normative z-score and standard deviation of normative z-scores and use those values to compute a final set of z-scores that we can use to make placement decisions. Using the procedure described previously, we find that the mean normative z-score is about 0.70 and the standard deviation is about 0.47. Therefore, we compute the final z-scores for the Stanford math subscale by subtracting 0.70

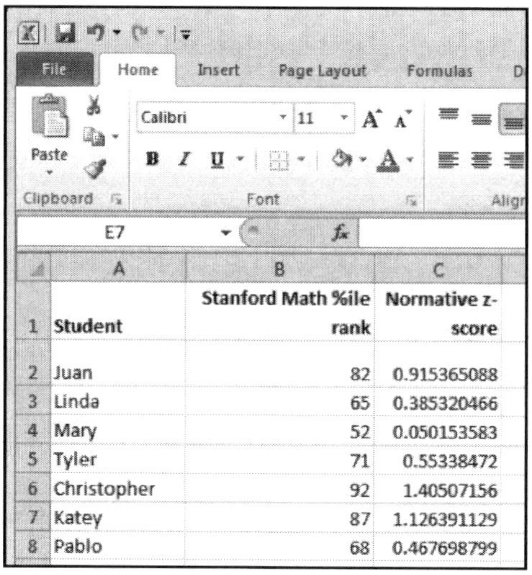

	A	B	C
1	Student	Stanford Math %ile rank	Normative z-score
2	Juan	82	0.915365088
3	Linda	65	0.385320466
4	Mary	52	0.050153583
5	Tyler	71	0.55338472
6	Christopher	92	1.40507156
7	Katey	87	1.126391129
8	Pablo	68	0.467698799

Figure 9.6. Transforming percentile ranks to z-scores based on the normal distribution.

for each student's normative z-score and then dividing by 0.47. The results are shown in Figure 9.7.

Once all of the pieces of evidence are on a common scale, the scores can be combined. Because this school district wants to use a rank-ordered system to select the best 25 students out of the 40 in the talent pool, the only choice is the "mean" rule. The use of rank ordering also means that it is not necessary to set an identification cutoff.

Placing all of the scores on a common z-score metric implicitly gave all of the scores the same weight. In many cases, however, not all criteria are equally important for predicting success in the program. However, looking at the assessments, two of the six assessments are math tests (on-level and out-of-level) and a third is math GPA (which measures both achievement and motivation). Two of the six are direct measures of motivation, and only one of the six is a measure of intelligence. Although each assessment might be equally weighted, the differential number of assessments in each category means that the CogAT scores carry less weight in the mean.

The team determined that prior knowledge is most important, followed by motivation, followed by intelligence. Furthermore, the team decides that the out-of-level math test should be weighted more heavily than the grade-level math test, and also that the teacher-reported motiva-

	A	B	C	D
1	Student	Stanford Math %ile rank	Normative z-score	Final math z-score
2	Juan	82	0.915365088	0.458223591
3	Linda	65	0.385320466	-0.669530923
4	Mary	52	0.050153583	-1.38265195
5	Tyler	71	0.55338472	-0.311947405
6	Christopher	92	1.40507156	1.500152256
7	Katey	87	1.126391129	0.907215168
8	Pablo	68	0.467698799	-0.494257874

Figure 9.7. Transforming normative z-scores to "local" z-scores.

tion scores should be weighted more that the student-reported motivation scores. The team arrives at the following weights:

- Math test (out of level): 4
- Math test (grade level): 2
- Math GPA: 2
- Teacher-reported motivation: 2
- Student-reported motivation: 1
- CogAT score: 2

The total of the weights are 13. The out-of-level math test will carry (3/13 ≅ 23%) of the weight in the mean score, the CogAT score will carry about 15%, and so on. As a category, the math achievement tests carry about 46% of the weight while grades and motivation measures carry about 38%.

The weights can be any positive number. For rank-ordered systems, the only requirement is that the pattern of weights follow the emphasis that you want to place on each assessment. If the mean scores are to be compared against a cutoff z-score, it would be important to scale the weights so that they sum to one. To implement the weights, all you do is multiply the z-scores for each assessment by the weight. Using the weights provided above, for example, the out-of-level math z-scores would be multiplied by four. Once all of the weights are applied, you just compute the mean of all the weighted z-scores. In the final step, sort the dataset by the mean scores you computed in the previous step, and prepare to welcome those top 25 students to the program.

One final note about the "mean" combination rule. If a cutoff is to be used, it is important to note that the cutoff, which should also be expressed on a z-score metric, needs to be adjusted. When the mean is computed for a set of measurements whose true scores are not perfectly correlated (such as what happens when you compute the mean of scores on math achievement and the CogAT score, for example), the variance of the resulting mean is reduced or "shrunken." If you set the z-score cutoff for program entry at a value that corresponds with, say, the 90th percentile, the *effective* cutoff relative to those mean scores will be higher than intended because of the shrinkage. The equations for adjusting for shrinkage are too technical to present in this book but are available in McBee et al. (in press).

Conclusion

Although "using" multiple measures is suggested as best practice, how these multiple measures are used is critical and often insufficiently considered. Depending on how the same few measures are combined, program size could be triple what it is under an alternate method. The pool of identified students could be very similar or extremely diverse. This has significant implications for programming. Many qualified students could be missed, or many unqualified students could be selected The decision of how to combine multiple measures should be made based on the potential for risk of an appropriate placement as well as the measurement criteria discussed throughout this chapter. It should be clear that an effective multicriteria system is not a simple thing to design and implement.

Conclusion

10

We hope by now our message is clear: identification should best match instruction and content with student need. If ever there becomes a place where student needs are consistently assessed and met—the world of perfect differentiation—then programs such as gifted education or advanced academics can cease to exist. Until then, programs for exceptional learners will be needed at both ends of the ability spectrum. As we discussed at length in Chapters 1 and 2, what "need" actually means is a complex question. It involves an understanding of a student's current level of mastery but also knowledge about existing "standard" curriculum and just how far a teacher can effectively differentiate that curriculum. No matter how advanced the students, the scope of the standard curriculum, or the talents of teachers, there will always be some students in *every* school whose advanced academic needs are not being met. This is not a fault of the school or the teacher; instead, it is a side effect of the diversity of students in American schools. With so many different kinds of diversity comes a need to gather a great deal of information in order to conduct effective instruction.

A news article in *The New York Times* (Anderson, 2013) discussed a situation in New York City Public Schools where some high-income parents spend large sums of money to prepare their 4-year-old children to take the gifted entrance test. These students spend hours each week studying and practicing so that they could be identified as gifted. The result of this has been increasing numbers of very high test scores. Certainly some of these concerned parents just want their kids to get into the best schools, but we have also seen many similar scenarios where parents just want their kids to "be" gifted. Such a scenario illustrates an important point we wish to make: the identification or label is meaningless. Educators and parents need to focus on whether or not a student is having his or her educational needs met by the child's current educational placement and content. As we said way back in Chapter 1, "gifted" or advanced academics in our perspective all comes down to need. If there is a need on the advanced end of the content spectrum, then some kind of service is required. A label or identification system is only necessary to the extent that it helps educators locate and address that need. If an assessment system or test is being used in schools but does not result in greater student learning, then it has no reason to exist. The same is true with gifted education or advanced academics. Educators and policy makers use assessment and identification to make the best educational decisions. Identification must serve to make more effective decisions about instruction. Everyone involved in education should keep this in mind, lest we stray and begin again to focus on labels for their own sake.

We believe, and have personally experienced, that discussions of meeting student need are much easier to have with parents of advanced students as well as school officials than are conversations about "giftedness." The question of "I see my student has scored at the 99th percentile in reading. How is that being addressed in the classroom?" is much more straightforward than "I have a gifted kid. What are you going to do about that?" It also provides specific diagnostic information in a content area, and can serve as a springboard to advanced academic programming. The construct of gifted is simply too complex and is interpreted in too many different ways for it to yield meaningful information about instruction. It also dredges up too many political issues of race and equality that only serve as roadblocks that further delay some students from receiving a proper education.

The last point we want to reaffirm is that the programs designed to serve advanced or gifted students need not be limited to those that are academic in nature. In this book, we have focused on those skills and domains because they are the most universal across schools. This does not mean that a school or district could not decide to offer advanced agriculture courses, for example, due to the values of the local community and the range of needs and abilities of the students. Even under state mandates, there remains flexibility in the range of domains that can be addressed by gifted education, and this is even more true within the broader category we have called advanced academics. Schools should be encouraged to reach out into these areas that might be unique to their students in any way they see fit, provided that identification systems proposed to locate students in need are well-designed and are closely connected to the program.

As we said at the beginning of the book, we did not set out to provide a canned process or program for gifted education or even for advanced academic identification and programming. The primary purpose of this book was to show where the field of gifted education is and how we believe it should change in order to best bring about the education of advanced learners. What's more, as we highlighted in Chapter 4, such a goal does not happen in isolation. Without a consistent application of differentiation in every classroom, more and more students will require supplementary programs on both ends of the achievement spectrum. For this reason, K–12 educational systems as a whole need to be designed so that student need is always considered when making instructional decisions. We hope that our perspective on identification as the assessment of student need, with an eye toward providing advanced academic programming, will provide a useful paradigm for teachers and administrators who want to build defensible advanced academic programs and increase the educational achievement of all students.

References

Adelson, J. L., McCoach, D. B., & Gavin, M. K. (2012). Examining the effects of gifted programming in math and reading using the ECLS-K. *Gifted Child Quarterly, 56,* 25–39.

American Educational Research Association, American Psychological Association, & National Council on Measurement in Education. (1999). *Standards for educational and psychological testing.* Washington, DC: Authors.

Anastasi, A., & Urbina, S. (1997). *Psychological testing* (7th ed.). Upper Saddle River, NJ: Prentice Hall.

Anderson, J. (2013, February 18). Schools ask: Gifted or just well-prepared? *The New York Times,* A12. Retrieved from http://www.nytimes.com/2013/02/18/nyregion/new-york-city-schools-struggle-to-separate-the-gifted-from-the-just-well-prepared.html?pagewanted=all&_r=0

Anderson, L. W., & Krathwohl, D. R. (Eds.). (2001). *A taxonomy for learning, teaching and assessing: A revision of Bloom's taxonomy of educational objectives.* New York, NY: Longman.

Assouline, S. G., Colangelo, N., Lupkowski-Shoplik, A., Lipscomb, J., & Forstadt, L. (2009). *Iowa Acceleration Scale: A guide for whole-grade acceleration K–8* (3rd ed.). Tucson, AZ: Great Potential Press.

185

Baldwin, A. (1984). *The Baldwin Identification Matrix 2 for identification of gifted and talented.* Unionville, NY: Trillium Press

Borland, J. (2005). Gifted education without gifted children. In R. J. Sternberg & J. E. Davidson (Eds.), *Conceptions of giftedness* (pp. 1–19). Cambridge, UK: Cambridge University Press.

Bracken, B. A., & McCallum, R. S. (1998). *The Universal Nonverbal Ability Test.* Austin, TX: PRO-ED.

Briggs, C. J., Reis, S. M., & Sullivan, E. E. (2008). A national view of promising programs and practices for culturally, linguistically, and ethnically diverse gifted and talented students. *Gifted Child Quarterly, 52,* 131–145.

Brown, L., Sherbenou, R. J., & Johnson, S. K. (2010). *Test of Nonverbal Intelligence* (4th ed.). Austin, TX: PRO-ED.

Brulles, D., Peters, S. J., & Saunders, R. (2012). Schoolwide mathematics achievement within the gifted cluster grouping model. *Journal of Advanced Academics, 23,* 200–216. doi:10.1177/193202X12451439

Brulles, D., Saunders, R., & Cohn, S. J. (2010). Improving performance for gifted students in a cluster grouping model. *Journal for the Education of the Gifted, 34,* 327–350.

Bui, S. A., Craig, S. A., & Imberman, S. A. (2011). *Is gifted education a bright idea? Assessing the impact of gifted and talented programming on achievement* (National Bureau of Economic Research Working paper 17089). Washington, DC: National Bureau of Economic Research.

Callahan, C. M., Hertberg-Davis, H., Izzo, R. T., Azano, A. P., Germundson, A. J., Meyer, K. E. . . . Matthews, M. S. (2013). *The AP challenge program.* Charlottesville: The University of Virginia.

Camilli, G. (2006). Test fairness. In R. L. Brennan (Ed.), *Educational measurement* (4th ed., pp. 221–256). Westport, CT: American Council on Education/Praeger.

Carnoy, M., & Rothstein, R. (2013). *What do international tests show about U.S. student performance?* Washington, DC: Economic Policy Institute.

Castellano, J. A., & Frazier, A. D. (Eds.). (2010). *Special populations in gifted education: Understanding our most able students from diverse backgrounds.* Waco, TX: Prufrock Press.

Colangelo, N., Assouline, S. G., & Gross, M. U. M. (Eds.). (2004). *A nation deceived: How schools hold back America's brightest students.* Iowa City: University of Iowa, The Connie Belin and Jaqueline N. Blank International Center for Gifted Education and Talent Development.

Colangelo, N., Assouline, S. G., Marron, M. A., Castellano, J. A., Clinkenbeard, P. R., Rogers, K., . . . Smith, D. (2010). Guidelines for developing an academic acceleration policy. *Journal of Advanced Academics, 21,* 180–203.

Cooper, H., Nye, B., Charlton, K., Lindsay, J., & Greathouse, S. (1996). The effects of summer vacation on achievement test scores: A narrative and meta-analytic review. *Review of Educational Research, 66,* 227–268.

Davis, G. A., Rimm, S. B., & Siegle, D. (2011). *Education of the gifted and talented* (6th ed.). Boston, MA: Allyn & Bacon.

Delisle, J. R. (1992). *Guiding the social and emotional development of gifted youth.* New York, NY: Longman.

Feldhusen, J. F., Asher, J. W., & Hoover, S. M. (1984). Problems in the identification of giftedness, talent, or ability. *Gifted Child Quarterly, 28,* 149–151. doi:10.1177/001698628402800402

Feldhusen, J., Proctor, T. B., & Black, K. N. (1986). Guidelines for grade advancement of precocious children. *Roeper Review, 9,* 9–10.

Firmender, J. M., Reis, S. M., & Sweeny, S. M. (2012). Reading comprehension and fluency levels ranges across diverse classrooms: The need for differentiated reading instruction and content. *Gifted Child Quarterly, 57,* 3–14. doi:10.1177/0016986212460084

Gavin, M. K., Casa, T. M., Adelson J. L., Carroll, S. R., Sheffield, L. J., & Spinelli, A. M. (2007). Project M³: Mentoring Mathematical Minds: Challenging curriculum for talented elementary students. *Journal of Advanced Academics, 18,* 566–585.

Gentry, M. (2006). No Child Left Behind: Neglecting excellence. *Roeper Review, 29,* 24–27.

Gentry, M., & MacDougall, J. (2009). Total school cluster grouping: Model, research, and practice. In J. S. Renzulli, E. J. Gubbins, S. K. McMillen, R. D. Eckert, & C. A. Little (Eds.), *Systems and models for developing programs for the gifted and talented* (2nd ed., pp. 211–234). Waco, TX: Prufrock Press.

Gentry, M., & Mann, R. L. (2009). *Total school cluster grouping and differentiation: A comprehensive, research-based plan for raising student achievement and improving teacher practices.* Waco, TX.

Gentry, M., & Owen, S. V. (1999). An investigation of the effects of total school flexible cluster grouping on identification, achievement, and classroom practices. *Gifted Child Quarterly, 43,* 224–243. doi:10.1177/001698629904300402

Georgia Department of Education. (2012). *Georgia resource manual for gifted education services*. Retrieved from http://www.doe.k12. ga.us/Curriculum-Instruction-and-Assessment/Curriculum-and-Instruction/Pages/Gifted-Education.aspx

Griggs v. Duke Power, 401 U.S. 424 (1971).

Hansen, J. B., & Feldhusen, J. F. (1994). Comparison of trained and untrained teachers of gifted students. *Gifted Child Quarterly, 38,* 115–121. doi:10.1177/001698629403800304

Horowitz, F. D., Subotnik, R. F., & Matthews, D. J. (Eds.). (2009). *The development of giftedness and talent across the life span.* Washington, DC: American Psychological Association.

Illinois State Board of Education. (2009). *Illinois Standards Achievement Test technical manual.* Retrieved from http://www.isbe.net/assessment/pdfs/isat_tech_2010.pdf

Institute for Research on Acceleration Policy, National Association for Gifted Children, & Council of State Directors of Programs for the Gifted. (2009). *Guidelines for developing an acceleration policy.* Iowa City: University of Iowa, Institute for Research on Acceleration Policy.

Jairrels, J. (2009). *African Americans and standardized tests: The real reason for low test scores.* Sauk Village, IL: African American Images.

Joint Committee on Testing Practices. (2004). *Code of fair testing practices in education.* Washington, DC: American Psychological Association.

Krisel, S., & Cowan, R. (1997, December). Georgia's journey toward multiple-criteria identification of gifted students. *Roeper Review, 20*(Gifted Education Supplement), A1–A3.

Lee, S.-Y., Matthews, M. S., & Olszewski-Kubilius, P. (2008). A national picture of talent search and talent search educational programs. *Gifted Child Quarterly, 52,* 55–69. doi:10.1177/001698620731115

Lee, S.-Y., Olszewski-Kubilius, P., & Peternel, G. (2010). The efficacy of academic acceleration for gifted minority students. *Gifted Child Quarterly, 54,* 189–208. doi:10.1177/0016986210369256

Lee, S.-Y., Olszewski-Kubilius, P., & Thomson, D. T. (2012). Academically gifted students' perceived interpersonal competence and peer relationships. *Gifted Child Quarterly, 56,* 90–104. doi:10.1177/0016986212442568

Lohman, D. F. (2005a). An aptitude perspective on talent: Implications for identification of academically gifted minority students. *Journal for the Education of the Gifted, 28,* 333–360.

Lohman, D. F. (2005b). Review of Naglieri and Ford (2003): Does the Naglieri Nonverbal Ability Test identify equal proportions of high-scoring White, Black, and Hispanic students? *Gifted Child Quarterly, 49,* 19–26. doi:10.1177/001698620504900103

Lohman, D. F. (2005c). The role of nonverbal ability tests in identifying academically gifted students: An aptitude perspective. *Gifted Child Quarterly, 49,* 111–138. doi:10.1177/001698620504900203

Lohman, D. F. (2006). *Identifying academically talented minority students* (RM05216). Storrs: University of Connecticut, The National Research Center on the Gifted and Talented.

Lohman, D. (2009). Identifying academically talented students: Some general principles, two specific procedures. In L. V. Shavinina (Ed.), *International handbook on giftedness* (pp. 971–997). Heidelberg, Germany: Springer.

Lohman, D. F., & Hagen, E. P. (2001). *Cognitive Abilities Test–Form 6.* Itasca, IL: Riverside.

Lohman, D. F., & Korb, K. (2006). Gifted today but not tomorrow? Longitudinal changes in ITBS and CogAT scores during elementary school. *Journal for the Education of the Gifted, 29,* 451–484.

Lohman, D. F., Korb, K. A., & Lakin, J. M. (2008). Identifying academically gifted English-language learners using nonverbal tests: A comparison of the Raven, NNAT, and CogAT. *Gifted Child Quarterly, 52,* 275–296.

Lohman, D. F., & Lakin, J. (2008). Nonverbal test scores as one component of an identification system: Integrating ability, achievement, and teacher ratings. In J. L. Van Tassel-Baska (Ed.), *Alternative assessments with gifted and talented students* (pp. 41–66). Waco, TX: Prufrock Press.

Matthews, M. S. (2006). Benefits and drawbacks of state-level assessments for gifted students: NCLB and standardized testing. *Duke Gifted Letter, 7*(1) [electronic version]. Retrieved from http://www.tip.duke.edu/node/827

Matthews, M. S. (2007). Talent search programs. In C. M. Callahan & J. A. Plucker (Eds.), *Critical issues and practices in gifted education* (pp. 641–653). Waco, TX: Prufrock Press.

Matthews, M. S., & Kirsch, L. (2011). Evaluating gifted identification practice: Aptitude testing and linguistically diverse learners. *Journal of Applied School Psychology, 27,* 155–180. doi:10.1080/15377903.2011.565281

McBee, M. (2006). A descriptive analysis of referral sources by race and socioeconomic status. *Journal of Secondary Gifted Education, 17,* 103–111.

McBee, M. (2010a). Examining the probability of identification for gifted programs for students in Georgia elementary schools: A multilevel path analysis study. *Gifted Child Quarterly, 54,* 283–297.

McBee, M. (2010b). Modeling outcomes with floor or ceiling effects: An introduction to the Tobit model. *Gifted Child Quarterly, 54,* 314–320. doi:10.1177/001698621037909

McBee, M. T., McCoach, D. B., Peters, S. J., & Matthews, M. S. (2012). The case for a schism: Commentary on Subotnik, Olszewski-Kubilius, and Worrell (2011). *Gifted Child Quarterly, 56,* 210–214.

McBee, M. T., Peters, S. J., & Waterman, C. (in press). Combining scores in multiple-criteria assessment systems: The impact of combination rule. *Gifted Child Quarterly.*

McCall, R. B., Appelbaum, M. I., & Hogarty, P. S. (1973). Developmental changes in mental performance. *Monographs of the Society for Research in Child Development, 38*(3, Serial No. 150), 1–84. doi:10.2307/1165768

Naglieri, J. A. (2003). *Naglieri Nonverbal Ability Test* (2nd ed.). San Antonio, TX: Pearson.

Naglieri, J. A., & Ford. D. Y. (2003). Addressing underrepresentation of gifted minority children using the Naglieri Nonverbal Ability Test (NNAT). *Gifted Child Quarterly, 47,* 155–160.

Naglieri, J. A., & Ford, D. Y. (2005). Increasing minority children's participation in gifted classes using the NNAT: A response to Lohman. *Gifted Child Quarterly, 49,* 29–36. doi:10.1177/001698620504900104

National Association for Gifted Children. (2008). *The role of assessment in the identification of gifted students.* Washington, DC: Author. Retrieved from http://www.nagc.org/index.aspx?id=4022

National Association for Gifted Children. (2010a). *NAGC pre-K–grade 12 gifted education programming standards: A blueprint for quality gifted education programs.* Washington, DC: Author. Retrieved from http://www.nagc.org/ProgrammingStandards.aspx

National Association for Gifted Children. (2010b). *Redefining giftedness for a new century: Shifting the paradigm.* Washington, DC: Author. Retrieved from http://www.nagc.org/index2.aspx?id=6404

National Association for Gifted Children, & Council of State Directors of Programs for the Gifted. (2011). *State of the states in gifted education:*

2010–2011. Washington, DC: Author. Retrieved from http://www.nagc.org/stateofthestatesreport.aspx

National Center for Educational Statistics. (2011). *The nation's report card: Science 2009* (NCES 2011-451). Washington, DC: Institute for Educational Sciences, U.S. Department of Education.

Northwest Evaluation Association. (2011a). *2011 normative data.* Portland, OR: Author. Retrieved from http://decatur.schoolfusion.us/modules/groups/homepagefiles/cms/138407/File/Technology%20Documents/NWEA%20documents/2011norm%20rits.pdf?sessionid=840d41c4f13563e0fd3bd1e299dac71

Northwest Evaluation Association. (2011b). *RIT scale norms: For use with Measures of Academic Progress (MAP®) and MAP® for primary grades.* Portland, OR: Author.

Ohio Department of Education. (2013). *Kindergarten.* Retrieved from http://education.ohio.gov/GD/Templates/Pages/ODE/ODEDetail.aspx?page=3&TopicRelationID=778&ContentID=2167&Content=124271

Palmer, J. G. (2009, Fall). Mentorships for gifted high school students. *Teaching for High Potential,* 14–15.

Park, G., Lubinski, D., & Benbow, C. P. (2012). When less is more: Effects of grade skipping on adult STEM productivity among mathematically precocious adolescents. *Journal of Educational Psychology.* Advance online publication. doi:10.1037/a0029481

Pearson Education. (2003). *Otis-Lennon School Ability Test: Technical manual* (8th ed.). San Antonio, TX: Pearson.

Pereles, D. A., Omdal, S., & Baldwin, L. (2009). Response to Intervention and twice-exceptional learners: A promising fit. *Gifted Child Today, 32*(3), 40–51.

Peters, S. J. (2012). The importance of multi-group validity evidence in the identification of exceptionalities. *Gifted and Talented International, 26*(1), 99–104.

Peters, S. J., & Gentry, M. (2010). Multigroup construct validity evidence of the HOPE Scale: Instrumentation to identify low-income elementary students for gifted programs. *Gifted Child Quarterly, 54,* 298–313. doi:10.1177/0016986210378332

Peters, S. J., & Gentry, M. (2012). Group-specific norms and teacher rating scales: Implications for underrepresentation. *Journal of Advanced Academics, 23,* 125–144.

Peters, S. J., & Mann, R. L. (2009). Getting ahead: Current secondary and post-secondary acceleration options for high ability students in Indiana. *Journal of Advanced Academics, 20*, 630–657.

Peters, S., & McBee, M. (2012, November). *The potential pitfalls and possibilities of involving teachers in gifted education identification.* Presented at the annual meeting of the National Association for Gifted Children, Denver, CO.

Peterson, J. S. (1999). Gifted—through whose cultural lens? An application of the postpositivistic mode of inquiry. *Journal for the Education of the Gifted, 22*, 354–383.

Pfeiffer, S., & McClain, M.-C. (2012). Identification of gifted students in the United States today: A look at state definitions, policies, and practices. *Journal of Applied School Psychology, 28*, 59–88. doi:10.1080/15377903.2012.643757

Plucker, J. A., Burroughs, N., & Song, R. (2010). *Mind the (other) gap! The growing excellence gap in K–12 education.* Bloomington, IN: Center for Evaluation and Education Policy.

Reis, S. M., Burns, D. E., & Renzulli, J. S. (1991). *Curriculum compacting: The complete guide to modifying the regular curriculum for high ability students.* Waco, TX: Prufrock Press.

Reis, S. M., Gentry, M., & Maxfield, L. R. (1998). The application of enrichment clusters to teachers' classroom practices. *Journal for Education of the Gifted, 21*, 310–324.

Renzulli, J. (2005). The three-ring conception of giftedness: A developmental model for promoting creative productivity. In R. J. Sternberg & J. E. Davidson (Eds.), *Conceptions of giftedness* (pp. 246–279). Cambridge, UK: Cambridge University Press.

Rollins, K., Mursky, C. V., Shah-Coltrane, S., & Johnsen, S. K. (2009). RtI models for gifted students. *Gifted Child Today, 32*(3), 21–30.

Rudner, L. M. (1994). Questions to ask when evaluating tests. *Practical Assessment, Research & Evaluation, 4*(2). Retrieved from http://PAREonline.net/getvn.asp?v=4&n=2

Sander, R. H., & Taylor, S., Jr. (2012). *Mismatch: How affirmative action hurts students it's intended to help, and why universities won't admit it.* New York, NY: Basic Books.

Shaunessy, E., & Matthews, M. S. (2008). *Accounting for gifted education: Making a case for reporting and transparency* [Policy brief]. Tampa: University of South Florida, David C. Anchin Center.

Southern, W. T., & Jones, E. (2004). *Acceleration in Ohio: A summary of findings from a statewide study of district policies and practices.* Retrieved from http://www.ode.state.oh.us/GD/Templates/Pages/ ODE/ODEDetail.aspx?page=3&TopicRelationID=964&ContentID=6163 &Content=41228

Stanley, J. C. (1978). SMPY's DT-PI model: Diagnostic testing followed by prescriptive instruction. *Intellectually Talented Youth Bulletin, 4*(10), 7–8.

Stanley, J. C. (1990). Leta Hollingworth's contributions to above-level testing of the gifted. *Roeper Review, 13,* 166–171.

State of Maryland, Education Article §7-101, COMAR 13A.08.01.02. Retrieved from http://www.dsd.state.md.us/comar/getfile.aspx?file= 13a.08.01.02.htm

Steenbergen-Hu, S., & Moon, S. M. (2011). The effects of acceleration on high-ability learners: A meta-analysis. *Gifted Child Quarterly, 55,* 39–53. doi:10.1177/0016986210383155

Subotnik, R. F., Olszewski-Kubilius, P., & Worrell, F. C. (2011). Rethinking giftedness and gifted education: A proposed direction forward based on psychological science. *Psychological Science in the Public Interest, 12,* 3–54.

Terman, L. M. (1922). A new approach to the study of genius. *Psychological Review, 29,* 310–318.

U.S. Census Bureau. (2012). *Income, poverty, and health insurance coverage in the United States: 2009.* Current Population Reports, series P60-238, and Historical Tables—Tables 2 and 6. Retrieved from http://www.census.gov/compendia/statab/cats/income_expenditures_poverty_wealth/poverty.html

U.S. Department of Education. (1993). *National excellence: The case for developing America's talent.* Washington, DC: U.S. Government Printing Office.

Valencia, R. R., & Suzuki, L. A. (2001). *Intelligence testing and minority students.* Thousand Oaks, CA: Sage.

Vandenberg, R. J., & Lance, C. E. (2000). A review and synthesis of the measurement invariance literature: Suggestions, practices, and recommendations for organizational research. *Organizational Research Methods, 3,* 4–70.

Vygotsky, L. S. (1978). *Mind in society: The development of higher psychological processes* (M. Cole, V. John-Steiner, S. Scribner, & E. Souberman, Trans.). Cambridge, MA: Harvard University Press.

Wisconsin Administrative Rule PI 8.01(2)(t)2, 2012.

Wisconsin Department of Public Instruction. (2011). *Wisconsin Knowledge and Concepts Examination: Fall 2010 WKCE technical report.* Retrieved from http://oea.dpi.wi.gov/oea_publications

Wisconsin Information Network for Successful Schools. (n.d.). *Data analysis.* Retrieved from http://data.dpi.state.wi.us/data

Worrell, F. (2009). Myth 4: A single test score or indicator tells us all we need to know about giftedness. *Gifted Child Quarterly, 53,* 242–244.

Wyner, J. S., Bridgeland, J. M., & DiIulio, J. J. (2009). *Achievement trap: How America is failing millions of high-achieving students from lower-income families* (Rev. ed.). Washington, DC: The Jack Kent Cooke Foundation.

Xiang, Y., Dahlin, M., Cronin, J., Theaker, R., & Durant, S. (2011). *Do high flyers maintain their altitude? Performance trends of top students.* Washington, DC: Thomas B. Fordham Institute.

Yoon, S., & Gentry, M. (2009). Racial and ethnic representation in gifted programs: Current status of and implications for gifted Asian American students. *Gifted Child Quarterly, 53,* 121–136.

Appendix A
NAGC Pre-K–Grade 12 Gifted Education Programming Standards

Gifted Education Programming Standard 1: Learning and Development

Introduction

To be effective in working with learners with gifts and talents, teachers and other educators in PreK-12 settings must understand the characteristics and needs of the population for whom they are planning curriculum, instruction, assessment, programs, and services. These characteristics provide the rationale for differentiation in programs, grouping, and services for this population and are translated into appropriate differentiation choices made at curricular and program levels in schools and school districts. While cognitive growth is important in such programs, affective development is also necessary. Thus many of the characteristics addressed in this standard emphasize affective development linked to self-understanding and social awareness.

Standard 1: Learning and Development

Description: *Educators, recognizing the learning and developmental differences of students with gifts and talents, promote ongoing self-understanding, awareness of their needs, and cognitive and affective growth of these students in school, home, and community settings to ensure specific student outcomes.*

Student Outcomes	Evidence-Based Practices
1.1. Self-Understanding. Students with gifts and talents demonstrate self-knowledge with respect to their interests, strengths, identities, and needs in socio-emotional development and in intellectual, academic, creative, leadership, and artistic domains.	1.1.1. Educators engage students with gifts and talents in identifying interests, strengths, and gifts. 1.1.2. Educators assist students with gifts and talents in developing identities supportive of achievement.
1.2. Self-Understanding. Students with gifts and talents possess a developmentally appropriate understanding of how they learn and grow; they recognize the influences of their beliefs, traditions, and values on their learning and behavior.	1.2.1. Educators develop activities that match each student's developmental level and culture-based learning needs.
1.3. Self-Understanding. Students with gifts and talents demonstrate understanding of and respect for similarities and differences between themselves and their peer group and others in the general population.	1.3.1. Educators provide a variety of research-based grouping practices for students with gifts and talents that allow them to interact with individuals of various gifts, talents, abilities, and strengths. 1.3.2. Educators model respect for individuals with diverse abilities, strengths, and goals.
1.4. Awareness of Needs. Students with gifts and talents access resources from the community to support cognitive and affective needs, including social interactions with others having similar interests and abilities or experiences, including same-age peers and mentors or experts.	1.4.1. Educators provide role models (e.g., through mentors, bibliotherapy) for students with gifts and talents that match their abilities and interests. 1.4.2. Educators identify out-of-school learning opportunities that match students' abilities and interests.

Student Outcomes	Evidence-Based Practices
1.5. Awareness of Needs. Students' families and communities understand similarities and differences with respect to the development and characteristics of advanced and typical learners and support students with gifts and talents' needs.	1.5.1. Educators collaborate with families in accessing resources to develop their child's talents.
1.6. Cognitive and Affective Growth. Students with gifts and talents benefit from meaningful and challenging learning activities addressing their unique characteristics and needs.	1.6.1. Educators design interventions for students to develop cognitive and affective growth that is based on research of effective practices. 1.6.2. Educators develop specialized intervention services for students with gifts and talents who are underachieving and are now learning and developing their talents.
1.7. Cognitive and Affective Growth. Students with gifts and talents recognize their preferred approaches to learning and expand their repertoire.	1.7.1. Teachers enable students to identify their preferred approaches to learning, accommodate these preferences, and expand them.
1.8. Cognitive and Affective Growth. Students with gifts and talents identify future career goals that match their talents and abilities and resources needed to meet those goals (e.g., higher education opportunities, mentors, financial support).	1.8.1. Educators provide students with college and career guidance that is consistent with their strengths. 1.8.2. Teachers and counselors implement a curriculum scope and sequence that contains person/social awareness and adjustment, academic planning, and vocational and career awareness.

Gifted Education Programming Standard 2: Assessment

Introduction

Knowledge about all forms of assessment is essential for educators of students with gifts and talents. It is integral to identification, assessing each student's learning progress, and evaluation of programming. Educators need to establish a challenging environment and collect multiple types of assessment information so that all students are able to demonstrate their gifts and talents. Educators' understanding of non-biased, technically adequate, and equitable approaches enables them to identify students who represent diverse backgrounds. They also differentiate their curriculum and instruction by using pre- and post-, performance-based, product-based, and out-of-level assessments. As a result of each educator's use of ongoing assessments, students with gifts and talents demonstrate advanced and complex learning. Using these student progress data, educators then evaluate services and make adjustments to one or more of the school's programming components so that student performance is improved.

Standard 2: Assessment

Description: *Assessments provide information about identification, learning progress and outcomes, and evaluation of programming for students with gifts and talents in all domains.*

Student Outcomes	Evidence-Based Practices
2.1. Identification. All students in grades PK–12 have equal access to a comprehensive assessment system that allows them to demonstrate diverse characteristics and behaviors that are associated with giftedness.	2.1.1. Educators develop environments and instructional activities that encourage students to express diverse characteristics and behaviors that are associated with giftedness. 2.1.2. Educators provide parents/guardians with information regarding diverse characteristics and behaviors that are associated with giftedness.
2.2. Identification. Each student reveals his or her exceptionalities or potential through assessment evidence so that appropriate instructional accommodations and modifications can be provided.	2.2.1. Educators establish comprehensive, cohesive, and ongoing procedures for identifying and serving students with gifts and talents. These provisions include informed consent, committee review, student retention, student reassessment, student exiting, and appeals procedures for both entry and exit from gifted program services.

Student Outcomes	Evidence-Based Practices
	2.2.2. Educators select and use multiple assessments that measure diverse abilities, talents, and strengths that are based on current theories, models, and research.
	2.2.3 Assessments provide qualitative and quantitative information from a variety of sources, including off-level testing, are nonbiased and equitable, and are technically adequate for the purpose.
	2.2.4. Educators have knowledge of student exceptionalities and collect assessment data while adjusting curriculum and instruction to learn about each student's developmental level and aptitude for learning.
	2.2.5. Educators interpret multiple assessments in different domains and understand the uses and limitations of the assessments in identifying the needs of students with gifts and talents.
	2.2.6. Educators inform all parents/guardians about the identification process. Teachers obtain parental/guardian permission for assessments, use culturally sensitive checklists, and elicit evidence regarding the child's interests and potential outside of the classroom setting.

Student Outcomes	Evidence-Based Practices
2.3. Identification. Students with identified needs represent diverse backgrounds and reflect the total student population of the district.	2.3.1. Educators select and use non-biased and equitable approaches for identifying students with gifts and talents, which may include using locally developed norms or assessment tools in the child's native language or in nonverbal formats. 2.3.2. Educators understand and implement district and state policies designed to foster equity in gifted programming and services. 2.3.3. Educators provide parents/guardians with information in their native language regarding diverse behaviors and characteristics that are associated with giftedness and with information that explains the nature and purpose of gifted programming options.
2.4. Learning Progress and Outcomes. Students with gifts and talents demonstrate advanced and complex learning as a result of using multiple, appropriate, and ongoing assessments.	2.4.1. Educators use differentiated pre- and post- performance-based assessments to measure the progress of students with gifts and talents. 2.4.2. Educators use differentiated product-based assessments to measure the progress of students with gifts and talents. 2.4.3. Educators use off-level standardized assessments to measure the progress of students with gifts and talents. 2.4.4. Educators use and interpret qualitative and quantitative assessment information to develop a profile of the strengths and weaknesses of each student with gifts and talents to plan appropriate intervention. 2.4.5. Educators communicate and interpret assessment information to students with gifts and talents and their parents/guardians.

Student Outcomes	Evidence-Based Practices
2.5. Evaluation of Programming. Students identified with gifts and talents demonstrate important learning progress as a result of programming and services.	2.5.1. Educators ensure that the assessments used in the identification and evaluation processes are reliable and valid for each instrument's purpose, allow for above-grade-level performance, and allow for diverse perspectives. 2.5.2. Educators ensure that the assessment of the progress of students with gifts and talents uses multiple indicators that measure mastery of content, higher level thinking skills, achievement in specific program areas, and affective growth. 2.5.3. Educators assess the quantity, quality, and appropriateness of the programming and services provided for students with gifts and talents by disaggregating assessment data and yearly progress data and making the results public.
2.6. Evaluation of Programming. Students identified with gifts and talents have increased access and they show significant learning progress as a result of improving components of gifted education programming.	2.6.1. Administrators provide the necessary time and resources to implement an annual evaluation plan developed by persons with expertise in program evaluation and gifted education. 2.6.2. The evaluation plan is purposeful and evaluates how student-level outcomes are influenced by one or more of the following components of gifted education programming: (a) identification, (b) curriculum, (c) instructional programming and services, (d) ongoing assessment of student learning, (e) counseling and guidance programs, (f) teacher qualifications and professional development, (g) parent/guardian and community involvement, (h) programming resources, and (i) programming design, management, and delivery. 2.6.3. Educators disseminate the results of the evaluation, orally and in written form, and explain how they will use the results.

Gifted Education Programming Standard 3: Curriculum Planning and Instruction

Introduction

Assessment is an integral component of the curriculum planning process. The information obtained from multiple types of assessments informs decisions about curriculum content, instructional strategies, and resources that will support the growth of students with gifts and talents. Educators develop and use a comprehensive and sequenced core curriculum that is aligned with local, state, and national standards, then differentiate and expand it. In order to meet the unique needs of students with gifts and talents, this curriculum must emphasize advanced, conceptually challenging, in-depth, distinctive, and complex content within cognitive, affective, aesthetic, social, and leadership domains. Educators must possess a repertoire of evidence-based instructional strategies in delivering the curriculum (a) to develop talent, enhance learning, and provide students with the knowledge and skills to become independent, self-aware learners, and (b) to give students the tools to contribute to a multicultural, diverse society. The curriculum, instructional strategies, and materials and resources must engage a variety of learners using culturally responsive practices.

Standard 3: Curriculum Planning and Instruction

Description: *Educators apply the theory and research-based models of curriculum and instruction related to students with gifts and talents and respond to their needs by planning, selecting, adapting, and creating culturally relevant curriculum and by using a repertoire of evidence-based instructional strategies to ensure specific student outcomes.*

Student Outcomes	Evidence-Based Practices
3.1. Curriculum Planning. Students with gifts and talents demonstrate growth commensurate with aptitude during the school year.	3.1.1. Educators use local, state, and national standards to align and expand curriculum and instructional plans. 3.1.2. Educators design and use a comprehensive and continuous scope and sequence to develop differentiated plans for PK–12 students with gifts and talents. 3.1.3. Educators adapt, modify, or replace the core or standard curriculum to meet the needs of students with gifts and talents and those with special needs such as twice-exceptional, highly gifted, and English language learners. 3.1.4. Educators design differentiated curricula that incorporate advanced, conceptually challenging, in-depth, distinctive, and complex content for students with gifts and talents. 3.1.5. Educators use a balanced assessment system, including pre-assessment and formative assessment, to identify students' needs, develop differentiated education plans, and adjust plans based on continual progress monitoring. 3.1.6. Educators use pre-assessments and pace instruction based on the learning rates of students with gifts and talents and accelerate and compact learning as appropriate. 3.1.7. Educators use information and technologies, including assistive technologies, to individualize for students with gifts and talents, including those who are twice-exceptional.
3.2. Talent Development. Students with gifts and talents become more competent in multiple talent areas and across dimensions of learning.	3.2.1. Educators design curricula in cognitive, affective, aesthetic, social, and leadership domains that are challenging and effective for students with gifts and talents. 3.2.2. Educators use metacognitive models to meet the needs of students with gifts and talents.

Student Outcomes	Evidence-Based Practices
3.3. Talent Development. Students with gifts and talents develop their abilities in their domain of talent and/or area of interest.	3.3.1. Educators select, adapt, and use a repertoire of instructional strategies and materials that differentiate for students with gifts and talents and that respond to diversity. 3.3.2. Educators use school and community resources that support differentiation. 3.3.3. Educators provide opportunities for students with gifts and talents to explore, develop, or research their areas of interest and/or talent.
3.4. Instructional Strategies. Students with gifts and talents become independent investigators.	3.4.1. Educators use critical-thinking strategies to meet the needs of students with gifts and talents. 3.4.2. Educators use creative-thinking strategies to meet the needs of students with gifts and talents. 3.4.3. Educators use problem-solving model strategies to meet the needs of students with gifts and talents. 3.4.4. Educators use inquiry models to meet the needs of students with gifts and talents.
3.5. Culturally Relevant Curriculum. Students with gifts and talents develop knowledge and skills for living and being productive in a multicultural, diverse, and global society.	3.5.1. Educators develop and use challenging, culturally responsive curriculum to engage all students with gifts and talents. 3.5.2. Educators integrate career exploration experiences into learning opportunities for students with gifts and talents, e.g. biography study or speakers. 3.5.3. Educators use curriculum for deep explorations of cultures, languages, and social issues related to diversity.
3.6. Resources. Students with gifts and talents benefit from gifted education programming that provides a variety of high quality resources and materials.	3.6.1. Teachers and administrators demonstrate familiarity with sources for high quality resources and materials that are appropriate for learners with gifts and talents.

Gifted Education Programming Standard 4: Learning Environments

Introduction

Effective educators of students with gifts and talents create safe learning environments that foster emotional well-being, positive social interaction, leadership for social change, and cultural understanding for success in a diverse society. Knowledge of the impact of giftedness and diversity on social-emotional development enables educators of students with gifts and talents to design environments that encourage independence, motivation, and self-efficacy of individuals from all backgrounds. They understand the role of language and communication in talent development and the ways in which culture affects communication and behavior. They use relevant strategies and technologies to enhance oral, written, and artistic communication of learners whose needs vary based on exceptionality, language proficiency, and cultural and linguistic differences. They recognize the value of multilingualism in today's global community.

Standard 4: Learning Environments

Description: *Learning environments foster personal and social responsibility, multicultural competence, and interpersonal and technical communication skills for leadership in the 21st century to ensure specific student outcomes.*

Student Outcomes	Evidence-Based Practices
4.1. Personal Competence. Students with gifts and talents demonstrate growth in personal competence and dispositions for exceptional academic and creative productivity. These include self-awareness, self-advocacy, self-efficacy, confidence, motivation, resilience, independence, curiosity, and risk taking.	4.1.1. Educators maintain high expectations for all students with gifts and talents as evidenced in meaningful and challenging activities. 4.1.2. Educators provide opportunities for self-exploration, development and pursuit of interests, and development of identities supportive of achievement, e.g., through mentors and role models. 4.1.3. Educators create environments that support trust among diverse learners. 4.1.4. Educators provide feedback that focuses on effort, on evidence of potential to meet high standards, and on mistakes as learning opportunities. 4.1.5. Educators provide examples of positive coping skills and opportunities to apply them.
4.2. Social Competence. Students with gifts and talents develop social competence manifested in positive peer relationships and social interactions.	4.2.1. Educators understand the needs of students with gifts and talents for both solitude and social interaction. 4.2.2. Educators provide opportunities for interaction with intellectual and artistic/creative peers as well as with chronological-age peers. 4.2.3. Educators assess and provide instruction on social skills needed for school, community, and the world of work.
4.3. Leadership. Students with gifts and talents demonstrate personal and social responsibility and leadership skills.	4.3.1. Educators establish a safe and welcoming climate for addressing social issues and developing personal responsibility. 4.3.2. Educators provide environments for developing many forms of leadership and leadership skills. 4.3.3. Educators promote opportunities for leadership in community settings to effect positive change.

Student Outcomes	Evidence-Based Practices
4.4. Cultural Competence. Students with gifts and talents value their own and others' language, heritage, and circumstance. They possess skills in communicating, teaming, and collaborating with diverse individuals and across diverse groups[1]. They use positive strategies to address social issues, including discrimination and stereotyping.	4.4.1. Educators model appreciation for and sensitivity to students' diverse backgrounds and languages. 4.4.2. Educators censure discriminatory language and behavior and model appropriate strategies. 4.4.3. Educators provide structured opportunities to collaborate with diverse peers on a common goal.
4.5. Communication Competence. Students with gifts and talents develop competence in interpersonal and technical communication skills. They demonstrate advanced oral and written skills, balanced biliteracy or multiliteracy, and creative expression. They display fluency with technologies that support effective communication.	4.5.1. Educators provide opportunities for advanced development and maintenance of first and second language(s). 4.5.2. Educators provide resources to enhance oral, written, and artistic forms of communication, recognizing students' cultural context. 4.5.3. Educators ensure access to advanced communication tools, including assistive technologies, and use of these tools for expressing higher-level thinking and creative productivity.

1 *Differences among groups of people and individuals based on ethnicity, race, socioeconomic status, gender, exceptionalities, language, religion, sexual orientation, and geographical area.*

Gifted Education Programming Standard 5: Programming

Introduction

The term programming refers to a continuum of services that address students with gifts and talents' needs in all settings. Educators develop policies and procedures to guide and sustain all components of comprehensive and aligned programming and services for PreK-12 students with gifts and talents. Educators use a variety of programming options such as acceleration and enrichment in varied grouping arrangements (cluster grouping, resource rooms, special classes, special schools) and within individualized learning options (independent study, mentorships, online courses, internships) to enhance students' performance in cognitive and affective areas and to assist them in identifying future career goals. They augment and integrate current technologies within these learning opportunities to increase access to high level programming such as distance learning courses and to increase connections to resources outside of the school walls. In implementing services, educators in gifted, general, special education programs, and related professional services collaborate with one another and parents/guardians and community members to ensure that students' diverse learning needs are met. Administrators demonstrate their support of these programming options by allocating sufficient resources so that all students within gifts and talents receive appropriate educational services.

Standard 5: Programming

Description: *Educators are aware of empirical evidence regarding (a) the cognitive, creative, and affective development of learners with gifts and talents, and (b) programming that meets their concomitant needs. Educators use this expertise systematically and collaboratively to develop, implement, and effectively manage comprehensive services for students with a variety of gifts and talents to ensure specific student outcomes.*

Student Outcomes	Evidence-Based Practices
5.1. Variety of Programming. Students with gifts and talents participate in a variety of evidence-based programming options that enhance performance in cognitive and affective areas.	5.1.1. Educators regularly use multiple alternative approaches to accelerate learning. 5.1.2. Educators regularly use enrichment options to extend and deepen learning opportunities within and outside of the school setting. 5.1.3. Educators regularly use multiple forms of grouping, including clusters, resource rooms, special classes, or special schools. 5.1.4. Educators regularly use individualized learning options such as mentorships, internships, online courses, and independent study. 5.1.5. Educators regularly use current technologies, including online learning options and assistive technologies to enhance access to high-level programming. 5.1.6. Administrators demonstrate support for gifted programs through equitable allocation of resources and demonstrated willingness to ensure that learners with gifts and talents receive appropriate educational services.
5.2. Coordinated Services. Students with gifts and talents demonstrate progress as a result of the shared commitment and coordinated services of gifted education, general education, special education, and related professional services, such as school counselors, school psychologists, and social workers.	5.2.1. Educators in gifted, general, and special education programs, as well as those in specialized areas, collaboratively plan, develop, and implement services for learners with gifts and talents.
5.3. Collaboration. Students with gifts and talents' learning is enhanced by regular collaboration among families, community, and the school.	5.3.1. Educators regularly engage families and community members for planning, programming, evaluating, and advocating.

Student Outcomes	Evidence-Based Practices
5.4. Resources. Students with gifts and talents participate in gifted education programming that is adequately funded to meet student needs and program goals.	5.4.1. Administrators track expenditures at the school level to verify appropriate and sufficient funding for gifted programming and services.
5.5. Comprehensiveness. Students with gifts and talents develop their potential through comprehensive, aligned programming and services.	5.5.1. Educators develop thoughtful, multi-year program plans in relevant student talent areas, PK–12.
5.6. Policies and Procedures. Students with gifts and talents participate in regular and gifted education programs that are guided by clear policies and procedures that provide for their advanced learning needs (e.g., early entrance, acceleration, credit in lieu of enrollment).	5.6.1. Educators create policies and procedures to guide and sustain all components of the program, including assessment, identification, acceleration practices, and grouping practices, that is built on an evidence-based foundation in gifted education.
5.7. Career Pathways. Students with gifts and talents identify future career goals and the talent development pathways to reach those goals.	5.7.1. Educators provide professional guidance and counseling for individual student strengths, interests, and values. 5.7.2. Educators facilitate mentorships, internships, and vocational programming experiences that match student interests and aptitudes.

Gifted Education Programming Standard 6: Professional Development

Introduction

Professional development is essential for all educators involved in the development and implementation of gifted programs and services. Professional development is the intentional development of professional expertise as outlined by the NAGC-CEC teacher preparation standards and is an ongoing part of gifted educators' professional and ethical practice. Professional development may take many forms ranging from district-sponsored workshops and courses, university courses, professional conferences, independent studies, and presentations by external consultants and should be based on systematic needs assessments and professional reflection. Students participating in gifted education programs and services are taught by teachers with developed expertise in gifted education. Gifted education program services are developed and supported by administrators, coordinators, curriculum specialists, general education, special education, and gifted education teachers who have developed expertise in gifted education. Since students with gifts and talents spend much of their time within general education classrooms, general education teachers need to receive professional development in gifted education that enables them to recognize the characteristics of giftedness in diverse populations, understand the school or district referral and identification process, and possess an array of high quality, research-based differentiation strategies that challenge students. Services for students with gifts and talents are enhanced by guidance and counseling professionals with expertise in gifted education.

Standard 6: Professional Development

Description: *All educators (administrators, teachers, counselors, and other instructional support staff) build their knowledge and skills using the NAGC-CEC Teacher Standards for Gifted and Talented Education and the National Staff Development Standards. They formally assess professional development needs related to the standards, develop and monitor plans, systematically engage in training to meet the identified needs, and demonstrate mastery of standard. They access resources to provide for release time, funding for continuing education, and substitute support. These practices are judged through the assessment of relevant student outcomes.*

Student Outcomes	Evidence-Based Practices
6.1. Talent Development. Students develop their talents and gifts as a result of interacting with educators who meet the national teacher preparation standards in gifted education.	6.1.1. Educators systematically participate in ongoing, research-supported professional development that addresses the foundations of gifted education, characteristics of students with gifts and talents, assessment, curriculum planning and instruction, learning environments, and programming. 6.1.2. The school district provides professional development for teachers that models how to develop environments and instructional activities that encourage students to express diverse characteristics and behaviors that are associated with giftedness. 6.1.3. Educators participate in ongoing professional development addressing key issues such as anti-intellectualism and trends in gifted education such as equity and access. 6.1.4. Administrators provide human and material resources needed for professional development in gifted education (e.g. release time, funding for continuing education, substitute support, webinars, or mentors). 6.1.5. Educators use their awareness of organizations and publications relevant to gifted education to promote learning for students with gifts and talents.
6.2. Socio-emotional Development. Students with gifts and talents develop socially and emotionally as a result of educators who have participated in professional development aligned with national standards in gifted education and National Staff Development Standards.	6.2.1. Educators participate in ongoing professional development to support the social and emotional needs of students with gifts and talents.

Student Outcomes	Evidence-Based Practices
6.3. Lifelong Learners. Students develop their gifts and talents as a result of educators who are life-long learners, participating in ongoing professional development and continuing education opportunities.	6.3.1. Educators assess their instructional practices and continue their education in school district staff development, professional organizations, and higher education settings based on these assessments. 6.3.2. Educators participate in professional development that is sustained over time, that includes regular follow-up, and that seeks evidence of impact on teacher practice and on student learning. 6.3.3. Educators use multiple modes of professional development delivery including online courses, online and electronic communities, face-to-face workshops, professional learning communities, and book talks. 6.3.4. Educators identify and address areas for personal growth for teaching students with gifts and talents in their professional development plans.
6.4. Ethics. Students develop their gifts and talents as a result of educators who are ethical in their practices.	6.4.1. Educators respond to cultural and personal frames of reference when teaching students with gifts and talents. 6.4.2. Educators comply with rules, policies, and standards of ethical practice.

This appendix was reprinted from *NAGC Pre-K-Grade 12 Gifted Programming Standards: A Blueprint for Quality Gifted Education Programs* by the National Association for Gifted Children (2010), Washington, DC: National Association for Gifted Children. Copyright 2010 by the National Association for Gifted Children. Reprinted with permission.

Appendix B
Code of Fair Testing Practices in Education: Prepared by the Joint Committee on Testing Practices

The Code of Fair Testing Practices in Education (***Code***) is a guide for professionals in fulfilling their obligation to provide and use tests that are fair to all test takers regardless of age, gender, disability, race, ethnicity, national origin, religion, sexual orientation, linguistic background, or other personal characteristics. Fairness is a primary consideration in all aspects of testing. Careful standardization of tests and administration conditions helps to ensure that all test takers are given a comparable opportunity to demonstrate what they know and how they can perform in the area being tested. Fairness implies that every test taker has the opportunity to prepare for the test and is informed about the general nature and content of the test, as appropriate to the purpose of the test. Fairness also extends to the accurate reporting of individual and group test results. Fairness is not an isolated concept, but must be considered in all aspects of the testing process.

The ***Code*** applies broadly to testing in education (admissions, educational assessment, educational diagnosis, and student placement) regardless of the mode of presentation, so it is relevant to conventional paper-and-pencil tests, computer based tests, and performance tests. It is not designed to cover employment testing, licensure or certification testing, or other types of testing outside the field of education. The ***Code*** is directed pri-

215

marily at professionally developed tests used in formally administered testing programs. Although the *Code* is not intended to cover tests made by
teachers for use in their own classrooms, teachers are encouraged to use the
guidelines to help improve their testing practices.

The *Code* addresses the roles of test developers and test users separately. Test developers are people and organizations that construct tests, as
well as those that set policies for testing programs. Test users are people
and agencies that select tests, administer tests, commission test development services, or make decisions on the basis of test scores. Test devel-
oper and test user roles may overlap, for example, when a state or local
education agency commissions test development services, sets policies that
control the test development process, and makes decisions on the basis of
the test scores.

Many of the statements in the *Code* refer to the selection and use of
existing tests. When a new test is developed, when an existing test is modified, or when the administration of a test is modified, the *Code* is intended
to provide guidance for this process.

The Code is not intended to be mandatory, exhaustive, or definitive,
and may not be applicable to every situation. Instead, the Code is intended
to be aspirational, and is not intended to take precedence over the judgment of those who have competence in the subjects addressed.

The *Code* provides guidance separately for test developers and test
users in four critical areas:

- Developing and Selecting Appropriate Tests
- Administering and Scoring Tests
- Reporting and Interpreting Test Results
- Informing Test Takers

The *Code* is intended to be consistent with the relevant parts of the
Standards for Educational and Psychological Testing (American Educational
Research Association [AERA], American Psychological Association
[APA], and National Council on Measurement in Education [NCME],
1999). The *Code* is not meant to add new principles over and above those
in the *Standards* or to change their meaning. Rather, the *Code* is intended
to represent the spirit of selected portions of the *Standards* in a way that is
relevant and meaningful to developers and users of tests, as well as to test
takers and/or their parents or guardians. States, districts, schools, organizations and individual professionals are encouraged to commit themselves

to fairness in testing and safeguarding the rights of test takers. The Code is intended to assist in carrying out such commitments.

The **_Code_** has been prepared by the Joint Committee on Testing Practices, a cooperative effort among several professional organizations. The aim of the Joint Committee is to act, in the public interest, to advance the quality of testing practices. Members of the Joint Committee include the American Counseling Association (ACA), the American Educational Research Association (AERA), the American Psychological Association (APA), the American Speech-Language-Hearing Association (ASHA), the National Association of School Psychologists (NASP), the National Association of Test Directors (NATD), and the National Council on Measurement in Education (NCME).

A. Developing and Selecting Appropriate Tests

Test Developers	Test Users
Test developers should provide the information and supporting evidence that test users need to select appropriate tests.	Test users should select tests that meet the intended purpose and that are appropriate for the intended test takers.
A-1. Provide evidence of what the test measures, the recommended uses, the intended test takers, and the strengths and limitations of the test, including the level of precision of the test scores.	A-1. Define the purpose for testing, the content and skills to be tested, and the intended test takers. Select and use the most appropriate test based on a thorough review of available information.
A-2. Describe how the content and skills to be tested were selected and how the tests were developed.	A-2. Review and select tests based on the appropriateness of test content, skills tested, and content coverage for the intended purpose of testing.
A-3. Communicate information about a test's characteristics at a level of detail appropriate to the intended test users.	A-3. Review materials provided by test developers and select tests for which clear, accurate, and complete information is provided.
A-4. Provide guidance on the levels of skills, knowledge, and training necessary for appropriate review, selection, and administration of tests.	A-4. Select tests through a process that includes persons with appropriate knowledge, skills, and training.
A-5. Provide evidence that the technical quality, including reliability and validity, of the test meets its intended purposes.	A-5. Evaluate evidence of the technical quality of the test provided by the test developer and any independent reviewers.

Test Developers	Test Users
A-6. Provide to qualified test users representative samples of test questions or practice tests, directions, answer sheets, manuals, and score reports.	A-6. Evaluate representative samples of test questions or practice tests, directions, answer sheets, manuals, and score reports before selecting a test.
A-7. Avoid potentially offensive content or language when developing test questions and related materials.	A-7. Evaluate procedures and materials used by test developers, as well as the resulting test, to ensure that potentially offensive content or language is avoided.
A-8. Make appropriately modified forms of tests or administration procedures available for test takers with disabilities who need special accommodations.	A-8. Select tests with appropriately modified forms or administration procedures for test takers with disabilities who need special accommodations.
A-9. Obtain and provide evidence on the performance of test takers of diverse subgroups, making significant efforts to obtain sample sizes that are adequate for subgroup analyses. Evaluate the evidence to ensure that differences in performance are related to the skills being assessed.	A-9. Evaluate the available evidence on the performance of test takers of diverse subgroups. Determine to the extent feasible which performance differences may have been caused by factors unrelated to the skills being assessed.

B. Administering and Scoring Tests

Test Developers	Test Users
Test developers should explain how to administer and score tests correctly and fairly.	Test users should administer and score tests correctly and fairly.
B-1. Provide clear descriptions of detailed procedures for administering tests in a standardized manner.	B-1. Follow established procedures for administering tests in a standardized manner.
B-2. Provide guidelines on reasonable procedures for assessing persons with disabilities who need special accommodations or those with diverse linguistic backgrounds.	B-2. Provide and document appropriate procedures for test takers with disabilities who need special accommodations or those with diverse linguistic backgrounds. Some accommodations may be required by law or regulation.
B-3. Provide information to test takers or test users on test question formats and procedures for answering test questions, including information on the use of any needed materials and equipment.	B-3. Provide test takers with an opportunity to become familiar with test question formats and any materials or equipment that may be used during testing.

Test Developers	Test Users
B-4. Establish and implement procedures to ensure the security of testing materials during all phases of test development, administration, scoring, and reporting.	B-4. Protect the security of test materials, including respecting copyrights and eliminating opportunities for test takers to obtain scores by fraudulent means.
B-5. Provide procedures, materials and guidelines for scoring the tests, and for monitoring the accuracy of the scoring process. If scoring the test is the responsibility of the test developer, provide adequate training for scorers.	B-5. If test scoring is the responsibility of the test user, provide adequate training to scorers and ensure and monitor the accuracy of the scoring process.
B-6. Correct errors that affect the interpretation of the scores and communicate the corrected results promptly.	B-6. Correct errors that affect the interpretation of the scores and communicate the corrected results promptly.
B-7. Develop and implement procedures for ensuring the confidentiality of scores.	B-7. Develop and implement procedures for ensuring the confidentiality of scores.

C. Reporting and Interpreting Test Results

Test Developers	Test Users
Test developers should report test results accurately and provide information to help test users interpret test results correctly.	Test users should report and interpret test results accurately and clearly.
C-1. Provide information to support recommended interpretations of the results, including the nature of the content, norms or comparison groups, and other technical evidence. Advise test users of the benefits and limitations of test results and their interpretation. Warn against assigning greater precision than is warranted.	C-1. Interpret the meaning of the test results, taking into account the nature of the content, norms or comparison groups, other technical evidence, and benefits and limitations of test results.
C-2. Provide guidance regarding the interpretations of results for tests administered with modifications. Inform test users of potential problems in interpreting test results when tests or test administration procedures are modified.	C-2. Interpret test results from modified test or test administration procedures in view of the impact those modifications may have had on test results.

Test Developers	Test Users
C-3. Specify appropriate uses of test results and warn test users of potential misuses.	C-3. Avoid using tests for purposes other than those recommended by the test developer unless there is evidence to support the intended use or interpretation.
C-4. When test developers set standards, provide the rationale, procedures, and evidence for setting performance standards or passing scores. Avoid using stigmatizing labels.	C-4. Review the procedures for setting performance standards or passing scores. Avoid using stigmatizing labels.
C-5. Encourage test users to base decisions about test takers on multiple sources of appropriate information, not on a single test score.	C-5. Avoid using a single test score as the sole determinant of decisions about test takers. Interpret test scores in conjunction with other information about individuals.
C-6. Provide information to enable test users to accurately interpret and report test results for groups of test takers, including information about who were and who were not included in the different groups being compared, and information about factors that might influence the interpretation of results.	C-6. State the intended interpretation and use of test results for groups of test takers. Avoid grouping test results for purposes not specifically recommended by the test developer unless evidence is obtained to support the intended use. Report procedures that were followed in determining who were and who were not included in the groups being compared and describe factors that might influence the interpretation of results.
C-7. Provide test results in a timely fashion and in a manner that is understood by the test taker.	C-7. Communicate test results in a timely fashion and in a manner that is understood by the test taker.
C-8. Provide guidance to test users about how to monitor the extent to which the test is fulfilling its intended purposes.	C-8. Develop and implement procedures for monitoring test use, including consistency with the intended purposes of the test.

D. Informing Test Takers

Under some circumstances, test developers have direct communication with the test takers and/or control of the tests, testing process, and test results. In other circumstances the test users have these responsibilities.

Test developers or test users should inform test takers about the nature of the test, test taker rights and responsibilities, the appropriate use of scores, and procedures for resolving challenges to scores.
D-1. Inform test takers in advance of the test administration about the coverage of the test, the types of question formats, the directions, and appropriate test-taking strategies. Make such information available to all test takers.
D-2. When a test is optional, provide test takers or their parents/guardians with information to help them judge whether a test should be taken—including indications of any consequences that may result from not taking the test (e.g., not being eligible to compete for a particular scholarship) —and whether there is an available alternative to the test.
D-3. Provide test takers or their parents/guardians with information about rights test takers may have to obtain copies of tests and completed answer sheets, to retake tests, to have tests rescored, or to have scores declared invalid.
D-4. Provide test takers or their parents/guardians with information about responsibilities test takers have, such as being aware of the intended purpose and uses of the test, performing at capacity, following directions, and not disclosing test items or interfering with other test takers.
D-5. Inform test takers or their parents/guardians how long scores will be kept on file and indicate to whom, under what circumstances, and in what manner test scores and related information will or will not be released. Protect test scores from unauthorized release and access.
D-6. Describe procedures for investigating and resolving circumstances that might result in canceling or withholding scores, such as failure to adhere to specified testing procedures.
D-7. Describe procedures that test takers, parents/guardians, and other interested parties may use to obtain more information about the test, register complaints, and have problems resolved.

Note: The membership of the Working Group that developed the ***Code of Fair Testing Practices in Education*** and of the Joint Committee on Testing Practices that guided the Working Group is as follows:

Peter Behuniak, PhD

Lloyd Bond, PhD

Gwyneth M. Boodoo, PhD

Wayne Camara, PhD

Ray Fenton, PhD

John J. Fremer, PhD (Co-Chair)

Sharon M. Goldsmith, PhD

Bert F. Green, PhD

William G. Harris, PhD

Janet E. Helms, PhD

Stephanie H. McConaughy, PhD

Julie P. Noble, PhD

Wayne M. Patience, PhD

Carole L. Perlman, PhD

Douglas K. Smith, PhD (deceased)

Janet E. Wall, EdD (Co-Chair)

Pat Nellor Wickwire, PhD

Mary Yakimowski, PhD

Lara Frumkin, PhD, *of the APA served as staff liaison.*

The Joint Committee intends that the Code be consistent with and supportive of existing codes of conduct and standards of other professional groups who use tests in educational contexts. Of particular note are the Responsibilities of Users of Standardized Tests (Association for Assessment in Counseling, 1989), APA Test User Qualifications (2000), ASHA Code of Ethics (2001), Ethical Principles of Psychologists and Code of Conduct (1992), NASP Professional Conduct Manual (2000), NCME Code of Professional Responsibility (1995), and Rights and Responsibilities of Test Takers: Guidelines and Expectations (Joint Committee on Testing Practices, 2000).

Appendix C
NAGC Position Statement: The Role of Assessments in the Identification of Gifted Students

Assessments can be used for a variety of purposes, including identifying students for gifted programs; providing ongoing feedback to guide the instructional process; and to determine to what extent students have obtained intended goals (e.g., academic, affective) within a gifted program. The purpose of this position paper is to provide parents, teachers, and other advocates of gifted students with best practices endorsed by NAGC related to the first purpose--the role of assessments in identifying students for gifted programs.

NAGC believes that the process of identifying students for gifted and talented programs must be based on defensible measurement practices, including the process of selecting psychometrically sound assessments aligned with a program's goals and objectives; the administration and interpretation of the assessments by individuals with appropriate credentials or training; and the ethical application of decisions regarding gifted program placement. Further, NAGC believes that there are specific practices that are supportive of these measurement practices.

In recent years, there have been significant discussions regarding the role of traditional assessments in identifying students who are typically under-represented in gifted programs, including culturally and linguistically diverse and low-income gifted students, and the use of alternative assessments with these students such as nonverbal ability tests (Lohman, 2005). NAGC believes that assessments selected for use in the identification of gifted students must be sensitive to and appropriate for the characteristics of the students being assessed and must aim to be inclusive of students from different cultures, races, and economic circumstances. Program administrators should choose the most psychometrically sound assessments with appropriate norms for their population of students and programs and use them appropriately for selection (see Lohman, 2005). However, it is also imperative that test users and policymakers understand that alternative-type assessments are not panaceas to the issue of under-representation, each come with limitations in terms of reliability and validity, and that these types of assessments should never be used in isolation to identify gifted children.

Another issue that warrants consideration in the identification of gifted students is the decision to use group versus individual testing, which is often determined by the availability of resources and the characteristics of the children to be evaluated. More accurate assessment data may be obtained via one-on-one testing with very young children and children with special characteristics and needs such as those with dual exceptionalities. For these children it is important to have a tester who is sensitive to and experienced with the group being assessed as well as the training in the administration of the assessments.

NAGC believes that because the use of assessments is an integral part of the identification process, test users have a responsibility to ensure that all testing is conducted in a fair and ethical manner. Such practices include the appropriate storing of testing materials before, during, and after testing; training all personnel involved with the administration and/or scoring of assessments; utilizing assessments that are developmentally appropriate and for only the purposes for which they were developed; interpreting assessment results to the appropriate audiences; and maintaining the confidentiality of students at all times.

While NAGC advocates for the use of multiple assessments in the identification of gifted students, NAGC also believes that combining disparate data from multiple assessments must be done in such a way as to identify not only those students who are in immediate need of instruction beyond the regular curriculum, but also those students who display the potential for high-level learning beyond the regular curriculum.

In order to best implement defensible assessment practices for the purposes of gifted program identification, NAGC supports the collaboration of multiple stakeholders, including teachers, parents, and other advocates of gifted children, as well as general education administration at the district and state levels. This collaboration works to ensure that the application of defensible measurement practices results in the equitable and consistent use of assessments for the purposes of gifted program identification.

Research-Based Practices Regarding the Use of Assessments for Identification Purposes

Regardless of the type of assessments used for identification or whether students are assessed in groups or individually, there are five non-negotiable practices in the use of assessments as identification tools. First, the choice of assessment tools must match the definition of giftedness that has been determined by the state, district, or school. The degree to which the assessment tool is aligned with the definition of giftedness is an important aspect of validity. Further, any assessments used in the identification process also should be aligned with the gifted program's goals and objectives and desired outcomes for students as a result of participation in the program (Feldhusen, Asher, & Hoover, 1984). Program administrators must carefully consider the program's goals and objectives as well as the aptitudes, achievement levels, and other characteristics of students (e.g., motivation, persistence, interest) needed for success in the program in order to select instruments that provide the most reliable and valid data regarding students' potential for success.

Second, identification of gifted and talented students should not be based on a single assessment. Rather, multiple pieces of evidence should be collected that measure different constructs and characteristics aligned to the gifted program's definition, goals, and objectives (Callahan, Tomlinson, & Pizzat, 1993), ideally including a variety of format types (e.g., paper-and-pencil; performance assessment). Multiple pieces of psychometrically sound data obtained from a variety of sources result in a more comprehensive and thus, more accurate picture of the student on which to base selection. For example, if trying to measure mathematical ability, appropriate choices might include a selected-response, domain-specific mathematics achievement test (e.g., a multiple-choice assessment) and a constructed-response assessment (e.g., performance assessment) where the student solves problems in an authentic context. However, when multiple assessments are used, it is important that the assessments provide different types of information as well as measure the construct, i.e. mathematical reasoning ability, differently. For example, although multiple pieces of information are being collected, administering assessments that follow the same response format may unfairly penalize some students while benefiting others. Program administrators should consider the use of a variety of format types when considering the specific assessments that will be used in an identification process and choose assessments sensitive to the inclusion of under-represented groups, culturally and linguistically diverse, and twice-exceptional students.

Third, the assessment conditions should mimic as closely as possible a natural setting in which the student can fully demonstrate his or her knowledge, skills, and abilities. The greater the unfamiliarity of the assessment setting, the greater the potential for undue negative influences on a student's performance (American Educational Research Association, American Psychological Association, National Council on Measurement in Education, 1999). For example, testing some of a district's second-grade students in a high school cafeteria on a given Saturday, while other second graders are administered the assessments within their classroom context, unfairly penalizes those students who are assessed outside their natural setting.

Fourth, school system personnel have the responsibility to be well-informed consumers regarding the technical documentation of each assessment used for identification (Joint Committee on Testing Practices, 2004). Assessment developers or publishers should include information on an instrument's psychometric properties (e.g., reliability and validity) and only assessments with adequate psychometric properties should be used in the identification of gifted students. In the absence of this information, responsible persons should determine an instrument's reliability and validity for diverse populations prior to using the instrument in an identification process.

Fifth, school system personnel have the responsibility to ensure that persons who administrator and score assessments used for identification are appropriately trained and that placement decisions are driven by defensible data and not based on personal relationships, political associations, or parental pressure.

The Variety of Assessment Types

Assessments differ on dimensions such as: the degree to which they are standardized (e.g., using large national samples versus local samples); the type of response format (e.g., producing a response as opposed to selecting a response from a predefined set); the ways in which the material is presented (e.g., paper-and-pencil, computerized, oral); and the content (e.g., mathematics) or constructs (e.g,. creativity) being assessed. NAGC believes that regardless of the type of assessment, only assessments that provide psychometrically sound information on students, regardless of language, culture, gender, race, or socio-economic status, should be used. The following are three types of assessments often used in identifying students for participation in programs and services for gifted learners.

1. *Objective-type instruments*: These types of selected-response assessments used for identification purposes range from standardized, nationally normed paper-and-pencil or computerized tests to locally developed and normed tests, including most of the aptitude and achievement tests used in schools as well as IQ tests (see NAGC position paper; "Use of WISC-IV for Gifted Identification"). When using these types of assessments, users should be fully aware of the test's purposes and have evidence of sufficient reliability of the test scores. In addition, test users should use assessments that have a sufficient ceiling for measuring students' aptitudes or achievement, lack item bias, and have support for the validity of the types of decisions that will be made based on the results of the assessment (Joint Committee, 2004).

2. *Performance assessments*: Performance assessments, authentic assessments, and portfolios are constructed-response assessments that may be used in the identification process. These types of assessments directly measure the domain-specific construct of interest. Examples of performance assessments include open-ended or extended-response items. For example, students might be asked to present arguments for or against a particular position on an issue, write in response to a prompt, or conduct and write a report of

a scientific investigation. Portfolios are examples of another type of performance assessment in which students present their 'best pieces' highlighting the strengths of each piece or a 'work in progress' where students illustrate their improvement over time. When using these types of assessments, test users have the responsibility of ensuring that high-quality training procedures for scoring students' responses or rating students' work are in place in order to achieve a sufficient standard for exact rater agreement (Moon & Hughes, 2002). The acceptable standard for rater agreement is 80% exact agreement between two raters evaluating the same student response.

3. *Rating Scales, Interviews*: Classroom observations of students' behaviors, collected by the use of rating scales designed to assess student characteristics or behaviors, and student interviews can provide useful supplemental data, particularly on students whose talents may not be evident on traditional aptitude or achievement tests. NAGC believes that the use of rating scales and interviews should play only a supplementary role in the identification process. Collecting these types of information is very difficult to do well because all individuals are affected by bias and prejudice, even if only at a subconscious level. If these types of data are collected, it is important that one recognize that different genders, cultures, races, ethnicities, and social classes have different ways of communicating which may impact an observer's/interviewer's perspective on what behaviors constitute giftedness. It is also essential to recognize one's own views and predispositions relative to these differing subgroups of the population. To guard against the introduction of observer/interviewer bias into the identification process, educators should use structured tools with inclusive, but specific and clear, criteria to guide the data collection process (Oosterhof, 2003). Program administrators have the responsibility to ensure that individuals collecting these types of data have sufficient training in both the use of the instrument as well as the manifestation of giftedness in differing subgroups.

Implications for Practice

Program administrators are responsible for ensuring that:
*   the identification process and the assessments used are aligned with the program's definition of giftedness;
*   the process includes the use of multiple assessments that are combined in a reasoned way that is not biased against any particular subgroup of students (VanTassel-Baska, 2007);
*   the types of assessments used have sufficient psychometric evidence supportive of decisions about students' readiness for gifted programming;
*   all individuals involved in the assessment process have sufficient training in the administration and use of the assessments;
*   they themselves are fully informed about best practices in the field of testing as well as the latest research regarding the identification of gifted students; and
*   there is a process in place whereby the identification process is periodically evaluated to ensure it is reflective of best practices in the identification of gifted students.

Approved October 2008

Annotated Bibliography

American Educational Research Association, American Psychological Association, National Council on Measurement in Education. (1999). *Standards for educational and psychological testing.* **Washington, DC: American Educational Research Association.**
This reference outlines the standards associated with the testing process. The reference provides the criteria for the evaluation of tests, testing practices, and the consequences of using tests and is applicable for those who develop tests; those who select or review tests; those who administer and score tests; and those who use the results from tests for decision-making purposes, among others.

Callahan, C. M., Tomlinson, C. A., & Pizzat, P. M. (Eds.). (1993). *Contexts for promise: Noteworthy practices and innovations in the identification of gifted students.* **Charlottesville: National Research Center on the Gifted and Talented, University of Virginia.**

This report is based on a National Research Center on the Gifted and Talented study that involved the collection and evaluation of instruments and processes used in identification processes from districts across the nation. The work includes many of the projects that have been funded by the Jacob K. Javits Gifted and Talented Students Education Act.

Feldhusen, J. F., Asher, J. W., & Hoover, S. M. (1984). Problems in the identification of giftedness, talent, or ability. In J. S. Renzulli (Ed.) (2004), *Identification of students for gifted and talented programs* **(pp. 79-85), Thousand Oaks, CA: Corwin Press.**

This article, first appearing in Gifted Child Quarterly in 1984, discusses five steps associated with the identification of students for gifted programs: defining of program goals and the types of students to be served; procedures for nomination; procedures for assessment; individual differentiation; and validation of the identification process.

Joint Committee on Testing Practices. (2004). *Code of fair testing practices in education.* **Washington, DC: American Psychological Association.**

The reference is a collaborative effort among the American Counseling Association, the American Educational Research Association, the American Psychological Association, the American Speech-Language-Hearing Association, the National Association of School Psychologists, the National Association of Test Directors, and the National Council on Measurement in Education. The Code serves as a guide for individuals who are test developers as well as test users and focuses on the (1) development and selection of assessments; (2) administration and scoring of assessments; (3) reporting and interpreting assessment results; and (4) informing of test takers.

Lane, S., & Stone, C. A. (2006). Performance assessment. In R. L. Brennan (Ed.), *Educational Measurement* **(4th ed.), (pp. 387-432).**

National Council on Measurement in Education & American Council on Education. Westport, CT: Praeger Publishers.
This chapter provides an overview on the design, use, and validity of performance assessments for large-scale educational testing.

Lohman, D. F. (2005). The role of nonverbal ability tests in identifying academically gifted students: An aptitude perspective. *Gifted Child Quarterly, 49,* **111-138.**
This article presents an overview of the different types of nonverbal ability tests, from individually administered to group administered and how selecting students on the basis of these types of assessments alone excludes many students who would profit from gifted and talented programs and includes many students for whom gifted and talented programs would be an ill fit.

Moon, T. R., & Hughes, K. R. (2002). Training and scoring issues involved in large-scale writing performance assessments. *Educational Measurement: Issues and Practice, 21*(2), **15-19.**
This study investigated the amount of error introduced into students' scores from constructed-response items based upon the type of training raters received as well as the type of scoring used for evaluating student responses.

Oosterhof, A. (2003). *Developing and using classroom assessments.* **Upper Saddle River, NJ: Pearson Education.**
This text provides a thorough and succinct discussion of the issues involved with using assessments in an educational environment, from development of to the uses of to the interpretation of various types of assessments as well as the issues that need to be taken into consideration when using each type of assessment.

VanTassel-Baska, J. (2007). *Alternative assessments with gifted and talented students.* **Waco, TX: Prufrock Press.**
This text provides an introductory guide to the methods used in educational settings for identifying gifted students as well as discussion for the need to identify students from under-represented populations for gifted and talented programs. It also focuses on ways to assess the learning of gifted student through alternative means.

Author Note

This appendix was reprinted from *NAGC Pre-K-Grade 12 Gifted Programming Standards: A Blueprint for Quality Gifted Education Programs* by the National Association for Gifted Children (2010), Washington, DC: National Association for Gifted Children. Copyright 2010 by the National Association for Gifted Children. Reprinted with permission.

About the Authors

Scott J. Peters, Ph.D., is assistant professor of educational foundations at the University of Wisconsin–Whitewater, where he teaches courses related to measurement and assessment, research methodology, and gifted education. He received his Ph.D. from Purdue University specializing in gifted and talented education with secondary areas in applied research methodology and English education. His research work focuses on educational assessment with regard to policy and practice, identification of student exceptionalities—particularly those from low-income or underrepresented groups—and gifted and talented programming outcomes. He has published in *Teaching for High Potential, Gifted Child Quarterly, Journal of Advanced Academics, Gifted and Talented International, Gifted Children, Journal of Career and Technical Education Research, Educational Leadership,* and *Pedagogies.* He is the past recipient of the Feldhusen Doctoral Fellowship in Gifted Education, the NAGC Research and Evaluation Network Dissertation Award, the NAGC Doctoral Student of the Year Award, and the UW-Whitewater College of Education Innovation Award. He has served as the assistant program chair and program chair of the AERA Research on Giftedness, Creativity, and Talent SIG, on the board of directors of the Wisconsin Association for Talented and Gifted, and as the National Association for Gifted Children Research and Evaluation network secretary.

Michael S. Matthews, Ph.D., is associate professor of gifted education and graduate coordinator for the Academically & Intellectually Gifted program at the University of North Carolina at Charlotte. He is widely published in gifted education; this is his fifth book. Dr. Matthews is coeditor of the *Journal of Advanced Academics*, and is an active member of the Research and Evaluation network of the National Association for Gifted Children. He has held several offices in the SIG-Research on Giftedness, Creativity, and Talent of the American Educational Research Association, and has served as vice president and conference co-chair of the North Carolina Association for the Gifted & Talented. In 2010, he was awarded the NAGC Early Scholar Award, and in 2012, he and his coauthors received from the AERA SIG-RCGT the Michael Pyryt Collaboration Award for their article, "Parental Influences on the Academic Motivation of Gifted Students: A Self-Determination Theory Perspective." Dr. Matthews' research focuses on the areas of gifted education identification and policy; gifted education in science and mathematics; motivation and underachievement; the role of parents in the development of their children's abilities; and the assessment and identification of learners from diverse backgrounds, especially those who are English language learners.

Matthew T. McBee, Ph.D., is assistant professor of experimental psychology at East Tennessee State University where he teaches courses on statistics, experimental design, and quantitative research methodology. He is interested in many aspects of gifted and talented education, with a particular focus on the identification of gifted students. He has also contributed statistical expertise to research in disciplines such as autism spectrum disorders, reading and writing, pediatric obesity, and transfusion medicine. His publications have appeared in *Gifted Child Quarterly, Journal of Advanced Academics, Roeper Review, Journal of Secondary Gifted Education, Reading and Writing, Annals of Dyslexia, Journal of Autism and Developmental Disorders, Research in Autism Spectrum Disorders, Transfusion, Contemporary Clinical Trials,* and *Journal of the American Animal Hospital Association.*

D. Betsy McCoach, Ph.D., is an associate professor in the Measurement, Evaluation and Assessment program at the University of Connecticut. Betsy has published more than 75 journal articles, book chapters, and books, including *Motivating Gifted Students* with Del Siegle and *Multilevel Modeling of Educational Data* with Ann O'Connell. Her newest book, *Instrument Development in the Affective Domain* (3rd ed.), coauthored with Robert K. Gable and John P. Madura, will be released in 2013. Betsy served as the founding coeditor for the *Journal of Advanced Academics*, and she is the current coeditor of *Gifted Child Quarterly*. She is also an associate editor of *Frontiers in Measurement and Quantitative Psychology*. Betsy serves as a coprincipal investigator and research methodologist on several federally funded research grants, including Project Early Vocabulary Intervention, funded by the Institute of Education Sciences, and School Structure and Science Success: Organization and Leadership Influences on Student Success, funded by the National Science Foundation. In addition, she has served as the research methodologist for the National Research Center on the Gifted and Talented for the last 6 years. Her research interests include gifted education, underachievement, and assessing academic growth and achievement.